Measuring
the Success of
Leadership
Development

A Step-by-Step Guide for Measuring Impact and Calculating ROI

PRESS

ROI INSTITUTE™

Patricia Pulliam Phillips, PhD
Jack J. Phillips, PhD
Rebecca Ray, PhD

Chapter 12 was originally published as "Measuring ROI in Safety Management for Project Leaders," chap. 13 in *Measuring ROI in Environment, Health, and Safety* (Beverly, MA: Scrivener Publishing, 2014), and is reprinted with permission.

ATD Press is an internationally renowned source of insightful and practical information on talent development, workplace learning, and professional development.

ATD Press
1640 King Street
Alexandria, VA 22314 USA

Ordering information: Books published by ATD Press can be purchased by visiting ATD's website at www.td.org/books or by calling 800.628.2783 or 703.683.8100.

Library of Congress Control Number: 2015934621

ISBN-10: 1-56286-942-6
ISBN-13: 978-1-56286-942-7
e-ISBN: 978-1-60728-239-6

ATD Press Editorial Staff:
Director: Kristine Luecker
Manager: Christian Green
Community of Practice Manager, Senior Leaders and Executives: Cynthia Schoeppel
Associate Editor: Melissa Jones
Cover Design: Maggie Hyde
Interior Design: Bey Bello
Printed by United Graphics, Mattoon, IL, www.unitedgraphicsinc.com

Table of Contents

Preface vii

Part I: **The ROI Methodology: A Credible Approach to**
Evaluating Your Leadership Development Programs

Chapter 1   Leadership Development Is as Important
as Leadership Itself 3
The Top Executive View 3
Status of Leadership Development 6
Measuring the Results .11
Final Thoughts 11

Chapter 2   System for Accountability 13
High-Performing Culture and Measurement 13
How and Why Leadership Development Fits With ROI 14
Types of Data for the ROI Methodology 17
Selecting Programs for ROI Analysis 21
ROI Process Model 24
Final Thoughts 24

Chapter 3   Alignment of Programs and Evaluation Planning 27
Achieving the Proper Alignment 27
Evaluation Planning 36
Case Study 36
Final Thoughts 42

Chapter 4   Data Collection at Five Levels 43
Quantitative and Qualitative Inquiry 43
Questionnaires and Surveys 44
Testing 47
Interviews 47
Focus Groups 48
Observations 48
Action Plans and Performance Agreements 49
Monitoring Performance .54
Improving the Response Rate for Data Collection 55
Sources of Data 56

Timing for Data Collection .57
Final Thoughts 59

Chapter 5   Data Analysis That Is Practical and Credible 61
Isolating the Effects. 61
Converting Data to Monetary Units 67
Costs of the Program 70
Calculating the Return 72
Intangibles 74
Final Thoughts 77

Chapter 6   Reporting Results to Appropriate Audiences. 79
Guidelines for Communicating Results 79
The Cautions of Communicating Results 82
The Complete Report 83
Using Meetings. 85
The Joan Kravitz Story: Presenting the Results of an ROI Study
    to Senior Management .86
Routine Communication Tools. 92
Routine Feedback on Progress 93
The Communication Plan 94
Final Thoughts 95

Chapter 7   Implementing and Sustaining ROI 97
The Importance of Sustaining the Use of ROI 97
Implementing the Process: Overcoming Resistance 98
Assessing the Climate. 99
Developing Roles and Responsibilities. 99
Establishing Goals and Plans 101
Revising or Developing Guidelines and Procedures 102
Preparing the Team 104
Initiating ROI Studies 105
Preparing the Clients and Executives 106
Removing Obstacles 107
Monitoring Progress 109
Final Thoughts 109

Part II: **Evaluation in Action: Case Studies Describing the Evaluation of Leadership Development Programs**

Chapter 8   Measuring ROI in Leadership for Performance
            for Store Managers. 113

Chapter 9   Measuring ROI in a Supervisory Leadership
            Development Program. 137

Chapter 10 Measuring ROI in Fundamentals of Business Leadership. .155

Chapter 11 Measuring ROI in a Selection and Onboarding Program
            for New Leaders 179

Chapter 12 Measuring ROI in Safety Leadership for Construction
            Project Leaders. 201

Chapter 13 Measuring ROI in an Operations Manager
            Development Program. 225

            About the ROI Institute 241
            About the Authors 243
            Index 247

Preface

A large gold-mining company based in North America with mines in three continents was facing a typical challenge. Survey data taken from its employees indicated that the first level of management needed leadership help—the engagement survey results were much lower than expected and pointed to a need for formal leadership development. The chief operating officer (COO) agreed, and approved a project that involved 14 days of leadership development coupled with 360-degree feedback processes, and a team of individuals to make it successful. In all, nearly 1,000 managers would be trained at a cost of more than $6 million. The COO was willing to make this investment if the human resource function could show the financial return on investment (ROI)—"How can I spend this amount of money and not show my shareholders the return on this investment?" This request presented a challenge to the HR executives, who had never pursued an ROI study for any of their previous projects.

This case study highlights three developing trends:

Globally, a record amount of money is being invested in leadership development, as confirmed by several benchmarking reports.

A record number of requests are being made for accountability for leadership development, including showing impact and ROI for major programs.

Human resource professionals, particularly those involved in the soft skill area, must be prepared to step up to this challenge, not only when impact and ROI are requested, but ideally, before the request is made. HR professionals around the world are doing just that by developing the skills to become certified ROI professionals (CRP).

The outcome of this case study is detailed in chapter 9 of this book.

SNEAK PREVIEW

Measuring the Success of Leadership Development will address the issues outlined in the case study above. It will demonstrate how leadership development can be evaluated, including measuring impact and ROI. This method represents a significant change in leadership development because this process begins with the end in mind—such as the business impact, if it is going to be evaluated at that level. This shift in thinking about leadership development, which often begins with seeking new behaviors, moves the discussion to business improvement. These new behaviors are sought and needed for a reason, which often involves driving the performance of a group of people.

This book will take you through the necessary steps to make this development and points to other resources for more detail if necessary. The information in the first half is complemented by the case studies in the second part, which amplify, with real-life examples, how this challenge is being met. *Measuring the Success of Leadership Development* is an essential resource for the leadership development team, chief learning officer, and chief human resources officer.

THE FLOW OF THE BOOK

This book begins with a chapter about the status of leadership development and the challenge of showing its worth to the organization. The following six chapters present the ROI Methodology, which is the most documented and used evaluation system in the world, and fits perfectly with leadership development. Many practitioners are using this approach to clearly show the value of leadership using data that top executives appreciate and understand. Part II presents six case studies that offer a variety of settings, programs, and content.

Measuring the Success of Leadership Development complements an earlier book of ours, *Measuring Leadership Development: Quantify Your Program's Impact and ROI on Organizational Performance*, which was released by McGraw-Hill in 2012. That book provides much more detail on the methodology of showing leadership development value. This new book contains a condensed explanation of the methodology and case studies. We envision the two books as companions that can easily be used together— one for a quick reference with case studies and the other a more detailed how-to.

TARGET AUDIENCE

The principal audience for this book will be individuals involved in leading the human resource or the learning and development function. Whether their title is chief learning officer or the chief human resources officer, these individuals need to understand that major leadership programs are not only necessary, but can provide impressive business results. When this value is shown, it improves support, respect, and critical funding for future leadership development programs.

A second audience will be leadership development directors, organizers, coordinators, and consultants charged with implementing leadership development in organizations. These practitioners need to know how to set up leadership development programs to deliver value from the beginning; how to keep the focus on the business impact throughout the process; how to follow up to see if the business impact has been delivered; and when needed or requested, how to show the financial ROI directly from the leadership development program. This book shows how to achieve this with excellent examples.

A third audience will be individuals who are involved in or support leadership in some way. This group includes the participants of the program, managers who have some of their own team involved, advisors to the leadership development team, leadership development facilitators, external consultants and designers and developers of leadership development programs. For individuals in any of these roles, this book provides further evidence that leadership development is making a difference and satisfying the appetites of the executive group.

CASE STUDIES

The case studies presented here represent a cross-section of leadership development programs with different levels of participants and in different types of organizational settings. We appreciate the organizations that allowed their projects to be included. The authors of the case studies are experienced, professional, knowledgeable, and on the leading edge of leadership development. Collectively, they represent practitioners, consultants, researchers, and professors.

ACKNOWLEDGMENTS

Rebecca Ray

I remain deeply appreciative of the opportunity to continue the important discussion about the role and impact of leadership development, this time through the detailed examination of real challenges and solutions articulated in this book. A special thanks to the executives who shared their stories with us and who see leadership development—lifting people to their highest potential and ensuring the continued success of an organization—as a noble calling. Over the years, the leaders I've worked with, the teams I've been part of, and the challenges I've had the good fortune to tackle have taught me many things, some of them about the subject matter, but many more of them about myself as a leader. One of my greatest professional pleasures is to partner with Jack and Patti—their insights make me smarter, their ability to inspire thousands to tackle and master a sometimes daunting challenge is humbling, and their generosity of spirit is boundless. I am very fortunate. How often does one get an opportunity to learn from legends? Finally, I wish to thank my muse.

Patti and Jack

We want to thank all the leaders we have worked with during the last 20 years in our work at the ROI Institute. Most of our projects take us to the middle and top leadership teams of organizations. We have had the pleasure of working with thousands of organizations and have witnessed what great leadership can do. The successful implementation of ROI in an organization is a direct result of great leadership for that function. We have seen firsthand that leaders can make a positive difference, and that they add value. We thank them for their efforts and applaud their accomplishments.

We also would like to acknowledge the great work of Rebecca Ray, executive vice president, knowledge organization and human capital lead at The Conference Board. Rebecca is an outstanding leader, who has led teams for learning and development and human resources in very high-profile organizations. She is also an outstanding teacher, speaker, writer, and researcher. She brings those skill sets quite effectively to The Conference Board. We are delighted to be working with her on another publication.

Finally, we want to thank the efforts of Hope Nicholas, director of publications for ROI Institute. Hope manages a very hectic schedule as we produce eight to 10 books each year with major publishers. Her great work shines through this manuscript; we are fortunate to have her with us and delighted to work with her again on another project.

Comments and Suggestions

As always, we welcome your comments, suggestions, and recommendations. This is the fifth book in the series and we have many more planned. Please send your thoughts directly to the authors or to ROI Institute at info@roiinstitute.net.

Patti Phillips
patti@roiinstitute.net

Jack Phillips
jack@roiinstitute.net

Rebecca Ray
Rebecca.Ray@conference-board.org

Atlanta, Georgia, and New York, New York

Part I

The ROI Methodology

A Credible Approach to Evaluating Your Leadership Development Programs

1

Leadership Development Is as Important as Leadership Itself

The famous British banker Nathan Rothschild once noted that great fortunes are made when cannonballs fall in the harbor, not when violins play in the ballroom. Rothschild understood that the more unpredictable the environment, the greater the opportunity—if you have the leadership skills to capitalize on this (Schoemaker, Krupp, and Howland 2013). This opening chapter outlines some of the current issues surrounding leadership development, the status of leadership development, and some of the challenges involved. It also sets the stage for the rest of the book by emphasizing the importance of leadership and leadership development.

THE TOP EXECUTIVE VIEW

Ask CEOs and C-suite leaders around the world about the top challenges they face and they will readily tell you that customer relationships, operational excellence, and innovation top their list of never-ending challenges. Human capital not only remains at the top, but is also seen as the lever, when managed effectively, with which to address other top challenges. Ask executive leadership how critical effective leaders are and they will tell you that without them, they cannot expand the business into new markets, drive innovation, achieve operational efficiency, retain customers, increase market share, or retain key talent. The Conference Board's 2014 CEO Challenge (Mitchell, Ray, and van Ark 2014) surveyed executive leaders and found that they planned to focus on the following human capital strategies during the next year:

1. Provide employee training and development.
2. Raise employee engagement.
3. Improve performance management processes and accountability.
4. Increase efforts to retain critical talent.
5. Improve leadership development programs.
6. Focus on internally developed talent to fill key roles.
7. Enhance the effectiveness of the senior management team.
8. Improve effectiveness of frontline supervisors and managers.
9. Improve corporate brand and employee value propositions to attract talent.
10. Improve succession planning for current and future needs.

Four of those strategies are focused on leaders or their development: Improve leadership development programs, enhance effectiveness of senior management teams, improve effectiveness of frontline supervisors and managers, and improve succession planning for current and future needs. Effective leaders, in turn, execute against the other strategies chosen by CEOs. Few would question the wisdom of having strong leaders and an adequate pipeline of future leaders; few would doubt that an agile and capable workforce is necessary to compete and win in an increasingly volatile, uncertain, complex, and ambiguous (VUCA) world. Indeed, there is a lot riding on the CEO's bet that leaders can create a high-performance organization that remains competitive. Are the leaders prepared and ready?

The Conference Board and Development Dimensions International (DDI) teamed up to determine the answer to that question. Together, they conducted the world's largest leadership development study, the *Global Leadership Forecast 2014/2015*, which surveyed more than 13,000 business leaders and more than 1,500 HR executives from more than 2,000 companies (Sinar, Wellins, Ray, Abel, and Neal 2014). Business leaders were asked to assess their own readiness to step up to the challenges identified by their CEOs. The results were dismal; no self-assessment broke the halfway mark—only 45 percent felt ready to address customer relationships, 33 percent felt ready to address operational excellence issues, 26 percent felt ready to take on the challenge of innovation, and only 27 percent felt they were able to address the human capital challenge. This is particularly bleak given the amount of time and resources that most organizations devote to developing leaders at the top of the organization, as well as helping managers be successful in their efforts to hire, develop, engage, and retain employees. Not only do these leaders have little confidence in their abilities, but organizations are spending a great deal of money with little to show for it. According to the Association for Talent Development's *2013 State of the Industry* report, investment in leadership and management development programs and initiatives in the United States alone is estimated to be more than 10 percent of the $164 billion spent on all employees, with another 4 percent focused on executive development (ASTD 2013).

In the 2014 CEO Challenge survey, CEOs were asked to select the leadership characteristics they felt were critical to future success (Mitchell, Ray, and van Ark 2014). On a global basis (and with a great deal of regional alignment), the attributes and behaviors they selected were integrity, leading change, managing complexity, entrepreneurial mindset, and retaining and developing talent. While one can argue that integrity cannot be trained, the other qualities must be mastered during a leader's rise to increasing levels of responsibility and reach.

The stakes continue to rise in this high-risk VUCA world. In 2015, CEOs again listed human capital as the top challenge on a global basis; they again selected four leadership development–related strategies among the top 10. In fact, two of the challenges—enhance effectiveness of the senior management team and improve succession planning for current and future needs—rose in importance as ranked by the Conference Board's 2015 CEO Challenge (Mitchell, Ray, and van Ark 2015). If we were to ask leaders to rate their own effectiveness in addressing the challenges that matter most to CEOs, it is not likely that their level of faith would be radically different. Therein lies the dilemma—CEOs may set a strategy in motion without the requisite leadership cadre to effectively execute it. And, all too often, that realization comes after the organization has already set the strategy in motion.

Recently, Accenture surveyed 1,300 C-suite and senior-suite executives in 13 industries in 16 countries. The goal was to understand what leaders are doing to face the critical and important changes facing their industries. Agile leaders are needed to address these many issues. Figure 1-1 is a summary of their research, which emphasizes what leaders must do and are doing to adjust to these changing environments (Smith, Silverstone, Brecher, and Upadhyaya 2015). This research underscores that the top-performing organizations are fully prepared for these changes, whereas the low performing organizations are falling woefully short.

FIGURE 1-1. Leadership Imperatives for an Agile Business

Vision and strategy	Relationship between leaders and followers	Driving results
Develop a long-term strategy built for change.	**Use an ensemble approach to building management teams.**	**Speed up decision making and the execution of those decisions.**
Leaders of top-performing companies are more likely to see uncertainty as an opportunity, not only a threat. They are able to balance short-term needs with long-term perspectives.	Leaders build effective teams by deploying executives and managers in a network that can flexibly shift and re-form to address challenges and opportunities as they arise.	Leaders establish a culture of making critical decisions at speed and then implement decisions with the scale, buy-in, and accountability needed to make it all stick.
Involve unconventional thinkers.	**Develop leadership skills at all levels of the organization.**	**Establish accountability.**
Leaders regularly bring thinkers from outside the mainstream into management meetings as a way to encourage new ideas.	Companies that are most adept at managing through uncertainty and volatility are those that are developing leaders at every level.	Leaders clarify expectations, roles, and responsibilities. They take action immediately when issues arise. They reward results, not just activity.

Source: Smith, Silverstone, Brecher, and Upadhyaya (2015).

STATUS OF LEADERSHIP DEVELOPMENT

We know that leadership matters. Leadership development matters, too. Some companies have built leadership development ecosystems that enable them to consistently develop the right leaders at the right time to execute the right strategy. Some of these successful organizations have earned a reputation as an "academy" company for leaders. What do they do that is different? What in their DNA sets them apart? Those were the central questions that shaped the report *DNA of Leaders: Leadership Development Secrets* (Ray and Learmond 2013).

There was no silver bullet for many of the world's best companies for leaders profiled in the study, including Shell, Wipro, Siemens, Unilever, Accenture, the Coca-Cola Company, American Express, Intel, BASF, Hewlett-Packard, Procter & Gamble, General Mills, Caterpillar, L'Oreal, McDonald's, Cardinal Health, and IBM. It was a combination of dedication to leadership development programs in good times and bad, active involvement of senior leaders beginning with the CEO, an integrated talent management strategy, and the relentless pursuit of quality outcomes and improvement. From that study, four overarching commonalities emerged. One in particular is especially germane to this conversation: "The success of leadership development programs and processes is increasingly measured by business linkage and impact" (Ray and Learmond 2013).

Since its initial offerings as a typical classroom session on the principles of leadership, the subject of leadership has evolved to become a critical part of organizational growth and development. How leaders are selected for programs and the specific ways in which programs are offered and structured are significant issues that define the current status.

How Leaders Are Selected for Development

Because leadership development can be one of the most expensive types of development and has so much potential for impact, selection must be a thoughtful process. At higher levels of the organization, participants in leadership development programs are often selected by the following methods:

- nomination by a manager
- cumulative data from performance management systems or past talent review discussions
- individual assessments and custom developmental plans based on their outcomes
- participation in an assessment center exercise
- behavioral or structured interviews.

At lower levels, participants are often selected versus screened out, and enter into a leadership development program by virtue of a promotion or a change in job title. For example, all new managers may be automatically enrolled in a particular program.

How Leaders Are Developed

In *Alice's Adventures in Wonderland*, Lewis Carroll wrote, "If you don't know where you are going, any road will get you there." This is also true with leadership development. Unless there is a clear road map, it may be a lovely journey, but one without a destination or committed travelers. The methods for development are varied and many are combined into programs and initiatives of infinite variety, including:

- formal training usually in a classroom (virtual or face-to-face)
- informal learning including self-guided or structured content
- action learning with a focus on strategic planning or innovation
- job shadowing
- coaching (either internal or external)
- mentoring
- experiential learning
- stretch assignments
- simulations
- community involvement
- community of practice or network involvement
- short-term rotational assignments
- long-term international assignments.

Years ago researchers created assignmentology, which is a way of mapping standard leadership competencies to specific opportunities for development, such as serving on a taskforce, chairing a major initiative, or assuming a role with a greatly expanded scope. The science of knowing what developmental experiences will result in specific competency improvements (and, by extension, what will not) is an extraordinary tool.

How Leadership Development Programs and Initiatives Are Structured

There will always be a need for a structured process of developing leaders. Simply dropping talented employees into the manager's chair robs them of the opportunity to continue being successful in completely new situations, and runs the risk of doing not only professional harm to the individual, but also organizational harm to those she works with. Deploying new leaders to different environments or challenging situations without careful planning and support is not a recipe for success either. Finally, simply hiring a new leader from the outside without considering the cultural assimilation challenges, internal communications, and talent implications is terribly short sighted.

This critical juncture should be carefully managed, and all stakeholders must be involved for mutual success. Most programs have one or more of these goals in mind for their leadership development programs and initiatives:

- Assess the bench strength of the current leadership and develop targeted plans to address deficiencies or placement issues for individuals, as well as organizational talent gaps that could impact strategy execution.
- Identify possible successors for critical roles.
- Enhance the effectiveness of current leaders by building specific competencies.
- Reduce the potential for derailers.
- Accelerate the development of high-potential and emerging leaders.
- Develop a strong leadership bench.
- Set standards of behavior and cultural norms.
- Leverage leaders' ability to develop and engage their employees, leading to increased levels of productivity, engagement, and retention.

Failure of Leadership Development Programs

The structure and effectiveness of leadership development (LD) programs is highly variable and, on the whole, disappointingly ineffective. In 2014 McKinsey surveyed 500 executives to explore the issues around the success of leadership development (Gurdjian, Halbeisen, and Lane 2014). This study uncovered some of the shortcomings of leadership development and identified four major reasons why leadership development fails:

1. **Overlooking context.** The context is a critical component because this reflects the job, the individual, and the current status of that individual. An executive may function extremely well in one environment, but have difficulties in another.

2. **Decoupling reflection from real work.** Leadership development programs often use skill-building activities, simulations, and skill practices, as well as provide ample opportunities to reflect on the current status and the changes needed in the future. However, while they look good and feel good in the classroom or virtual format, they may be disconnected from the real work environment.

3. **Underestimating mindsets.** Leaders come to leadership development programs with established mindsets. While they usually understand that the changes are needed, many programs fail to change their mindsets in a meaningful way.

4. **Failing to measure results.** Leadership development is often measured at Level 1 (reaction), Level 2 (learning), and sometimes at Level 3 in terms of skill application or competencies used on the job. However, leadership development needs to be connected to key business measures in the beginning and throughout the process. Measurements can reflect mismatches with the current context, the relevance of the program materials, and the current mindsets of the individuals.

The Myth of 70-20-10

The time devoted to learning about leadership is a critical issue. For decades, there has been an assumption that 70 percent of the time should be spent on the job with actual experiences; 20 percent learning from others, usually through coaching, mentoring, shadowing, and role modeling; and 10 percent in formal leadership development programs, the classroom, e-learning, or blended learning. This ratio comes from leaders who were asked to reflect on how they became effective leaders. Since leadership development has always included a small amount of time in the classroom, their input naturally reflected a small amount of formal learning. The rest was their best guess. The 70-20-10 theory was never meant to be a prescription for what should be done. A better approach is to ask leaders how *they* want to learn.

A recent study by The Conference Board and DDI, involving more than 13,000 leaders, 1,500 global human resource executives, and 2,000 participating companies, asked leaders about their optimal learning ratio (Sinar, Wellins, Ray, Abel, and Neal 2014; Figure 1-2). While 70-20-10 is the perception, this study found that, in reality, the ratio is 55-25-20. When the data were sorted for individuals with the highest quality leadership, the ratio became 52-27-21. This same group was asked to indicate how much additional time they would like to spend on leadership development per month. The leaders currently spend 5.4 hours per month on average, but they would prefer to spend 8.1 hours (nearly three hours more). When asked how they would prefer to spend their time, 76 percent said on formal learning, 71 percent said learning from others, and only 26 percent said on the job. These data clearly show that it is much better to plan the proper mix around the needs of the organizations and the needs of the leaders than to adhere to prescribed norms.

FIGURE 1-2. How and Where Leaders Are Developed

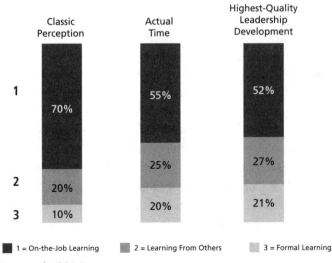

1 = On-the-Job Learning   2 = Learning From Others   3 = Formal Learning

Adapted from Sinar et al. (2014).

Managing Versus Leading

An important challenge for organizations is to increase the amount of time leaders spend leading instead of simply managing. Leaders spend much of their time on classic management skills, such as planning, organization, and control activities. Leading, on the other hand, involves skill sets that include interaction with employees. The following is a list of the critical skills from The Conference Board/DDI study:

- communicating and interacting with others
- building consensus and commitment
- coaching and developing others
- managing and successfully introducing change
- developing strong networks or partnerships
- identifying and developing future talent
- inspiring others toward a challenging future vision
- fostering employee creativity and innovation
- leading across generations
- integrating oneself into foreign environments
- intercultural communication
- leading across countries and cultures (Sinar et al. 2014).

These powerful skill sets can make a huge difference in an organization and many are critical to the organization's success.

This is a classic organizational issue, where the perception is that an organization typically values spending more time on managing and less time on leading. Among the surveyed executives, 41 percent of their time was spent on managing and only 25 percent on leading. However, they would have preferred the reverse (22 percent managing and 40 percent leading). The challenge for organizations is to encourage and build environments that support spending more time on leading, which is where most of the payoff would be.

Global Versus Local Leadership Programs

For global organizations, an important challenge is determining who controls the leadership and talent development programs. In some organizations, programs are dictated by corporate to ensure consistency with the organization's mission, vision, and values. The opposite extreme is when locally owned programs are developed in the countries where their leaders reside, addressing the needs and cultural issues in that area. Neither situation is ideal. The better approach is to have a good balance of corporate and local control. Corporate is more involved in mid-level to high-level leadership development; frontline leadership development is typically a balance between local and corporate control. Succession planning, on the other hand, is a local issue that involves candidates in those areas. This balancing process is an important consideration for human capital strategy.

MEASURING THE RESULTS

That brings us to the heart of this book, which examines the ways in which great programs for leadership development can be measured, articulated, and leveraged to advance the work being done to ensure the company's future. *Measuring the Success of Leadership Development* will provide step-by-step guidance for ROI and show the impact of leadership development programs and initiatives.

It is important to begin with an understanding of the big picture. Figure 1-3 presents the success factors for leadership development as identified by a survey of 232 leadership development directors (Phillips, Phillips, and Ray 2012). The factors, listed in the order they normally occur in the leadership development process, were developed from hundreds of studies on leadership development and through other research. They represent a solid design for increased accountability, particularly when impact and ROI measurements are desired.

FIGURE 1-3. Success Factors for Leadership Development

1.	Align the program to business measures in the beginning.	☐
2.	Identify specific behavior changes needed for the target audience.	☐
3.	Identify learning needs for the target audience.	☐
4.	Establish application and impact objectives for LD programs.	☐
5.	Involve the right kind of people at the right time.	☐
6.	Design leadership development for successful learning and application.	☐
7.	Create expectations to achieve results and provide data.	☐
8.	Address the learning transfer issue early and often.	☐
9.	Establish supportive partnerships with key managers.	☐
10.	Select the proper data sets for the desired evaluation level.	☐
11.	Build data collection into the process and position it as an application tool.	☐
12.	Isolate the effects of the program on impact data.	☐
13.	Be proactive and develop impact and ROI analyses for major programs.	☐
14.	Use data collected at different levels for adjustments and improvements.	☐

FINAL THOUGHTS

This opening chapter sets the stage for how to measure the success of leadership development. It reviewed the status of leadership development, how it is progressing, and the challenges along the way. It also provided examples of how leadership development is provided and some of the issues surrounding various types of programs. The clear concept throughout the process is that leadership development must be measured all the way to impact and sometimes even to ROI. The next chapter focuses on building accountability in leadership development.

REFERENCES

American Society for Training & Development (ASTD). 2013. *2013 State of the Industry*. Alexandria, VA: ASTD Press.

Gurdjian, P., T. Halbeisen, and K. Lane. 2014. "Why Leadership Development Programs Fail." *McKinsey Quarterly*, January.

Mitchell, C., R.L. Ray, and B. van Ark. 2014. *The Conference Board CEO Challenge 2014: People and Performance*. New York: The Conference Board.

Mitchell, C., R.L. Ray, and B. van Ark. 2015. *The Conference Board CEO Challenge 2015: Creating Opportunity Out of Adversity*. New York: The Conference Board.

Phillips, J.J., P.P. Phillips, and R.L. Ray. 2012. *Measuring Leadership Development: Quantify Your Program's Impact and ROI on Organizational Performance*. New York: McGraw-Hill.

Ray, R., and D. Learmond. 2013. *DNA of Leaders: Leadership Development Secrets*. New York: The Conference Board.

Schoemaker, P., S. Krupp, and S. Howland. 2013. "Strategic Leadership: The Essential Skills." *Harvard Business Review*, January.

Sinar, E., R.S. Wellins, R. Ray, A.L. Abel, and S. Neal. 2014. *Global Leadership Forecast 2014|2015 Ready-Now Leaders: Meeting Tomorrow's Business Challenges*. New York: The Conference Board; Pittsburgh, PA: Development Dimensions International.

Smith, D., Y. Silverstone, D. Brecher, and P. Upadhyaya. 2015. "Leadership Imperatives for an Agile Business." *Accenture Strategy*.

2

System for Accountability

While culture was once perceived as a vague concept, many organizations are recognizing its importance. The position of chief culture officer (CCO), which is held at a number of progressive organizations, is discussed in "The Rise of the Chief Culture Officer," an article in the July 2012 edition of *Fortune* magazine. The CCO's primary duty is to focus on maintaining the core parts of the culture that contribute to the organization's success.

While organizational culture is increasingly observed as a critical factor in success, the implications of measurement are also significant. To build a culture of measurement certain steps need to be taken, and it is in this context that the ROI Methodology is presented. In this chapter, we address using the ROI Methodology with leadership development, and how LD practitioners are a conduit of change in building a measurement culture.

HIGH-PERFORMING CULTURE AND MEASUREMENT

High-performing cultures have been associated with strong financial outcomes; however, these cultures also have strong employee motivation and performance. Research has shown that there are specific cultural characteristics directly related to organization effectiveness and outcomes. High-performance organizations tend to have cultures that share five common traits.

1. **Empowering Style Leadership:** Leaders communicate with respect and lead by example. Employees are empowered to use their judgment to make decisions and take action in their day-to-day jobs. Employees are not present to serve management or reinforce bureaucracy. Leadership is supportive of employees, with focus on helping to support employees so they can focus on caring for customers.

2. **Collaborative Environment:** This type of environment is inclusive; employees have a sense of belonging, with everyone sharing the responsibilities of identifying problems and coming up with solutions. These types of organizations are highly participatory.

3. **Strong Core Values:** Values of respect, loyalty, and integrity are embedded in leadership behaviors toward employees, and infuse the organization.

4. **Planning:** Employees know what the long-term plans are for the company and how to get there. Strategy is well-defined and priorities are clear. Plans are clearly articulated and there are specific measures to assess a plan's success. Employees know what is important for the organization and what is required to do their jobs effectively.

5. **Measurement and Feedback:** High-performing organizations not only plan and prioritize what is most important for the business, but also provide indicators and measures to know whether they are hitting the mark or not. *Data-driven organizations* is another way to describe this environment. Employees receive ongoing feedback so performance is collaboratively assessed as it relates to the business.

Organizational cultural characteristics play a pivotal role in organization effectiveness. Measurement and feedback is one of the components of a high-performing culture. There are many benefits for creating a measurement-oriented organization culture. The following are just a few at the top of the list:

1. **Measurement cultures lay the foundation for organization learning.** Information sharing is leveraged in the organization toward knowledge and growth. Data-driven organizations make this possible.

2. **Measurement cultures provide the way for departments to track their progress.** Managers have the ability to track progress toward department goals. What happens if the project that is implemented is a flop? Or if needs are not fully met? Tracking along the way allows for modifications if needed to move outcomes in a favorable direction.

3. **Measurement cultures make data-driven decisions.** The use of the hunch takes second place to making decisions based on data. If a project is not going in the direction it needs to go, then the data will validate this point. And collecting the right data should help pinpoint where things broke down.

HOW AND WHY LEADERSHIP DEVELOPMENT FITS WITH ROI

LD practitioners tend to be more socially driven (to help others) rather than financially driven. So what would drive an LD practitioner to pursue ROI? Perhaps this is best answered by considering how and why ROI helps the process, and ultimately, helps the client by showing how the intervention has yielded the desired change.

The LD Practitioner as a Change Agent

Practitioners often view their role as one who influences an individual, group, or organization toward desired change. The change agent plays a significant role in leading the change effort or collaborating with the team assigned to initiating change. Trying to create an environment that is measurement friendly also involves a change agent—someone to lead this effort and manage the change process within an organization.

It is important to remember that building a measurement culture should be a strategic change. The change agent must set the stage with the "why" behind building a measurement culture, make sure that the change effort is in sync with what's important for the organization, and include action planning and feedback to keep the momentum building. Involving people who are senior in the organization also helps because they have the clout necessary to pave the way for building a measurement culture.

Identify a System to Routinely Review Measures

Adopting a systematic way to plan, collect, analyze, and report on initiatives in the organization sets in motion the process of communicating and reinforcing what is important to the organization, while sending a clear message to key stakeholders as to what needs to change to improve outcomes. This is particularly true when measurement has been planned in advance to collect data points that will tell the story in a comprehensive way. The ROI Methodology is a proven approach to plan, collect, analyze, and communicate outcomes that measure organization development initiatives.

Table 2-1 shows a clear delineation between activity-based and results-based initiatives. The old "if you build it, they will come" mentality is challenged through a series of filtering questions.

- Is this initiative aligned with business impact or organization effectiveness outcomes?
- Is there an assessment of performance that shows a gap in performance?
- Is the work environment prepared to reinforce the implementation of leadership development?
- Have partnerships been established with key stakeholders to support this initiative?
- Are there specific measurable objectives for expected behavior change and business impact?

When leadership development programs are aligned with results-based initiatives or what's important to the organization, it becomes more likely that LD initiatives are easily measured and supported. The old adage rings true in this context: What gets measured gets done.

TABLE 2-1. Activity-Based Versus Results-Based Approach to Leadership Development

Activity-Based	Results-Based
Business need is not linked to the organization development initiative in terms of monetary impact.	Initiative is linked to specific business impact or organizational effectiveness measures.
Assessments of performance issues addressed in an organization development initiative are not captured in a quantifiable, measureable manner.	There is a gap assessment of performance effectiveness that needs to be closed.
Specific, measurable, quantifiable objectives are not clarified.	Specific, measurable objectives for behavior change and the related business impact are identified.
Employees are not fully engaged or prepared to participate in the project.	Results expectations are communicated with, and in partnership with, employees.
The work environment is not prepared to reinforce the application or implementation of the organization development initiative to ensure behavior change and business impact.	The work environment is prepared to reinforce the application or implementation of the organization development initiative to ensure behavior change and business impact.
Partnerships with key stakeholders to support the implementation have not been identified or developed.	Partnerships are established with key stakeholders prior to implementation to ensure participation and support.
Results or cost-benefit analysis in real, tangible, and objective measures—including monetary impact—are not captured.	Results and cost-benefit analysis are measured.
Planning and reporting is input focused.	Planning and reporting is outcome focused.

The ROI Methodology

The role of measurement and evaluation is crucial for establishing the impact and credibility of leadership. It is time for the field to fully accept its roots in a data-driven approach and understand the value inherent in measuring how and what we do.

Several features about return on investment make it an effective measure for leadership development:

- **To show bottom-line results for leadership development.** Return on investment represents the ultimate range of measurement—a comparison of the actual cost of a project to its monetary benefits. This is done by using the same standard ratio that accountants have used for years to show the return on investment for a variety of investments, such as technology, equipment, and buildings.

- **Return on investment has a rich history of application.** The ROI Methodology is not a passing trend used in today's organizations. It is a measure of accountability that has been in place for centuries. When resources are invested to address a business need, the ROI Methodology shows the financial impact of the investment.

- **To speak the same language as senior management.** Most managers in an organization have knowledge and skills about how to manage a business. Some have degrees in business administration. These managers understand the need for a process to establish solid business cases and calculating a return on investment. They use ROI for a variety of projects and are fluid in carrying on conversations that measure the monetary results from large investments.

- **Return on investment generates a high degree of attention among key stakeholders.** The positive ROI outcomes create buzz and attention, particularly when the ROI value exceeds expectations. Most stakeholders involved in leadership development projects intuitively believe that the interventions add value. Return on investment, as a measurement tool, confirms this hunch using a credible and valid process.

- **Using ROI Methodology forces the issue of strategic alignment.** By following the steps in the ROI process, conducting diagnostics with the multilevel framework for understanding business and performance needs, leadership development will be more closely aligned with the strategic and operational needs of the business.

Gone are the days of indiscriminately increasing human capital investments with no evidence as to their impact on the business. In times of budget cuts, human capital rises to the top of consideration and leadership development projects are no exception.

These five factors are foundational for executives and leadership development practitioners to rethink the use of ROI Methodology and to implement this type of evaluation in specific projects. Through the use of ROI Methodology, stakeholder groups receive a comprehensive set of significant and balanced information about the success of a leadership development intervention.

TYPES OF DATA FOR THE ROI METHODOLOGY

At the heart of the ROI Methodology is the variety of data collected throughout the process and reported at different intervals. Some of the data are assigned a level because they reflect a successive effect in which one type of data affects the next. The concept of levels is an old one. There are very logical steps of succession in a number of tasks and fields, and their use in a sequence can be linked to a variety of guidelines and models. The medical field uses levels in running and analyzing blood work. This not only helps the clinician to understand the categories represented by the levels, but also helps the patient understand the results. The ROI Methodology is based on levels of evaluation, as shown in Figure 2-1.

As the evaluation moves to the higher levels, the value ascribed to the data by the client increases. However, the degree of effort and cost of capturing the data for the higher levels of evaluation generally increase as well. With proper project planning and preparation, costs can be minimized.

Project Input Data

Level 0, inputs and indicators, represents a category of data that reveals the volume, time, and cost of leadership development programs. It includes the number of people involved and the time of their involvement, representing a fully loaded cost profile. It reflects all direct and indirect costs. Level 0 data do not represent outcome data, but they are important because they represent the investment in leadership.

Reaction Data

The first category of outcome data collected from a program is basic reaction data (Level 1 evaluation). This type of data represents the immediate reaction to the program from a variety of key stakeholders, particularly participants who have the responsibility to make it work. At this level, a variety of basic reaction measures are taken, often representing five to 15 separate measures to gain insight into the value, importance, relevance, and usefulness of the program.

Learning Data

As the program continues, new information is acquired and new skills are learned. This level of measurement (Level 2) focuses on the changes in knowledge and skill acquisition, and details what still needs to be learned. Some solutions have a high learning component, such as those involved in comprehensive, long-term leadership development programs. Others may have a low learning component, such as brief team-building sessions. In some cases, the focus is on organization learning or departmental skill development.

Application and Implementation Data

Application and implementation are key measures that show the extent to which behavior is changed or performance is improved. This type of data reflects how actions are taken, adjustments are made, new skills are applied, habits are changed, and steps in a new process are initiated as a result of the leadership development.

This is one of the most powerful categories of data because it uncovers not only the extent to which the leadership development is implemented, but also the reasons for lack of success. At this level, barriers and enablers to application and implementation are detailed, and a complete profile of performance change at the various steps of implementation is provided.

FIGURE 2-1. Six Categories of Data

Level	Measurement Focus	Typical Measures
0–Inputs and Indicators	• Inputs into the initiatives including indicators representing scope, volumes, times, costs, and efficiencies	• Types of topics or content • Number of programs • Number of people • Hours of involvement • Costs
1–Reaction and Planned Action	• Reaction to the initiative including the perceived value of the project	• Relevance • Importance • Usefulness • Appropriateness • Intent to use • Motivational • Recommended to others
2–Learning	• Knowledge gained, learning how to use the content and materials, including the confidence to use what was learned	• Skills • Learning • Knowledge • Capacity • Competencies • Confidences • Contacts
3–Application and Implementation	• Application, change in performance, use of content and materials in the work environment, including progress with implementation	• Behavior change • Extent of use • Task completion • Frequency of use • Actions completed • Success with use • Barriers to use • Enablers to use
4–Impact	• The impact of the use of the content and materials expressed as business impact and effectiveness measures	• Productivity • Revenue • Quality • Time • Efficiency • Accidents and incidents • Customer satisfaction • Employee engagement
5–ROI	• Comparison of monetary benefits from the program to program costs	• Benefit-cost ratio (BCR) • ROI (%) • Payback period

Business Impact Data

Behavior change or actions taken in application and implementation have consequences. These can be described in one or more measures representing an influence on the work environment, such as a direct impact to a given team or department, or as an impact to other parts of the organization.

This level of data (Level 4) reflects the specific business impact and may include measures such as output, quality, costs, time, job satisfaction, and customer satisfaction, which have been influenced by the application and implementation of the leadership development program. A direct link between the business impact and the program must be established for the program to drive business value. At this level of analysis, a technique must be used to isolate the effects of the program from other influences that may be driving the same measure. Answering the following question is imperative: "How do you know it was the leadership development program that caused the improvement and not something else?"

ROI Data

This level of measurement compares the monetary value of the business impact measures with the actual cost of the program. It is the ultimate level of accountability and represents the financial impact directly linked with the program, expressed as a benefit-cost ratio (BCR) or return-on-investment percentage. This measure is the fifth level of evaluation (Level 5). It requires converting business impact data to monetary value and comparing that value with the fully loaded cost of the program.

Intangible Data

Intangible data consist of measures that are not converted to monetary value. In some cases, however, converting certain measures to monetary values is not credible with a reasonable amount of resources. In these situations, data are listed as an intangible, but only if they are linked to the leadership development.

Satisfaction leads to learning, which leads to behavior change, which leads to business impact, and ultimately to return on investment. At the business impact level, the effects of the intervention must be isolated from other influences. In addition, business impact data are converted to monetary value and compared with the cost of the intervention to develop the return on investment. Stakeholders will more readily understand this chain of impact as they consider the long-term success of leadership development. It is a novel yet pragmatic way to show results.

The good news is that the ROI Methodology works extremely well in all types of environments and projects, particularly in leadership development. An initiative would likely be unsuccessful if an adverse reaction occurred, so the first level is critical. An element of learning is also required to make an initiative successful. Regardless of the type of initiative involved, those participating usually acquire knowledge and skills, and some projects even require significant skill development. However, learning does not guarantee success. Follow-up is needed to ensure that the knowledge and skills are used appropriately. Therefore, application and implementation are critical for effectiveness; failure in these areas is typically what causes project failure overall.

The most important data set for those who sponsor projects is the impact, the consequence of application, which is often expressed in business terms as output, quality, costs, and time. For some executives, showing the impact of an intervention isn't enough—they want to know something else, which pushes the evaluation to the ultimate level of accountability: return on investment. The return on investment converts the amount of the improvement at the impact level (attributed to the program) to money, and compares that with the cost of the program.

SELECTING PROGRAMS FOR ROI ANALYSIS

Every leadership development program should be evaluated in some way, even if it's only collecting reaction data from those involved in the program. Reaction data alone may be sufficient for evaluating some programs, but the challenge is to collect additional data at higher levels, and to do so when it is relevant and feasible.

Appropriate evaluation is usually determined when the program is initiated, recognizing that the evaluation level may change throughout the life of the program. For example, the UN raises awareness on gender equality, with an objective to increase awareness and advocacy for women. The awareness factors can be evaluated with reaction (Level 1) and learning (Level 2) data, ensuring that awareness and learning take place. Later, a follow-up may be implemented to determine whether the information provided in the intervention and actions were taken toward advocacy for women. This follow-up is an example of behavior change and performance evaluation (Level 3).

If the cost of this program increases, sponsors may ask to evaluate the impact (Level 4) and even ROI (Level 5) of the program. The important point is that during the life of a program, the desired level of evaluation may change. Because of the resources required and the realistic barriers for ROI implementation, ROI analysis is used only for those programs that meet several criteria, as outlined in the following pages.

Recommended Programs for Evaluation at Lower Levels

Reaction evaluation can suffice as the only level of evaluation for short interventions, such as briefings, policy introductions, and general information that is distributed. If reaction to the intervention is critical, however, ongoing assessment may be necessary. For example, if a leadership ethics briefing is measured at Level 1, it is important to capture the extent to which employees perceive the program as fair, appropriate, and helpful.

Learning evaluation (Level 2) is suitable when learning, knowledge, or skills are needed. With most leadership development programs, learning evaluation is important. For example, one organization offered a series of videos profiling how leaders achieved their success. The evaluation, which stopped at Level 2, assessed whether each participant took away key leadership principles.

Behavior change and performance evaluation (Level 3) is necessary when the target audience must perform or behave in a particular way as a result of the intervention. For example, most team leaders are required to use team leadership skills in directing their teams' use of new processes. Evaluation at Level 3 may be necessary to measure success. Observations may be used to ensure that they are using the desired behavior with their teams. Other methods are also available to evaluate key interventions at Level 3, depending on the needs and culture of the organization.

Deciding which type of evaluation to use is sometimes a trade-off depending on the resources available and the amount of disruption allowed collecting data. Because some data collection at this level may disrupt work at varying degrees or inconvenience those involved in some way, the evaluation needs to be balanced with the time, effort, and resources that can be committed to the process. Many organizations fall short of the ideal evaluation, instead settling for a feasible approach within existing constraints.

Recommended Programs for Impact and ROI Analysis

Programs taken to the levels of business impact and ROI analysis meet certain criteria; it's important to understand the contributions they make to the organization. Programs for this level of analysis must be carefully selected.

Expected Duration of the Program

The first criterion is the duration of the program. Some programs are brief, designed to react to a particular aspect of a team, and ROI analysis may not be necessary. Facilitating a one-hour Myers-Briggs Type Indicator session with an intact work team is an example of a short-cycle program. ROI evaluation at this level may not be necessary. On the other hand, some programs have a longer life cycle, such as a three-week executive leadership program. Consequently, at some point in the life cycle of this program, conducting a comprehensive analysis may be helpful.

Linkage to Strategic Initiatives

Strategic initiatives are those designed to address specific strategic objectives. These strategic initiatives are so important that they should be subjected to a high level of scrutiny. For example, a chain of retail stores implemented a leadership program to support a strategic goal that would transform the way the sales staff interacts with customers. The program was a multiyear change and became a candidate for ROI analysis because it was linked to this strategic initiative.

Cost of the Intervention

High-cost programs need to be evaluated in a comprehensive manner to ensure they are adding value—the higher the cost, the greater the need for ROI analysis. For example, an ROI analysis was warranted when a gold-mining company in Canada implemented a $6 million leadership development program for first-level managers.

Time Commitment

Programs that involve large amounts of time are also suitable candidates for business impact and ROI analysis. This is different than the duration criterion, because it's about the segments of time that participants are sacrificing to participate. If a significant amount of time is taken from their jobs to support the program, this is a good reason for pursuing the higher level of analysis. For example, executives from a pharmaceutical company questioned the value of a 360-degree feedback process because it required so much of the managers' time. The time involved ultimately led to an ROI study.

Visibility of the Intervention

Highly visible interventions lead to the need for accountability at higher levels. For example, a large South African electric utility conducted a two-week leadership program, the Leadership Challenge, each year for middle-level managers who were destined to be top executives. Extensive publicity made it a high-profile initiative; thus, it was important to show the business impact and monetary value of the program.

Management Interest

The extent of management interest is often the most critical issue in driving programs for impact and ROI analysis. Senior management has concerns about some programs, but not all of them. Sometimes, management interest may go hand-in-hand with visibility or costs associated with the program. For example, an impact study was conducted when executives at a financial services company questioned the impact of the program Seven Habits of Effective Managers, and how it contributed to improvement measures.

Client Requirement

Particularly since the global recession, sponsors of leadership development programs want to know the results. Executives are increasingly concerned about expenditures, so for major and significant programs, they may require an ROI calculation. For example, a major European oil company required an impact study for an executive leadership intervention developed by a prestigious university on the U.S. West Coast. The top executives said, "We must see results from this program because it takes a lot of time, money, and resources."

Programs Unsuitable for ROI Analysis

There are factors to consider that help filter out programs that are unsuitable for ROI analysis. Programs that are mandated are often not good candidates for ROI analysis. For example, take a series of performance tools, such as guides, tips, and notes, made available to all leaders. These are reinforcing tools that are unlikely to generate much behavior change, which makes evaluation questionable. Due to the limited resources for this level of analysis, the mandated leadership programs are typically not subject to ROI evaluation unless executives want to pursue it for some reason.

As noted, programs of short duration are also inappropriate for impact and ROI analysis. A change in behavior must take place for a program to add value, and brief programs do not typically drive this type of change.

ROI PROCESS MODEL

Measurement and evaluation must be systematic, following a routine process that can be duplicated to a variety of projects. The ROI Process Model is a 10-step process, illustrated in Figure 2-2. The process begins with the end in mind, by creating objectives, and proceeds until an impact report is generated. The model is highly adaptable to the needs of the project in question, as the evaluation can stop at any point along the process. The data collected during the intervention at Level 1 and Level 2, and data collected after the intervention at Levels 3 and 4, are steps along the way. This process will be explained in further detail in chapters 3 through 6.

FINAL THOUGHTS

This chapter has provided not only an explanation of a measurement culture but also presented why it is so important in the context of leadership development. Building on the premise that measurement culture matters, this chapter explored ways for leadership development practitioners to be change agents and build a measurement culture within the organizations in which they work. Finally, an introduction to the ROI Methodology was provided as a process to use in building measurement cultures.

FIGURE 2-2. ROI Methodology Process Model

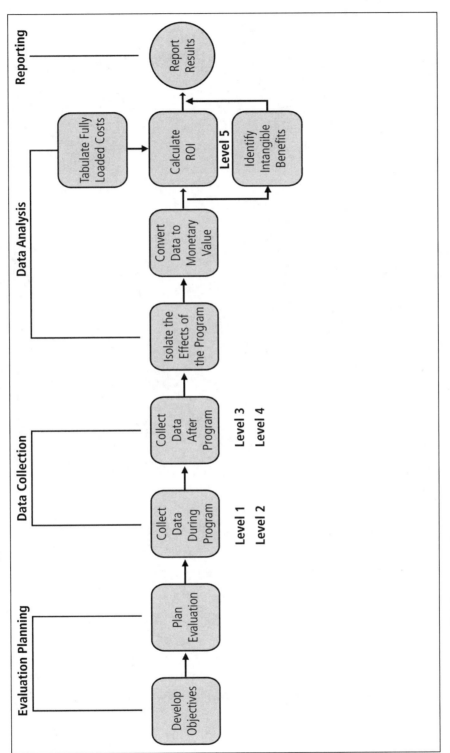

3

Alignment of Programs and Evaluation Planning

In far too many situations, leadership development programs are implemented without a complete picture of the reason for the program. Pursuing initiatives without knowing why and not identifying clear performance or business needs or measures up front can be disastrous in today's economic climate. Evaluation is too often an afterthought. This chapter explores why it is important to plan ahead, how to align programs with business needs using the V-Model, the process of integrating needs with the evaluation, and the steps and artifacts included in evaluation planning.

ACHIEVING THE PROPER ALIGNMENT

The basis for a leadership development program adding value rests on the rationale for its existence and the extent to which it relates to a specific business need. This fundamental concept requires thorough needs analysis, which is foundational to the beginning point in the ROI Methodology. As described earlier, conducting diagnosis or assessment of the organization's needs allows the leadership development practitioner to determine, with the help of the client, the necessary programs. This also sets the stage for collecting any necessary data and minimizing defensiveness and resistance.

While there are a variety of methods for doing a needs analysis, it is critical to integrate the ROI Methodology when measuring at higher levels of evaluation.

For example, let's assume that during the analysis phase two findings emerge: high turnover and low productivity. This is where the analysis phase moves to inquiring about what leadership behaviors, rewards, and helpful mechanisms may be contributing to the high turnover and decreased productivity. And in this case, we discover that leadership behavior is causing most of the problems, but that the organization's leaders are not aware of how profound the problem is. The solution in this case involves increasing awareness as well as developing leaders to behave in productive ways. Not only does this approach help to identify the right solution, but it sets into motion relevant goals and measures. Two key questions follow that will help to quantify the gap that exists: What is the ideal or desired state? What is the current state?

The V-Model (Figure 3-1) is a powerful method to ensure business alignment. The V-Model maps the connection of needs analysis from programs to objectives and evaluation. This figure shows the important links between the initial problem or opportunity that created the need for the program and its evaluation. It also shows the three points at which business alignment occurs: the beginning of the program, during the program, and during the follow-up evaluation in order to validate the alignment.

FIGURE 3-1. Alignment With the V-Model

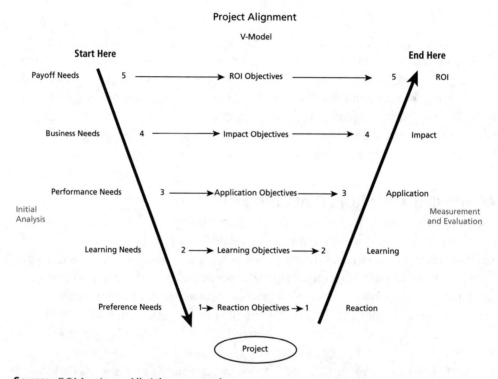

Source: ROI Institute. All rights reserved.

The V-Model is based on the concept of the five levels of evaluation. As we will explore throughout this book, leadership development is a natural candidate for the ROI Methodology and its alignment process.

It's best to think of the V-Model in terms of the evaluation side first. Evaluation moves through different levels of measurement:

- reaction to the program (Level 1)
- learning; skills and knowledge gained (Level 2)
- behavior change; application of skills and knowledge use (Level 3)
- impact measures linked to the program (Level 4)
- ROI; a comparison of monetary benefits with the cost of the program (Level 5).

From the viewpoint of key stakeholders, such as the clients or sponsors, the higher levels are more important, because most clients want to see the business contribution (Level 4) and even sometimes ROI (Level 5). In terms of evaluation, Level 4 is where an isolation technique is applied to specify how much improvement comes directly from the program. This step ensures that business alignment is confirmed.

The measures that are captured at each level are defined in the objectives. There are five corresponding levels of objectives, as illustrated in Figure 3-1. The objectives increase in importance as the levels progress, with Levels 4 and 5 often being the most valuable from a client's perspective. These objectives are developed during the needs assessment, which defines particular needs at each level. Here, the highest and most important level is the potential payoff of the program, followed by business, performance, learning, and preference needs.

Level 5, Payoff Needs

Needs assessment occurring at Level 5 addresses the potential payoff opportunity for an organization. This step examines the possibility for a return on investment before the program is pursued. The first part of the process is to determine whether the problem is worth solving or if the opportunity warrants serious consideration. This is obvious in cases where there are serious problems affecting the organization's operations and strategy. For example, at a hospital, an annual 32 percent turnover rate of critical talent is an obvious payoff opportunity. Another example is an organization in which new account growth is flat and customer loyalty is low, based on industry standards. These types of payoff opportunities make it clear that there is a problem that needs to be solved or an opportunity that should be pursued with a clearly identified business need.

Others represent not-so-obvious payoff opportunities, such as a request to implement a leadership development program or a succession management process. When this is the case, the business measures of importance become more evident during Level 4 analysis.

During Level 5 analysis, it is important to not only identify the business measures that need to improve, when possible, but also convert them into monetary values so the anticipated economic benefit of addressing the opportunity is evident. The monetary value of the payoff is useful not only in identifying the scope of the opportunity, but also in forecasting the potential ROI. When the solution(s) is identified and targets for improvement as a result of the solution are set, it is important to determine an approximate cost for the entire project. With the approximate program cost and the monetary value of the opportunity in hand, you can forecast the ROI in order to indicate the potential payoff for investing in a particular program. While this practice may not be feasible for some programs, it is often important with very expensive, strategic, or critical programs.

Level 4, Business Needs

At Level 4, business data that indicate movement toward addressing the payoff need are examined to determine which measures are in most need of improvement. Ideally, leadership development should improve the business measures listed in Tables 3-1 and 3-2. When cross-functional programs are anticipated, each participant could have a different business need. This may involve having participants bring one, two, or three measures (business needs) to improve, using the competencies with their teams. This is very powerful because leadership development is now customized to the participants at the impact level.

TABLE 3-1. Examples of Hard Data

OUTPUT	QUALITY	COSTS	TIME
• Completion rate	• Failure rates	• Shelter costs	• Cycle time
• Units produced	• Dropout rates	• Treatment costs	• Equipment
• Tons manufactured	• Scrap	• Budget variances	downtime
• Items assembled	• Waste	• Unit costs	• Overtime
• Money collected	• Rejects	• Cost by account	• On-time shipments
• Items sold	• Error rates	• Variable costs	• Time to project
• New accounts	• Rework	• Fixed costs	completion
generated	• Shortages	• Overhead costs	• Processing time
• Forms processed	• Product defects	• Operating costs	• Setup time
• Loans approved	• Deviation from	• Program cost	• Time to proficiency
• Inventory turnover	standard	savings	• Learning time
• Patients visited	• Product failures	• Accident costs	• Meeting schedules
• Applications	• Inventory	• Program costs	• Repair time
processed	adjustments	• Sales expense	• Efficiency
• Students	• Time card	• Participant costs	• Work stoppages
graduated	corrections		• Order response
• Tasks completed	• Incidents		• Late reporting
• Output per hour	• Compliance		• Lost time days
• Productivity	discrepancies		
• Work backlog	• Agency fees		
• Incentive bonus			

TABLE 3-2. Examples of Soft Data

WORK HABITS	CUSTOMER SERVICE	WORK CLIMATE/ SATISFACTION	EMPLOYEE DEVELOPMENT AND ADVANCEMENT
• Tardiness • Visits to the dispensary • Violations of safety rules • Communication breakdowns • Excessive breaks	• Customer complaints • Customer dissatisfaction • Customer impressions • Customer loyalty • Customer retention • Customer value • Lost customers	• Grievances • Discrimination charges • Employee complaints • Job satisfaction • Organization commitment • Employee engagement • Employee loyalty • Intent to leave • Stress	• Promotions • Capability • Intellectual capital • Programs completed • Requests for transfer • Performance appraisal ratings • Readiness • Networking

This may involve a review of organizational databases, examining all types of hard and soft data. Sometimes, the performance of one of the data items triggers the leadership development program. For example, the business measure is easily pinpointed when sales are not as much as they should be, operating costs are excessive, product quality is deteriorating, or productivity is low. These are key measures that come directly from data in the organization and are often found in the operating databases.

These business needs are arranged in categories of hard data to include output, quality, cost, and time. Examples are sales, production, errors, waste, accidental costs, downtime, project time, and compliance fines. These measures exist in any type of organization, even in the public sector and among nonprofits and nongovernment organizations (NGOs). They often attract the attention of executives and chief administrators because they represent business impact. An important goal is to connect the project to one or more of these measures. Impact measures can be subjective, such as customer service, image, work climate, customer satisfaction, job satisfaction, engagement, reputation, and teamwork.

In other cases, business alignment with leadership development may involve a review of HR measures, such as:
- talent retention, turnover, and turnover costs
- employee engagement
- job satisfaction
- employee complaints, grievances
- absenteeism, tardiness

- teamwork
- accidents, incidents
- performance ratings
- employee transfers, promotions.

These are examples of measures that may be relevant for a leadership develop-ment program. Although these measures are not as important as measures of output, quality, cost, and time, they are still important, and in some cases are the primary measures of interest for a leadership development program. Soft data are sometimes reported as a program's intangible benefits because they cannot always be converted to money credibly or with a minimum amount of resources. But they can be important business measures and, if improved, can help an organization take advantage of a payoff opportunity.

Level 3, Performance Needs

The Level 3 analysis involves determining performance needs or gaps that will contrib-ute to improving the business measures. The task is to determine what is causing the problem (or creating the opportunity) identified at Level 4 (for example, what is caus-ing the business to be below the desired level). What should the organization be doing more or less of? Is there something the organization should be doing differently? Per-formance tools or systems, inadequate technology, and broken or ineffective pro-cesses are all examples of performance needs.

The desired and current state should reveal performance needs. The reason for the inadequate performance is the basis for the solution or the project. For example, if customer complaints have increased, and it is discovered that the technology used by customer service is outdated and slow, then the technology that supports customer service representatives is the cause of the problem and needs to be resolved.

Performance needs can be uncovered using a variety of problem-solving or analy-sis techniques. This may involve the use of data collection techniques, such as surveys, questionnaires, focus groups, or interviews. The key is to determine the causes of the problem so that solutions can be developed. Sometimes one solution can address the performance need; other times there are multiple solutions and then a decision must be made as to which one to pursue, if pursuing all is not an option. ROI forecasting is one way to help make the decision.

Level 2, Learning Needs

During the Level 2 learning needs assessment, the specific information, knowledge, or skills that are required to address the performance needs are identified. Analysis may reveal learning deficiencies, in terms of knowledge and skills that can contribute to the problem. In other situations, the solution will need a learning component as employ-ees learn how to implement a new process, procedure, or technology. The learning typically involves the acquisition of knowledge or development of skills necessary to improve performance. In some cases, perceptions or attitudes may need to be altered to make a leadership development program successful. The extent of learning required will determine whether formalized training is needed, or if more informal, on-the-job methods can be used to build the necessary skills and knowledge.

Level 1, Preference Needs

Finally, Level 1 preference needs assessment describes the preferences for the leadership program. This involves determining the preferred way in which those involved in the process will need or want it to be implemented. Typical questions that surface include "Is this important?" "Is this necessary?" and "Is it relevant to me?" Preference needs may involve aspects of implementation, including decisions about when learning is expected, in what amounts, how it is presented, and the overall timeframe. Implementation involves timing, support, expectations, and other key factors.

Using the V-Model, Figure 3-2 shows an example of linking needs assessment with the evaluation of a leadership development program involving a team-based process for making improvements. The target audience is composed of team members and team leaders. As the figure shows, the first step is to see if the problem is worth pursuing.

These five levels of needs analysis develop a comprehensive profile for determining how best to address an opportunity or problem worth solving. They also serve as the basis for the intervention objectives.

FIGURE 3-2. Leadership Program Example With the V-Model

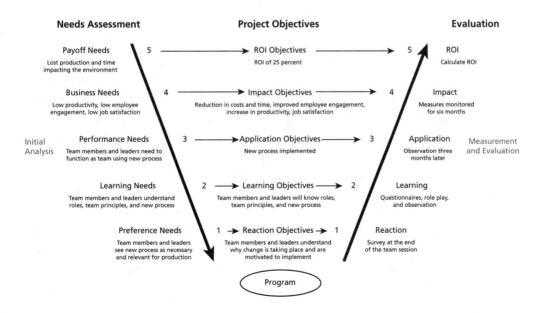

Objectives

Objectives keep the alignment between the leadership development program and the business by positioning that program with the outcomes in mind at every level. The levels of objectives are as follows.

- **Level 0 Input** objectives are those indicators generally tracked, such as the number of programs, people affected, hours, and so on. They are categorized as Level 0 because they do not reflect the outcome.
- **Level 1 Reaction** and planned action objectives describe expected immediate satisfaction with the leadership development program. They define important aspects including the relevance of the change and the importance of the information or content shared through the process.
- **Level 2 Learning** objectives describe the expected immediate outcomes in terms of knowledge acquisition, skill attainment, awareness, and insights gained through the leadership development program. These objectives set the stage for transitioning to performance and behavior change.
- **Level 3 Application** objectives describe the expected intermediate outcomes in terms of what behavior change is expected as a result of the leadership development program. Objectives may target specific steps to be taken or specific behaviors that need to change.
- **Level 4 Impact** objectives define the specific business measures that should improve as a result of the changed behavior. Improvements in these intermediate (and sometimes long-term) outcomes represent changes in output, quality, cost, and time measures, as well as customer satisfaction and employee satisfaction measures. Objectives at this level answer the question, "So what?" as it relates to the program. They describe to stakeholders the importance of the intervention.
- **Level 5 ROI** objectives define for stakeholders the intended financial outcome. This single indicator sets the expectation for how the benefits of the leadership development program will relate to its cost. Before an evaluation is conducted, these objectives must be identified and developed. Ideally, these are developed early in the process when the leadership development program is designed.

Each level represents a category of measures that describes how much progress is being made addressing the various levels of need. Specific measurable objectives serve as the blueprint for building the leadership development program. By aligning initiatives with the business through a thorough needs assessment and the development of measurable objectives, the implementation and evaluation of the leadership development program becomes more systematic and reliable. Identifying stakeholder needs and developing relevant objectives are the first two phases of business alignment and set the stage for planning the third phase, evaluation.

Case in Point

In this example, the payoff need is based on the problem of lost production time and damage to the work environment. To understand the impact (Level 4), the problem unfolds with more detail, and it becomes obvious that it is worth solving. The average production time is at an all-time high. However, productivity needs to improve and it has not increased in the last 18 months. The pressure of not meeting departmental and organization goals is putting stress on employees and has affected job satisfaction and employee engagement. When all these measures are considered, there is clearly a business problem—and to a certain extent, a great opportunity for improvement.

With the confirmation at Level 4 that there are business needs, a potential payoff can be projected. This involves estimating the cost of lost productivity and time. Next, the reduction that can come from the project is determined using standard values for production and time. This develops a profile of potential payoff and further demonstrates that the problem is worth solving.

At Level 3, the causes of the problem are explored using a variety of techniques. Each measure needs to be analyzed to see what factors are causing its current status (for example, why is productivity not improving, or what is the cause of the job dissatisfaction?). For this project, the analysts conducted interviews and focus groups to understand why business measures were at their current level.

The key principle, as in any analysis, is to identify the potential solution to the problem. A new team integration process was a viable option for organizing the work in teams. The potential impact was to dramatically reduce the time it took to produce new products. Of course, the program also needed to include the soft side as the employee base was not accustomed to working in teams. This meant that the team leaders and team members needed to learn new behaviors that were associated with team performance.

At Level 2, learning is explored. Do team leaders and members understand the new process? Are they clear about their new roles? The new process and team roles are at the heart of the learning needs.

At Level 1, the desired reaction needs to be considered. First, a realistic picture of the change involved must be shared so that teams understand the relevance of this approach. Adapting to change, motivation to implement, and the importance of the new process are factors that are critical to the success of launching this approach.

EVALUATION PLANNING

The evaluation must be planned—overall and individually—for each initiative. Not much planning is involved for an evaluation conducted only at the reaction levels, but as the evaluation moves up the value chain, increased attention and effort needs to be placed on planning. During the typical planning cycle, the purpose of the evaluation must be reviewed for specific solutions, and to determine where the evaluation will stop on the value chain. The feasibility of evaluating at different levels should also be explored.

Leadership development professionals understand the importance of planning for almost any type of undertaking. Most agree that thorough planning can lead to more effective implementation. The same holds true for ROI analysis. Careful planning for ROI analysis not only saves time and effort, but can also make a difference in the success or failure of the entire project. Planning involves the development of three documents:

- data collection plan
- ROI analysis plan
- communication and project plan.

These documents are described using the following case study.

CASE STUDY

A U.S.-based company operates in 12 countries with 21,000 employees. Revenues have increased during the past three years; however, profit margins show that given the expenses incurred, they are barely breaking even. The company has a solid, loyal customer base and works hard to align their business with client need. However the executive team is concerned about high turnover rates and low employee satisfaction.

Recent analysis of the main aspects of the business determined several key outcomes:

- Employees need to have a clearer understanding of career paths.
- To grow the business, more leaders need to take positions higher up in the company.
- The internal fill rate for leadership is 10 percent.

It would be beneficial to the company to groom more internal talent for higher positions. The cost for recruiting from the outside is high and not always effective, particularly in understanding the complexities of the business. Competencies have already been identified for leadership, including communication skills, business acumen, and the ability to align actions to customers' needs.

The leadership development team linked the competencies to business needs including talent retention, employee satisfaction, internal fill rate, and cost reduction.

In the meantime, managers throughout the company were asked to identify high-potential leaders who, based on their performance, would be suitable for leadership. The leadership development team worked with the executive team and agreed to implement a 360-degree feedback process, based on the leadership competencies, with the identified high-potential leader group. Due to several constraints, only half of the identified high-potential leader group could go through the 360-degree feedback process in the first year, with the remaining candidates slated to participate the following year. Thus the leadership development decided to set up the evaluation as a control group to isolate the effects of the 360-degree feedback process.

The 360-degree feedback involved several key steps. Before participating, the high-potential leaders completed a one-hour online session to learn about the process. The 360-degree feedback was administered online and collected input from the high-potential leaders, as well as their immediate supervisors, peers, direct reports, and in some cases, customers. This was followed by a feedback session conducted by a trained leadership development team member, along with a comprehensive report for each high-potential leader. The expected outcome was an action plan generated by the high-potential leader and his immediate supervisor.

Objectives
The organization development team created the following multilevel objectives for the leadership development:
- Participants will rate the leadership development program as relevant to their jobs.
- Participants will rate the leadership development as important to their career path.
- Participants must demonstrate acceptable performance on each major competency.
- Participants will use the competencies with team members on a routine basis.
- Participants will affect cost reduction, increase employee satisfaction, reduce turnover, and increase number of promotions.

Data Collection Plan
Figure 3-3 shows the completed data collection plan for a 360-degree feedback assessment. Defining the objectives and measures at each level, including return on investment, is vital. Measures can sometimes be looked at in different ways, so defining them up front eliminates confusion.

FIGURE 3-3. Data Collection Plan

Intervention: 360-Degree Feedback for High-Potential Leaders Program Responsibility: _____ Date: _____

Level	Objective(s)	Measures/Data	Data Collection Method	Data Sources	Timing	Responsibilities
1	**SATISFACTION/PLANNED ACTION** • Relevance to job • Importance to career path and promotion • Action items as a result of 360-degree feedback	• Average of 4 on 5-point scale	• Questionnaire	• High-potential leaders	• Immediately following receiving 360-degree feedback	• LD team
2	**LEARNING** • Uncovering strengths and weaknesses • Gaining business acumen • Communicating effectively • Enhancing leadership skills • Improving marketing skills	• Average of 4 on 5-point scale	• Questionnaire	• High-potential leaders	• Immediately following receiving 360-degree feedback	• Facilitator
3	**BEHAVIOR CHANGE** • Demonstrate competencies • Utilize the competencies with team members routinely as evidenced by scores on second administration of the 360-degree feedback	• Checklist for action plan • 4 out of 5 on a 5-point scale	• Action plan • 360-degree feedback	• High-potential leaders • Supervisors, direct reports, peers	• Six months after the 360-degree feedback, administer it a second time	• Facilitator • Store Training Coordinator

4	**BUSINESS IMPACT** • Talent retention • Employee satisfaction • Promotion • Cost reduction	• Reduce costs • Decrease in voluntary turnover • Increase in promotion • Increase employee satisfaction	• HR database • Operational database	• High-potential leaders	• Six months after the 360-degree feedback	• Store Training Coordinator
5	**ROI** • 25%	Comments: Action plans are provided and explained during the 360-degree feedback process. High-potential leaders commit to filling out action plans and sharing copy with LD team.				

The data collection methods are detailed here to correspond to the different levels of objectives, using a range of options described in the next chapter. Next, the data sources were identified. Data can be collected from existing organizational databases, or by those participating in the leadership development program. In some cases— as in the case of the 360-degree feedback assessment program—high-potential leaders, as well as their immediate supervisors, peers, direct reports, and customers provide data.

Timing is important for determining when data should be collected from the different sources for each level. During implementation, data often come directly from those involved in the program. In other situations, the follow-up can be determined based on when the program is operational and successful.

Finally, the responsibilities were detailed, outlining specifically who should be involved in the data collection process.

ROI Analysis Plan

Figure 3-4 shows the completed ROI analysis plan. This plan is connected through business impact data. The first column on this plan is the detailed definition of each impact data measure. The second column defines the method for isolating the effects of the intervention on each data item using one or more of the specific techniques available. The method of converting data to monetary values is listed in the third column using one or more available techniques.

The next column defines the cost categories for the specific program. Using a fully loaded cost profile, all the categories are detailed here. Completing this action during planning is helpful for determining whether specific cost categories need to be monitored during program implementation. The next column defines the intangible benefits that may be derived from this program. When listed here, the intangible benefits are only anticipated; they must be measured in some way to determine whether they have been influenced by the program. Finally, the other influences that may affect implementation are specified, along with any additional comments.

Communication and Implementation Plan

The communication and implementation plan details how the results will be communicated to various groups. It also details the specific schedule of events and activities connected to the other planning documents. The targets for communication identify the specific groups that will receive the information. The plan should also include the method of communicating, the content of the communication, and the timing for the communication.

This plan defines the rationale for communicating with the group and for anticipated payoffs, along with the individual responsibility for monitoring actions from the

Figure 3-4. ROI Analysis Plan

Program: High-Potential Leaders Program   Responsibility: _____   Date: _____

Data Items (Usually Level 4)	Methods for Isolating the Effects of the Program	Methods of Converting Data to Monetary Values	Cost Categories	Intangible Benefits	Communication Targets for Final Report	Other Influences/ Issues During Application	Comments
Cost reduction	• Control group • Participant estimates (for backup)	Standard value	• Diagnostics • 360-degree feedback fees • Time of those involved in process • Administrative overhead • Communication expenses • Facilities • Evaluation	• Increased job satisfaction • Increase in promotion	• Executives • Sponsors • LD team • Prospective participants for the 360-degree feedback	• An initiative that may influence the impact measures is the leadership development programs	

evaluation. It clearly delivers the information to the right groups to ensure that action occurs; in almost every impact study there are significant actions that can be taken.

FINAL THOUGHTS

This chapter explored the alignment of leadership development and evaluation planning. It described in detail when and how ROI analysis should be considered as a process improvement tool. Using the V-Model, a step-by-step explanation was provided to properly align leadership development projects with business needs. Special attention was paid to integrating needs analysis with the ROI Methodology, ensuring the leadership development practitioner has adequate tools and understanding to conduct a needs assessment and plan for the evaluation. Finally, the role of planning for an ROI project was presented, detailing the key steps in the process with the use of an actual case study, illustrating how planning documents are used.

4

Data Collection at Five Levels

For many leadership development practitioners with psychometrics and industrial psychology in their backgrounds, data collection is based on behavioral science methods. Data collection has relevance throughout the consulting cycle, beginning with diagnostics and ending with post-intervention. The primary objectives of data collection are to systematically gather information at three significant times: before, to understand organization problems and record hypotheses; during, to collect reaction and learning data; and after, to confirm the effectiveness of the intervention by collecting application and impact data. Data collection methods, principles, and timing are explored in this chapter. Particular attention is given to collecting data for ROI analysis, and introducing questions to gather estimates for ROI calculation.

QUANTITATIVE AND QUALITATIVE INQUIRY

There are advantages and disadvantages to both quantitative and qualitative methods of research. Before presenting the methods of data collection, it is helpful to discuss the types of data and research issues.

Advantages to Quantitative Data

Quantitative results have the advantage of being able to provide numerical value for large amounts of data as well as permitting the use of more powerful methods of mathematical and statistical analysis. Some professionals argue that the only data are quantitative data. They posit that everything is either a zero or one. Quantitative data can help form conclusions by assigning value from attributes to numerical scales and defined categories, and it is more easily analyzed with the use of software systems such as Excel or SPSS.

Advantages to Qualitative Data

Qualitative data also has advantages, such as allowing clients to use their own words to describe organization factors and problems. This method is helpful in situations in which the practitioner has a general sense of what to look for, but does not know details or specifics of an organization. That is why leadership development practitioners find qualitative interviews and focus groups particularly helpful when beginning a project. Qualitative data provide richness, depth, and complexity that may be unique

43

to the measurement culture. It is important to consider culture and its implication for data collection.

Organization Culture Implications

Organization culture may have implications for data collection methods. For some organizations, surveys are considered impersonal and bothersome. Some organizations are notorious for constantly surveying employees with no clear thought around the timing and methods for collecting data. Other organizations may be feedback deprived. This observation alone may be worth exploring, as there may be underlying assumptions about the means of communication within the organization.

Another consideration that relates to organization culture is providing confidential or anonymous surveys. Online surveys allow for anonymity in providing input, which could be a critical point to consider in the context of organization culture. Some groups have found that by offering anonymous questionnaires, it not only helps to improve response rates, but provides richer and more comprehensive data.

Mixing It Up

Mixed methodology allows for a combined qualitative and quantitative approach. This tactic is often used in creating questionnaires. In this case, the qualitative method precedes the quantitative by gathering important details that will help form the questions and response options for the questionnaire. For example, a leadership development practitioner working for a European cellular company conducted customer interviews to collect customer-specific perceptions and feedback. Once the interview data were organized and analyzed, the leadership development practitioner created a questionnaire based on the interview findings. In this way, the hypotheses could be confirmed and helped target the questionnaire to gather generalizable findings.

Resource Implications

Many companies today rely on quantitative methods because data collection and analysis processes are automated with the use of online-hosted survey systems. This implies more up-front work to create meaningful questions, but in cases with simple analysis and reporting, automating this process can drastically reduce the effort. Questionnaires also allow the practitioner to collect sample data that are representative of the populations, and with proper analytical tools, infer generalizations about the larger population or organization as a whole.

QUESTIONNAIRES AND SURVEYS

The most common method of data collection is the questionnaire. Ranging from short reaction forms to detailed follow-up tools, questionnaires are used to obtain subjective information about the organization or group involved, as well as objective data to measure business results for ROI analysis. With its versatility and popularity, the questionnaire is an optimal method for capturing the first four levels of data (reaction, learning, application, and business impact). Surveys represent a specific type of questionnaire to capture attitudes, beliefs, and opinions. The principles of survey construction and design are similar to questionnaire design. A questionnaire may include any of the following types of items:

- An open-ended question has an unlimited answer. The question is followed by ample blank space for the response.
- A checklist provides a list of items in which respondents are asked to check those that apply in the situation.
- A two-way question has alternate responses (yes/no) or other possibilities.
- A multiple-choice question asks the respondent to select the one most applicable response.
- A ranking scale requires the respondent to rank a list of items.

Questionnaire design is a straightforward, logical process. The following steps help develop a valid, reliable, and effective instrument:

1. Determine the specific information needed for each domain or level.
2. Secure input from subject matter experts.
3. Involve management in the process, when appropriate and feasible.
4. Decide on the method for returning the questionnaire.
5. Select the type(s) of questions. Keep in mind the time needed for analysis.
6. Choose the first question carefully.
7. Group related questions.
8. Begin with easy questions and build to the more complex.
9. Present the questions in the order of the results chain of impact.
10. Place sensitive questions at the end of the questionnaire.
11. Develop the questions with clarity and simplicity in mind.
12. Draft the questionnaire, checking the flow and total length.
13. Check the reading level and match it to the audience.
14. Design for ease of tabulation and analysis.
15. Be consistent in the visual presentation of the questions.
16. Use color and contrast to help respondents recognize the components of the questionnaire without distracting from the items themselves.
17. Avoid clutter and complexity in the question.
18. Develop the revised questionnaire.
19. Test the questions with a small group of individuals who are knowledgeable about the target audience.
20. Keep responses anonymous or confidential.
21. Finalize the completed questionnaire and prepare a data summary.
22. Use an existing user-friendly software tool, if feasible.

The areas of feedback used on reaction questionnaires depend on the purpose of the evaluation. Some forms are simple, while others are detailed and require considerable time to complete. When a comprehensive evaluation is planned, and impact and ROI are being measured, the reaction questionnaire can be simple, asking only questions that provide pertinent information about an individual's perception of the intervention. However, when a reaction questionnaire is the only means of collecting evaluation data, a more comprehensive list of questions is necessary. This feedback can be useful in making adjustments to an organization or assisting in predicting performance after the intervention, or both.

In most medium to large organizations with significant leadership development, reaction instruments are automated for analysis and reporting. Some organizations use direct input into a website to develop detailed reports and databases, which allows feedback data to be compared with other interventions.

Collecting learning data with a questionnaire is also common. Simple questions to measure learning can be developed for inclusion in the reaction questionnaire or in the form of a test.

Possible areas to explore on a questionnaire aimed at measuring learning are change in perception or attitude, knowledge gain, skill enhancement, ability, capability, and awareness.

Questions to gauge learning are developed using a format similar to the reaction part of the questionnaire. They measure the extent to which learning has taken place.

Questionnaires are also commonly used to collect post-program application and impact data. The following is a list of questionnaire content possibilities for capturing these follow-up data. Reaction and learning data may also be captured in a follow-up questionnaire to compare with similar data gathered immediately following the intervention. Most follow-up issues, however, involve application and implementation (Level 3) and business impact (Level 4):

- use of materials, guides, and technology
- application of knowledge and skills
- frequency of use of knowledge and skills
- success with use of knowledge and skills
- change in work or work behavior
- improvements and accomplishments
- monetary impact of improvements
- improvements linked to the intervention
- confidence level of data supplied
- perceived value of the investment
- linkage with output measures
- barriers to implementation
- enablers to implementation

- management support for implementation
- other benefits
- other possible solutions
- target audience recommendations.

TESTING

Testing can be important for measuring learning in leadership evaluations. Preprogram and post-program tests are an effective way to measure the change in learning. An improvement in test scores shows the change in skill, knowledge, or attitude attributed to the program. Performance testing, simulations, role plays, and business games are used to measure the extent of skills gained related to a program.

INTERVIEWS

Another helpful data collection method is the interview. The leadership development team or a third party usually conducts the interviews. Interviews can secure data not available in business or organization databases or data that may be difficult to obtain through written responses or observations. Interviews can also uncover success stories that can be useful in communicating evaluation results. Participants may be reluctant to describe their results in a questionnaire, but may be willing to volunteer the information to a skillful interviewer who uses probing techniques. The interview process can uncover reaction, learning, and impact data, but it is primarily used during diagnostics and post-program phases. It is particularly useful when gathering application or performance data. A major disadvantage of the interview is that it is time-consuming, because it requires interviewer preparation to ensure the process is consistent, as well as thematic analysis afterward.

Interviews are categorized into two basic types: structured and unstructured. A structured interview is much like a questionnaire. The interviewer asks specific questions that allow the interviewee little room to deviate from the menu of expected responses. The structured interview offers several advantages over the questionnaire. For example, an interview can ensure that the questions are answered and that the interviewer understands the responses supplied by the interviewee. The unstructured interview has built-in flexibility to allow the interviewer to probe for additional information. This type of interview uses a handful of core questions that can lead to more detailed information as important data are uncovered. The interviewer must be skilled in interviewing a variety of individuals and using the probing process. Interview design and steps for interviews are similar to those of the questionnaire. Preparing the interviewer, piloting the interview, providing clear instruction to the interviewee, and asking a set of core questions are critical steps in gathering useful data.

FOCUS GROUPS

Similar to interviews, focus groups are helpful when in-depth feedback is needed. The focus group involves a small group discussion conducted by an experienced facilitator. It solicits qualitative feedback on a planned topic. Group members are all invited to provide their thoughts, because individual input builds on group input.

Focus groups have several advantages over questionnaires, surveys, tests, or interviews. The basic premise of using focus groups is that when quality perspectives are subjective, several individual perspectives are better than one. The group process, whereby group members stimulate ideas in others, is an effective method for generating qualitative data. Focus groups are less expensive than individual interviews and can be quickly planned and conducted. They should be small (eight to 12 individuals) and should consist of a representative sample of the target population. Group facilitators should have expertise in conducting focus groups with a wide range of individuals. The flexibility of this data collection method makes it possible to explore organizational matters before the intervention, as well as to collect unexpected outcomes or application post-program. Barriers to implementation can also be explored through focus groups, while collecting examples and real concerns from those involved in the intervention.

Focus groups are particularly helpful when qualitative information is needed about the success of a program. For example, focus groups can be used to:

- Collect information contributing to diagnosis and the proposed solution.
- Gauge the overall effectiveness of program application.
- Identify the barriers and enablers to a successful implementation.
- Isolate the impact of an organization from other influences.

Focus groups are helpful when evaluation information is needed but cannot be collected adequately with questionnaires, interviews, or quantitative methods. It is an inexpensive and quick way to determine the strengths and weaknesses of HR interventions. For a complete evaluation, focus group information should be combined with data from other instruments.

OBSERVATIONS

Another potentially useful data collection method is observation. The observer may be a member of the leadership development team, an immediate manager, a member of a peer group, or an external party. The most common observer, and probably the most practical, is a member of the leadership development team.

To be effective, observations need to be systematic and well developed, minimizing the observer's influence and subjectivity. Observers should be carefully selected, fully prepared, and knowledgeable about how to interpret, score (if relevant), and report what they see.

This method is useful for collecting data on leadership development, management training, coaching, and executive education. For example, observation is used to provide 360-degree feedback as behavior changes are solicited from the direct reports, colleagues, internal customers, immediate managers, and self-input. This is considered a delayed report method of observation. This feedback process can be the actual intervention, or could be used before participating in another development initiative.

There are cases when observation is either invisible or unnoticeable. Invisible means that the person under observation is not aware that the observation is taking place, as in the case of a secret shopper. For example, Starbucks uses secret shoppers to observe their employees. A secret shopper goes to one of the stores, takes note of how long orders take to process, the demeanor of the server, whether the store and bathrooms are clean, and whether the server is familiar with new drink offerings. The observation continues immediately following the visit when the secret shopper checks the temperature of his drink order. This observation activity is supposed to be done in a way unbeknownst to the server. Another type of observation is unnoticeable, which means that although the person under observation may know that the observation is taking place, he does not notice it because it occurs over a longer period of time or at random times, as in listening in on customer service calls ("this call may be monitored for quality assurance purposes"), or in the case of a 360-degree feedback process.

ACTION PLANS AND PERFORMANCE AGREEMENTS

For many leadership development programs, business data are readily available. However, data won't always be easily accessible to the program evaluator. Sometimes, data are maintained at an individual, work unit, or department level and may not be known to anyone outside that area. Tracking down those data sets may be too expensive and time-consuming. In these cases, the use of action plans and performance agreements may be helpful in capturing data sets.

Action plans capture application and implementation data; however, this method can also be a useful way to collect business impact data. For business impact data, the action plan is more focused and often deemed more credible than a questionnaire. The performance agreement is an action plan with a preprogram commitment, so an action plan can easily be converted to a performance agreement with minor adjustments. The main difference between an action plan and a performance agreement is that performance agreements put the dialogue and agreement between a group member and his immediate manager. This can be a powerful process that can drive tremendous results, and is appropriate for leadership development programs where there is a need to achieve improvement. Not only do group members have the content to drive improvement, but they also have the support of their immediate managers and the extra efforts and attention of the facilitator to meet the performance target.

The basic design principles involved in developing and administering action plans are the same for collecting both application and business impact data. The following steps are recommended when an action plan is developed and implemented to capture business impact data and to convert the data to monetary values. The adjustments needed to convert action plans to performance agreements are described at the end of the section.

Set Goals and Targets

As shown in Figure 4-1, an action plan can be developed with a direct focus on business impact data. The plan presented in this figure requires an overall objective for the plan to be developed, which is usually the primary objective of the leadership development program. In some cases, an organization may have more than one objective, which requires additional action plans. In addition to the objective, the improvement measure is defined, along with the current and target levels of performance. This information requires that the individual anticipate the application of skills and sets goals for specific performances that can be realized.

The action plan is completed during the intervention, often with input and assistance from a leadership development team. The practitioner actually approves the plan, indicating that the action steps meet the requirements of being SMART: specific, motivating, achievable, realistic, and time-based. Each plan can be developed in a 30-minute timeframe and often begins with action steps related to the intervention. These action steps are Level 3 activities that detail the application and implementation of leadership development program content. These steps build support for and are linked to business impact measures.

Simplicity Rules the Day! Defining the Unit of Measure

The next step is to define the actual unit of measure. In some cases more than one measure may be used and will subsequently be contained in additional action plans. The unit of measure is necessary to break the process into the simplest steps so that its ultimate value can be determined. The unit may be output data, such as one unit produced or one closed sale. In terms of quality, the unit can be one reject, one error, or one rework. Time-based units are usually measured in minutes, hours, days, or weeks, such as one hour of process time. Other units are specific to their particular type of data, such as one grievance, one complaint, one absence, or one turnover. Here, simplicity rules the day by breaking down impact data into the simplest terms possible.

FIGURE 4-1. Sample Action Plan

Name: _____ Facilitator Signature: _____ Follow-Up Date: _____ Objective: _____

Evaluation Period: _____ to _____ Improvement Measure: _____

Current Performance: _____ Target Performance: _____

Action Steps	Analysis
1. _____	A. What is the unit of measure? _____
2. _____	B. What is the value (cost) of one unit? $ _____
3. _____	C. How did you arrive at this value? _____
4. _____	D. How much did the measure change during the evaluation period? (monthly value) _____
5. _____	E. List the other factors that have influenced this change. _____
6. _____	_____
7. _____	_____
	F. What percent of this change was actually caused by this program? _____ %
Intangible Benefits:	G. What level of confidence do you place on the above information? (100%=Certainty and 0%=No Confidence) _____ %

Comments: _____

Place a Monetary Value on Each Improvement

During the leadership development program, those involved are asked to locate, calculate, or estimate the monetary value for each improvement outlined in their plans. The unit value is determined using a variety of methods such as standard values, expert input, external databases, or estimates.

The process used in arriving at the value is described in the instructions for the action plan. When the actual improvement occurs, these values will be used to capture the annual monetary benefits of the plan. In the worst-case scenario, those participating in the leadership development program are asked to estimate the value. When estimates are necessary, it is important to collect the basis of their calculations. Space for this information should be provided. The preferred actions are using standard values or an expert. Also, the leadership development practitioner must be prepared to discuss values and reasonable methods in the session.

Implement the Action Plan

Ideally, the action plan is implemented post-program. Action plan steps are followed (Level 3), and subsequent business impact improvements are ensured (Level 4). The results are then forwarded to the leadership team.

Provide Specific Improvements

At the end of the specified follow-up period—usually three months, six months, nine months, or one year—group members indicate the specific improvements made, usually expressed as a daily, weekly, or monthly amount. This determines the actual amount of change that has been observed, measured, and recorded. Group members must understand the need for accuracy as data are recorded. In most cases, only the changes are recorded, because those amounts are needed to calculate the monetary values linked to the leadership development program. In other cases, before and after data may be recorded, which allows the evaluator to calculate the differences.

Isolate the Effects of the Program

Although the action plan is initiated because of the leadership development program, the actual improvements reported on the action plan may be influenced by other factors. The program usually shares the credit for the improvement gained. For example, an action plan to implement leadership skills for department managers could only be given partial credit for a business improvement because other variables in the work unit might have influenced the impact measures. While several ways are available to isolate the effects of a leadership development program, group member estimation is often used in the action planning process. Group members are asked to estimate the percentage of the improvement directly related to the leadership development program. This question can be asked on the action plan form or in a follow-up questionnaire, because sometimes it's beneficial to precede this question with a request to identify all other factors that may have influenced the results. This allows group members to think through the relationships before allocating a portion to this leadership program. Additional detail on methods to isolate the effects of leadership development programs is presented in chapter 5.

Provide a Confidence Level for Estimates

Isolating the amount of the improvement directly related to the intervention is not a precise process. Because it is an estimate, an error adjustment is made. Group members are asked to indicate their levels of confidence in their estimates using a scale of 0 to 100 percent—0 percent means no confidence and 100 percent means the estimates represent absolute certainty. The confidence estimate serves as an error discount factor.

Collect Action Plans

An excellent response rate is essential, so several steps may be necessary to ensure that the action plans are completed and returned. Usually, group members see the importance of the process and develop their plans during the program. Some organizations use follow-up reminders by mail or email. Others call group members to check on their progress. Still others offer assistance in developing the final plan. These steps may require additional resources, which need to be weighed against the importance of having more precise data. Specific ways to improve response rates are discussed later in this chapter.

Summarize the Data and Calculate the ROI

If developed properly, each action plan will have annualized monetary values that are associated with improvements. In addition, each individual will indicate the percentage of the improvement directly related to the leadership development program. Finally, group members will provide a confidence estimate expressed as a percentage to reflect their uncertainty with the estimates and the subjective nature of the data they provided.

Because this process involves estimates, it may not appear to be accurate. Several adjustments during the analysis make the process credible and more accurate. These adjustments reflect the guiding principles of the ROI Methodology, and are outlined as steps 1-6 below.

Step 1: For those group members who do not provide data, the assumption is that they had no improvement to report. This is a very conservative approach.

Step 2: Each value is checked for realism, usability, and feasibility. Extreme values are discarded and omitted from the analysis.

Step 3: Because improvement is annualized, the assumption is that the leadership development program had no improvement after the first year (for short-term programs). Some add value in years two and three.

Step 4: The new values are adjusted by the percentage of the improvement related directly to the program using multiplication. This isolates the effects of the program.

Step 5: The improvement from step 4 is then adjusted using the confidence estimate, multiplying it by the confidence percentage. The confidence estimate is actually an error percentage suggested by the group participants. The confidence estimate is multiplied by the amount of improvement connected to the leadership development program.

For example:

- A group participant indicates 80 percent confidence reflecting a 20 percent error possibility (100 – 80 = 20).
- In a $10,000 estimate with an 80 percent confidence factor, the group participant suggests that the value can be in the range of $8,000 to $12,000 (20 percent less to 20 percent more).
- To be conservative, the lower number, $8,000, is used.

Step 6: The monetary values determined in the previous five steps are totaled to arrive at the final program benefit. Since these values are already annualized, the total of these benefits becomes the annual benefits for the intervention. This value is placed in the numerator of the ROI formula to calculate the return on investment.

MONITORING PERFORMANCE

One of the more important methods of data collection is monitoring the organization's records. Performance data are available in every organization to report on impact measures such as output, quality, cost, time, job engagement, and customer satisfaction. In most organizations, performance data are available to measure the improvements from a leadership development program. If not, additional record-keeping systems must be developed for measurement and analysis. At this point, the question of economics arises. Is developing the record-keeping system necessary to evaluate the program economically? If the cost of developing and collecting the data is greater than the expected value for the data, then developing the systems to capture the data is meaningless.

The recommended approach is to use existing performance measures, if available. Performance measures should be reviewed to identify the items related to the proposed program objectives. Sometimes, an organization has several performance measures related to the same objective. For example, a new leadership program may be designed to increase productivity from the team, which could be measured in a variety of ways:

- team output (products, services, projects)
- individual output
- output per unit of time
- gross productivity (revenue per person)
- time savings (when the saved time is used on other productive work)
- fewer hours worked (with the same output)
- fewer team members (with the same output).

Each of these measures, in its own way, gauges the efficiency or effectiveness of the team. All related measures should be reviewed to determine those most relevant to the leadership development program.

IMPROVING THE RESPONSE RATE FOR DATA COLLECTION

One of the greatest challenges in data collection is achieving an acceptable response rate. Requiring too much information may result in a suboptimal response rate. The challenge, therefore, is to tackle data collection design and administration so as to achieve the maximum response rate. This is critical when the primary data collection method hinges on input obtained through questionnaires, surveys, and action plans. Here are a few ways to boost response rates:

- Provide advance communication about the questionnaire.
- Clearly communicate the reason for the questionnaire.
- Indicate who will see the results of the questionnaire.
- Show how the data will be integrated with other data.
- Keep the questionnaire as simple as possible.
- Keep questionnaire responses anonymous—or at least confidential.
- Make it easy to respond with email.
- Use two follow-up reminders.
- Have the introduction letter signed by a top executive.
- Send a summary of results to the target audience.
- Have a third party collect and analyze data.
- Communicate the time limit for submitting responses.
- Design questionnaire to attract attention, with a professional format.
- Let group members know what actions will be taken with the data.
- Provide options to respond (such as paper-based).
- Frame questions so group members can respond appropriately
  to relevant questions.

SOURCES OF DATA

An array of possible data sources is available to provide input on the success of a leadership development program. Six general categories are described here.

Business and Operational Databases

Perhaps the most useful and credible data sources for impact and ROI analysis are the databases and reports of the organization. Whether individualized or group-based, these records reflect performance in a work unit, department, division, region, or overall organization. Organization databases include all types of measures and are a preferred way to collect data for impact and ROI evaluation because these data sets usually reflect business impact data and are relatively easy to obtain. However, the old adage, "garbage in, garbage out," rings true here. Inconsistent and inaccurate data entry and data processing steps may complicate the task.

Participants

Perhaps the most widely used data source for an ROI analysis is from those participating in the leadership development program. Participants are frequently asked about reaction (Level 1), learning (Level 2), and how skills, knowledge, and procedures have been applied on the job (Level 3). Sometimes they are asked to explain the impact or consequence of those actions. Participants are a rich source of data for evaluation at the first four levels of data.

Participants are credible because they are involved in the program and are expected to make it successful. They also know the most about other factors that may influence results. The challenge is to find an effective, efficient, and consistent way to capture data from this important source to minimize the time required to provide input.

Participants' Immediate Managers

Another important data source is the immediate supervisors of the participants. Managers often have a vested interest in the evaluation process because they approve, support, or require the group members to become involved in the leadership development program in the first place. In many situations, they observe the participants as they attempt to make the intervention successful by applying their new learning.

Because of this, the managers are able to report on the successes linked to the program, as well as the difficulties and problems associated with application. Although manager input is usually best for application evaluation (Level 3), it is sometimes helpful for impact (Level 4) evaluation. The challenge is to make data collection convenient, efficient, and not disruptive.

Direct Reports

Because most leadership development programs involve supervisors, managers, and executives, their direct reports can be important sources of data. Direct reports can report perceived changes since the program was implemented. Input from direct reports is usually appropriate for application (Level 3) data. For example, in a 360-degree feedback program, comments from direct reports are perhaps the most credible source of data for changes in leadership behavior.

Team or Peer Group

Individuals who serve as team members or occupy peer-level positions in the organization are a source of data for some programs. Team or peer group members are usually a source of input for 360-degree feedback. In these situations, peer participants provide input on perceived changes since the program has been implemented. This source is appropriate when all team members participate in the intervention and, consequently, when they can report on the collective efforts of the group.

Internal or External Groups

In some situations, internal or external groups such as the leadership development team, intervention facilitators, coaches, mentors, expert observers, or external consultants may provide input on the success of the individuals when they learn and apply the skills and knowledge covered in the program. Sometimes expert observers or assessors may be used to measure learning. This source may be useful for on-the-job application (Level 3).

TIMING FOR DATA COLLECTION

Another important factor is the timing of data collection. In some cases, pre-change measurements are taken to compare with post-change measures, or multiple measures are taken. In other situations, pre-change measures are not available and specific follow-ups are still taken after the program. The important issue is to determine the timing for the follow-up evaluation.

The timing of data collection can vary. When a follow-up evaluation is planned after the program, determining the best time for data collection is critical. The challenge is to analyze the nature and scope of the application and implementation and determine the earliest time that a trend or pattern will evolve. This occurs when the application of skills becomes routine and the implementation is progressing properly. Deciding when to collect data often involves knowing the audience and general time it takes to see change. Collecting data as early as possible is important so that potential adjustments can still be made. At the same time, evaluations must allow for behavior changes to occur, so that the application of skills can be observed and measured. Two factors usually determine the routine use of skills: the complexity of the skill and the opportunity to use the skill. In leadership development programs spanning a considerable length of time for implementation, measures may be taken at three- to six-month intervals. This provides successive input on progress and clearly shows the extent of improvement, using effective measures at well-timed intervals.

The timing for impact data collection is based on the delay between application and consequence (the impact). Subject matter experts familiar with this situation will have to examine the content of the application and implementation and, when considering the context of the work environment, estimate how long it will take for the application to have an impact. In some situations, such as the use of new tools or procedures, the impact may immediately follow the application; in other processes, such as the use of complex leadership skills, the impact may be delayed for some time. For example, managers involved in a leadership development program to improve talent retention will have to learn to work more closely with the team, demonstrating increased caring for the group; assisting team members in achieving individual and professional goals; providing challenging assignments; and allowing team members to learn, grow, and develop. A mere change of behavior will not necessarily result in an immediate reduction in turnover of critical talent. There will be some lag between the new behavior and the corresponding increase in retention; however, the impact will usually occur in the timeframe of one to six months in most leadership development programs. The key is to move as quickly as possible to collect the impact data as soon as it occurs.

Convenience and constraints also influence the timing of data collection. Perhaps the group members are conveniently meeting in a follow-up session or at a special event. These would be excellent opportunities to collect data. Sometimes constraints are placed on data collection. Sponsors or other executives are eager to have the data so that they can make decisions about the leadership development program. So they move data collection to an earlier-than-ideal time. If it's too early, another, later data collection will be necessary.

Management's Time for Data Input

The time that a group member's immediate manager must allocate to data collection is another important issue when selecting a data collection method. Always strive to keep the managers' time requirements to a minimum. Some methods, such as focus groups, may require involvement from the manager prior to and after the intervention. Other methods, such as performance monitoring, may not require any manager time.

Disruption of Normal Work Activities

Another important factor in data collection is the amount of disruption created by the method selected. Routine work processes should be disrupted as little as possible. Some data collection techniques, such as business or operational databases, require little time or distraction from normal activities. Questionnaires generally do not disrupt the work environment and can often be completed in only a few minutes or even after normal work hours. Techniques such as focus groups and interviews may take more time for those involved.

Accuracy of Method

Accuracy is a factor to weigh when selecting a data collection method. Accuracy refers to the instrument's or the method's ability to correctly capture the data desired with minimum error. Some data collection methods are more accurate than others. For example, organization databases tend to be more accurate than an interview. If data are needed regarding on-the-job behavior, unobtrusive observation is a powerful option.

FINAL THOUGHTS

This chapter has provided an overview of data collection methods that can be used in ROI analysis. Leadership development practitioners and evaluators have the option to select from a variety of methods according to their resources, culture, and circumstances. Follow-up questionnaires and surveys are commonly used to collect data for application and impact analyses. Questionnaire design and ways to boost response rates were also explored. In the leadership development field, the use of action plans and performance agreements can be very effective. Next up, data analysis . . . after the data are collected, what do you do with them?

5

Data Analysis That Is Practical and Credible

Most leadership development practitioners will agree that data analysis and interpretation is one of the most challenging tasks of measurement and evaluation. A misunderstanding of the techniques as well as a fear of math and statistics confound this challenge. This chapter describes five key steps in simple terms.

The first part of the chapter addresses isolating the impact of a leadership development program. In almost every situation other variables will influence the impact of a leadership development program and these factors must be taken into account. The second part of the chapter discusses converting data to monetary values. It is one thing to collect the data, but it is a different process to assign a monetary value to it. The third part of the chapter is on the cost of the program. Since the ROI formula has two numbers—cost and benefit—the key elements to include when calculating the costs of programs are examined. The fourth part focuses on calculating the ROI, and presents common approaches to calculate values that can be used in comparison with other types of investment.

The final section is on intangibles, the impact measures that are not converted to money. Refer back to Figure 2-2 in chapter 2 for a visual depiction of the steps.

ISOLATING THE EFFECTS

The situation is not uncommon. An improvement is noted after a major leadership development program has been implemented. The two events appear to be related. An executive asks, "How much of this improvement was due to the leadership development program?" While this question is often asked, it is rarely answered with any degree of certainty. While the change in performance may be related to the leadership development program, other factors may also have contributed to the improvement. The leadership development program is only one of many variables that can influence performance. This section explores several techniques that can be used to answer the question, "What impact did the leadership development program have on performance?" with a much greater degree of certainty. Taking the time to carry out this step creates additional credibility for the process by focusing attention on other variables that may have influenced performance. The following section will describe isolation techniques and some examples.

Control Groups

The most credible approach for isolating the impact of a leadership development program is the use of control groups as in an experimental design process. This approach involves an experimental group that has the benefit of the leadership development program and a control group that does not have the intervention. The composition of both groups should be similar in characteristics and, if feasible, the selection of each group should be on a random basis. When this is possible, and both groups are subjected to the same environmental influences, the difference in the performance of the two groups can be attributed to the leadership development program. Figure 5-1 illustrates how the control group is set up. See the Case in Point sidebar for an example of using a control group in a leadership development program.

FIGURE 5-1. Use of Control Groups

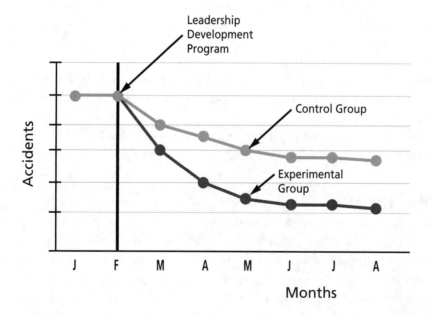

The use of control group arrangements has been around for a very long time. There is the story from biblical times in the Book of Daniel, dating back to 600 B.C. Daniel and his friends from Judah did not want to eat what the Babylonian royal court officials ate, so he proposed that he and his friends would eat vegetables and water for

10 days. When the 10 days were up, officials compared Daniel's group with the group that ate the royal food and found a significant difference in energy and health.

One major disadvantage for control groups is withholding the intervention from one group. Neil Rackham describes a case in which he used a control group, during which he observed $6 million in additional revenue from the group that participated in a leadership program. When he presented the results, the CEO asked why the other group was kept from the benefit of the program. There needs to be a solid business reason for using a control group.

Trend-Line Analysis

Another useful technique for approximating the impact of some leadership development programs is trend-line analysis. In this approach, a trend line is drawn on a graph from a point that represents the initial performance level of the target audience, and extends to a point that represents the anticipated performance level without the leadership development program. Upon completion of the leadership program, the actual performance is compared with the level the trend line predicted performance would be without the leadership development program. Any improvement of performance above what was predicted can be reasonably attributed to the leadership program. While this is not an exact process, it provides a reasonable estimation of the impact of a leadership development program.

Case in Point

A study focused on 500 managers who participated in a major leadership development program. The participants' performance and business impact metrics were compared with that of a control group of an approximately equivalent number of managers with similar characteristics. Performance and business measures were tracked for the two groups for nine months in categories of promotions, job satisfaction, number of complaints, turnover among direct reports, and turnover among the managers. The group who participated in the leadership development program had significantly more positive outcomes than the control group. Turnover and complaints were converted to monetary value using internal standards for those values. The results showed a 25 percent ROI.

Figure 5-2 shows an example of trend-line analysis taken from a logistics company. The data are slightly exaggerated to illustrate the process. The percentage of on-time shipments is presented before and after a leadership development program that was conducted in June. As shown in the figure, there was a downward trend on the shipment rate prior to conducting the leadership program. Although the leadership development program had a dramatic effect on the on-time shipments, the trend line shows that shipments would have continued downward, based on the trend that had been previously established. It is tempting to measure the improvement by comparing the average six-month shipping prior to the program with the average six months after the leadership development program. A more accurate comparison, however, is to compare month six after the program with the trend-line value at the same month. In this example, the difference is 27 percent (95 to 68).

FIGURE 5-2. Trend-Line Analysis

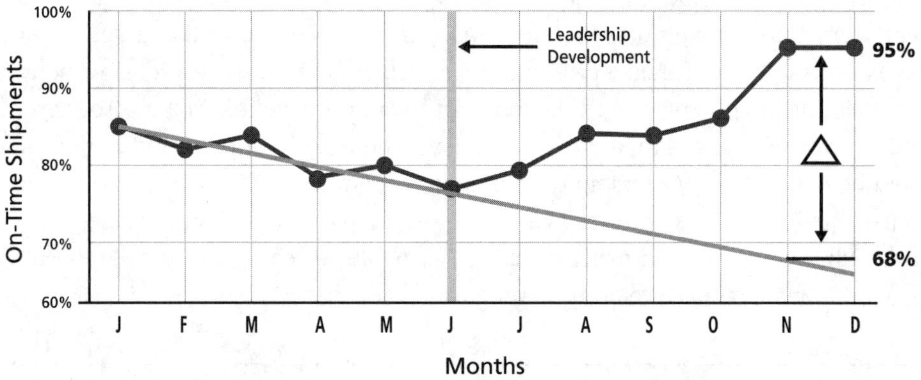

A primary disadvantage of this approach is that it is not necessarily accurate, although it may be as accurate as other methods described here. The use of this approach also assumes that the events that influenced the performance variable prior to the leadership development program are still in place after the program, except for the implementation of the leadership development program. Finally, this approach assumes that no new influences entered the situation. The trends that were established prior to the leadership development program will continue in the same relative direction. This may not always be the case.

The primary advantage of this approach is that it is simple and inexpensive, and takes very little effort. If historical data are available, a trend line can quickly be drawn and data estimated. While this process is not exact, it does provide a quick analysis of the program's impact.

Forecasting Methods

A more analytical approach to trend-line analysis is to use forecasting methods to predict the level of performance that might occur in the future if the leadership development program had not been undertaken. This approach represents a mathematical analysis of the trend-line analysis above. A linear equation is used to calculate a value of the anticipated performance improvement. A linear model is appropriate only when one other variable influenced the output performance.

The primary advantage of this process is that it can be an accurate predictor of the performance variables that would occur without implementing the leadership development program if appropriate data and models are available. The method is simple for linear relationships. However, a major disadvantage to this approach occurs when many variables enter the process. The process becomes more complex and requires the use of a more sophisticated statistical analysis. Even then, the data may not fit the model. Unfortunately, many organizations have not developed mathematical relationships for output variables as a function of one or more inputs. Without them, the forecasting method is difficult to use. If the numbers are available, they could provide useful evidence of the impact of training. The presentation of specific methods is beyond the scope of this book and is contained in other works (Phillips and Phillips 2015).

Participant Estimation

An easy method to isolate the impact of a leadership development program is to secure information directly from participants. This approach assumes that participants are capable of determining or estimating how much of a performance improvement is related to the leadership development program. As the source of the performance, participants may have reliable input on the issue. Because their actions produced the change, they should have some estimation as to how much of the change was caused by the leadership development program. Although their input is an estimate, it will usually have considerable credibility with management groups because participants are at the center of the change or improvement resulting from the leadership development program.

As an added enhancement to this method, management may be asked to approve the participants' estimates. For example, in a leadership development program participants estimated the amount of savings attributed to the leadership program. Table 5-1 shows a sample of these estimates. Managers at the next two levels above those participating reviewed and approved the estimates. So, in essence, the managers actually confirmed participants' estimates.

TABLE 5-1. Example of a Team Member's Estimates

Factor That Influenced Improvement	% of Improvement Caused by	Confidence Expressed as a %	Adjusted % of Improvement Caused by
LD Program	60%	80%	48%
Six Sigma	15%	70%	10.5%
Environmental Change	5%	60%	3%
System Change	20%	80%	16%
Other	__%	__%	__%
Total	**100%**		

The process has some disadvantages. It is an estimate and, consequently, it does not have the accuracy desired by some professionals. Also, the input data may be unreliable if individuals are uncomfortable with providing these types of estimates.

The approach has several advantages. It is a simple process and easily understood by participants and by others who review evaluation data, and there is an extensive body of research that suggests these estimates are accurate; there is wisdom in the crowds. It is inexpensive, takes little time and analysis, and results in an efficient addition to the evaluation process. Although it is an estimate, it originates from a credible source: the individuals who actually produced the improvement.

Manager's Estimation

In some cases, upper management may estimate the percent of improvement attributed to the leadership development program. Although the process is subjective, the source of the estimate is a group that usually allocates funds and has a sense of what the value should be. With this approach, the source of these estimates is not usually based on direct knowledge of the process.

Expert Estimation

Another approach to identifying factors that influence the impact of a leadership development program is to rely on external or internal experts to estimate what portion of results can be attributed to a leadership development program. With this process, the experts must be carefully selected based on their knowledge of the process, intervention, and situation. For example, an expert in quality might be able to provide estimates of how much quality improvement can be attributed to a leadership development program and what percent can be attributed to other factors. In another situation, an external expert can possibly estimate the extent to which improvement is made without the leadership program. This amount is subtracted from the improvement, and it is assumed that the remainder can be attributed to the leadership development program. This approach appears to be most effective when the expert has been involved in similar interventions and estimates the impact of those factors based on previous experience or the use of historical data.

CONVERTING DATA TO MONETARY UNITS

Chapter 4 presented the types of data collected for leadership development program evaluation. Before these data can be used to compare benefits with costs, it must be converted to monetary values. This section provides additional insight into practical ways to convert data to monetary values.

Converting Increased Output

Changes in output are the goal of many leadership development programs and in most situations the value of increased output can be easily calculated. For example, when implementing a program to increase sales, the change in output can easily be measured. The sales improvement after the leadership development program is calculated by being multiplied by the average profit per sale. In another example, consider packaging machine operators in a pharmaceutical plant. The operator packages drugs in boxes ready for shipment. Production managers participate in a leadership development program to learn how to increase production through better use of equipment and work procedures. The value of increased output is the operating profit margin. Fortunately, most of these conversions have been developed as standard values.

Converting Time Savings

Some leadership development programs are aimed at reducing the time to perform a task, deliver a service, or respond to a request. Time savings are important because employee time is money, in the form of wages, salaries, and benefits paid directly to the employee. The most common time savings result in reduced costs of effort for those involved in the leadership development program. The monetary savings are the hours saved multiplied by the effort cost per hour.

Converting Improved Quality

Quality improvement is an important and frequent target of leadership development programs. The cost of poor quality to an organization can be astounding. According to the late quality expert Phillip Crosby, an organization can probably increase its profits by 5 to 10 percent of sales if it concentrates on improving quality. To be effective, the measurable impact of a quality improvement program must be determined. To calculate the return on the intervention, the value of the quality improvement must be calculated.

The most obvious cost of poor quality is the scrap or waste generated by mistakes. Defective products, spoiled raw materials, and discarded paperwork are the results of poor quality. This scrap and waste translates into a monetary value that can be used to calculate the impact of an improvement in quality. For example, in a production environment, the cost of a defective product can be easily calculated; it is the total cost incurred at the point the mistake is identified minus the salvage value. The costs of paper and computer entry errors can be significant. For example, the cost of an error on a purchase order can be enormous if the wrong items are ordered.

Many mistakes and errors result in costly rework to correct the mistake. The most costly reworks occur when a product is delivered to a customer but must be returned for correction, or when an expensive intervention is implemented with serious errors. In determining the cost of rework, labor and direct cost are both significant. Maintaining a staff to perform rework is an additional overhead cost for the organization. In a manufacturing plant, the cost of rework is in the range of 15 to 70 percent of a plant's productivity. In banks, an estimated 35 percent of operating costs could be blamed on correcting errors.

Using Historical Costs

Occasionally an organization will develop and accumulate cost for specific data items. For example, some organizations monitor the cost of grievances. Although an extremely variable item, the average cost per grievance provides a basis for estimating the cost savings for a reduction in grievances. Because of their relative accuracy, historical costs, if available, should be used to estimate the value of data items, unless it takes too many resources.

Using Expert Input

Expert inputs, either internal or external, are sometimes used to estimate the value of soft data improvements. Internal experts are those employees who are proficient and knowledgeable in their fields. For example, a purchasing expert may estimate the salvage value of defective parts, an industrial engineer might estimate the time that it takes to complete a task or perform a function, and a marketing analyst might estimate the cost of a dissatisfied customer. Using internal experts provides excellent opportunities to recognize individuals in the organization. Chances are, their expert analysis will not be challenged because others in the organization have no better basis to make the estimate. External experts may also provide an estimate, depending on their expertise in a given field. One consultant may estimate the cost of work slowdowns and then use that figure with several organizations by providing an expert opinion.

External Studies

Extensive analyses of similar data in other organizations may be extrapolated to fit an internal situation. For example, many experts have attempted to calculate the cost of absenteeism. Although these estimates can vary considerably, they may serve as a rough estimate for other calculations with some adjustments for the specific organization. There are literally hundreds of studies covering the cost of variables such as absenteeism, turnover, tardiness, grievances, complaints, and loss of time due to accidents. Typical sources to pursue may include *Corporate Leadership Council, Academy of Management Journal, Journal of Applied Psychology, Personnel Psychology, Human Resources Management Review, OD Practitioner, Human Resource Development Quarterly*, and *Personnel Journal*.

Practitioners rarely venture into external studies, probably because there is not enough dialogue between the leadership development practitioners and the researchers. Each group seems to have a misunderstanding of the other's role, and they only mesh at times when it is convenient for both. Practitioners should learn more about research studies and publications and possibly influence future research.

Participant Estimation

Employees that are directly involved in a leadership development program may be capable of estimating the value of an improvement. Either during the leadership development program or in a follow-up, participants should be asked to estimate the value of the improvements. To provide further insight, participants should also be asked to furnish the basis for their estimate and their level of confidence in it. Estimations by participants are credible and may be more realistic than other sources because participants are usually directly involved with the improvement and are knowledgeable of the issues. If provided encouragement and examples, participants are often creative at estimating these values. For example, in one organization, in response to a special leadership development program, managers were asked to estimate the value of reducing the time to process a loan. Although their responses were not precise, they provided a credible estimate of this value.

Management Estimation

A final strategy for converting soft data to monetary values is to ask managers who are concerned about the intervention's evaluation to estimate the value of an improvement. Several management groups may be targets for this estimation, including supervisors of leadership development program participants, middle management, or even the C-suite.

These strategies are effective for converting soft data to monetary values when calculating the return on a leadership development program. One word of caution is in order. Whenever a monetary value is assigned to subjective information, it needs to be fully explained to the audience receiving the information. When there is a range of possible values, the most conservative one should be used to ensure credibility for the process.

COSTS OF THE PROGRAM

Analysis yields a need, and then the organization designs and develops a solution or acquires one and implements it. The leadership development team routinely reports to the client or sponsor throughout the process and then undertakes an evaluation to show the program's success. A group of costs also supports the process (such as administrative support and overhead costs). For costs to be fully understood, the project needs to be analyzed in these different categories.

The most important task is to define which specific costs are included in a tabulation of program costs. This step involves decisions that will be made by the leadership development team and, in most cases, approved by management. If appropriate, finance and accounting staff may need to approve the list. Table 5-2 shows the recommended cost categories for a fully loaded, conservative approach to estimating costs.

TABLE 5-2. Project Cost Categories

Cost Item	Prorated	Expensed
1. **Needs assessment**	✓	
2. **Design and development**	✓	
3. **Acquisition costs**	✓	
4. **Implementation costs**		
Salaries and benefits for coordination time		✓
Salaries and benefits for participant time		✓
Materials and supplies		✓
Use of facilities		✓
Travel, lodging, and meals		✓
5. **Maintenance and monitoring**		✓
6. **Administrative support and overhead**	✓	
7. **Evaluation and reporting**		✓

Needs Assessment Costs

One of the most overlooked cost items is the cost of conducting the initial assessment or diagnosis of the need for the leadership development program. In some projects, this cost is zero because the program is implemented without an initial assessment of need. However, as organizations focus increased attention on needs assessment, this item will become a more significant cost in the future.

While it's best to collect data on all costs associated with the needs assessment to the fullest extent possible, estimates are appropriate. These costs include the time of leadership development team members to conduct the assessment, direct fees, expenses for external consultants who conduct the diagnosis, and internal services and supplies used in the analysis. The total costs are usually prorated over the life of the project. Depending on the type and nature of the project, the life cycle should be kept to a reasonable number in the one- to two-year timeframe. The exception would be for expensive projects for which the needs are not expected to change significantly for several years.

Design and Development Costs

One of the most significant items is the cost of developing the intervention. This cost item includes internal staff and consultant time for development of software, CD-ROMs, job aids, and other support material directly related to the project. As with diagnostics costs, development costs are usually prorated, perhaps by using the same timeframe. Three to five years is recommended unless the project is expected to remain unchanged for many years and the development costs are significant.

Acquisition Costs

In lieu of development costs, many organizations purchase software or programs to use off the shelf or in a modified format. The acquisition costs for these programs include the purchase price and other costs associated with the rights to implement the program. These acquisition costs should be prorated, typically over three or five years, using the same rationale described earlier. If the organization needs to modify or further develop the program, those costs should be included as development costs. In practice, many programs have both acquisition costs and development costs.

Implementation Costs

Perhaps the most important segment of leadership development costs is implementation. Five major categories are included:

- **Salaries of coordinators and organizers.** The salaries of all individuals involved in coordination and direct support should be included. If a coordinator is involved in more than one program, the time should be allocated to the specific program under review. The key point is to account for all the direct time of internal employees or external consultants who work with the program. Include the employee benefits factor each time direct labor costs are involved.

- **Materials and supplies.** Specific project materials such as workbooks, handouts, brochures, guides, job aids, and CD-ROMs should be included in the delivery costs, along with license fees, user fees, and royalty payments.
- **Travel expenses.** Include direct costs of travel, if required, for participants, facilitators, and coordinators. Lodging, meals, and other expenses also fall under this category.
- **Facilities for sessions.** Take into account the direct cost of the meeting facilities. When external meetings are held, this item represents the direct charge from the conference center or hotel. If meetings are held internally, use of the meeting room represents a cost to the organization and should be included, even if it is not the practice to include facility costs in other cost reporting.
- **Participants' salaries and benefits.** The salaries plus employee benefits of group members for their time away from work represent an expense that should be included. Estimates are appropriate in the analysis.

Maintenance and Monitoring

This item includes all costs related to routine operation of the program. The category encompasses all costs in the same categories listed under implementation, plus perhaps equipment and services.

Overhead

A final charge is the cost of overhead: the additional costs of the leadership development function not directly charged to a particular program. The overhead category represents any leadership development function cost not considered in the previous calculations. Typical items include the cost of administrative support, administrative expenses, salaries of leadership development managers, and other fixed costs. A rough estimate developed through some type of allocation plan is usually sufficient.

Evaluation

The evaluation cost is included in the program costs to compute the fully loaded cost. For an ROI evaluation, the costs include developing the evaluation strategy and plans, designing instruments, collecting data, analyzing data, and preparing and presenting results. Cost categories include time, purchased services, materials, purchased instruments, and surveys.

CALCULATING THE RETURN

The return on investment is an intriguing and important calculation. Yet, it is a figure that must be used with caution and care because it can be interpreted or misinterpreted in many ways. This section presents some general guidelines to help calculate the return and interpret its meaning.

Defining the Return on Investment

The term *return on investment* may appear to be out of place in leadership development. The expression originates from finance and accounting and usually refers to the pretax contribution measured against controllable assets. It measures the anticipated profitability of an investment and is used as a standard measure of the performance of divisions and profit centers within a business.

In many situations, a group of employees is involved in a leadership development program, so the investment figure should be the total costs of analysis, development, implementation, operating, and evaluation lumped together for the bottom part of the equation. With these considerations for calculating the return on investment the following formula is used:

$$\text{ROI} = \frac{\text{Net Benefits}}{\text{Program Costs}} \times 100$$

The formula is multiplied by 100 to convert it to a percent. The net benefits are the benefits minus the costs.

To illustrate this calculation, consider a leadership development program designed to reduce error rates. Because of the program, the average daily error rate per employee dropped from 20 to 15. Before the program, an employee spent an average of 30 minutes correcting errors. If employees average $20 per hour and 20 employees completed the program, the weekly operational savings for this program using base pay savings only is $1,000 (5 x 0.5 x $20 x 20) = 40. The annual savings is $52,000. If the program costs $40,000, the return on investment after the first year is

$$\text{ROI} = \frac{\$52,000 - \$40,000}{\$40,000} \times 100 = 30 \text{ percent}$$

These figures may be more meaningful to managers who use ROI calculations for capital expenditures. ROI may be calculated prior to a program to estimate the potential cost effectiveness or after a program to measure the results achieved. The methods of calculation are the same.

Benefit-Cost Ratio

Another method for evaluating the investment is the benefit-cost ratio. Similar to the ROI, this ratio consists of the total of the benefits derived from the program expressed in monetary units, divided by the total cost of the program. A benefit-cost ratio greater than one indicates a positive return. A ratio of less than one indicates a loss. The benefits portion of the ratio is a tabulation of all the benefits derived from the program converted to monetary values as described earlier in this chapter. The total costs include all the cost categories as described earlier. The ratio has been used to evaluate projects, particularly in the public sector, beginning in the 20th century. Since then, it has been used for project evaluation in many different settings.

Benefit-cost ratio is often used by governments because it is not usually linked with standard accounting procedures. Although the benefits are converted to monetary values, steering away from the standard accounting terminology is a more comfortable approach. Sometimes there is a feeling that the accounting measures communicate a preciseness that is not always available when calculating the benefits or the cost portion of the equation.

Payback Period

A payback period is another method for evaluating a major expenditure. With this approach, the annual cash proceeds (savings) produced by investment are equated to the original cash outlay required by the investment to arrive at some multiple of cash proceeds equal to the original investment. Measurement is usually in terms of years and months. If the cost savings generated from a program is constant each year, the payback period is determined by dividing the total original cash investment (development costs, outside program purchase, and so on) by the amount of the expected annual savings. The savings that represent the net expenses are subtracted.

For example, if the intervention costs are $40,000, with a three-year useful life, and the benefits from the program are expected to be $52,000, then:

$$\text{Payback Period} = \frac{\text{Program Costs}}{\text{Annual Net Benefits}} \times 12 = \frac{\$40,000}{\$52,000} \times 12 = 9.23 \text{ months}$$

The program will "pay back" the original investment in 9.2 months. The payback period is simple to use but has the limitation of ignoring the time value of money.

INTANGIBLES

Perhaps the first step to understanding intangibles is to clearly define the difference between tangible and intangible assets in a business organization. As shown in Table 5-3, tangible assets are required for business operations; they are readily visible, rigorously quantified, and routinely represented as line items on balance sheets. Intangible assets are the key to competitive advantage. They are invisible, difficult to quantify, and not tracked through traditional accounting practices. With this distinction, it is easy to understand why intangible measures are more challenging to convert to money. This next section will highlight a handful of intangible measures that are relevant for leadership.

TABLE 5-3. Comparison of Tangible Assets

Tangible Assets (Required for Business Operations)	Intangible Assets (Key to Competitive Advantage in Knowledge)
Readily visible	Invisible
Rigorously quantified	Difficult to quantify
Part of the balance sheet	Not tracked through accounting practices
Investment produces known returns	Assessment based on assumptions
Can be easily duplicated	Cannot be bought or imitated
Depreciates with use	Appreciates with purposeful use
Has finite application	Multi-application without reducing value
Best managed with "scarcity" mentality	Best managed with "abundance" mentality
Best leveraged through control	Best leveraged through alignment
Can be accumulated	Dynamic: short shelf life when not in use

Organizational Commitment and Employee Engagement

Organizational commitment measures have complemented or replaced job satisfaction measures, going beyond employee satisfaction, and include the extent to which the employees identify with the organization's goals, mission, philosophy, value, policies, and practices. In recent years, the concept of involvement and engagement with the organization has become a key issue. Employee engagement is now the preferred measure. Employee engagement measures the extent to which employees are actively engaged in decisions and issues on the job. Organizational commitment and employee engagement measures closely correlate with productivity and other performance improvement measures, in contrast to employee satisfaction, which does not always correlate with improvements in productivity. As organization commitment and employee engagement scores improve (according to a standard index), a corresponding improvement in productivity should develop. Organizational commitment and employee engagement are often measured the same way that attitude surveys are, with a five- or seven-point scale taken directly from employees or groups of employees. Productivity is usually measured by revenue per employee.

Organizational commitment and employee engagement are rarely converted to monetary value. Although some relationships have been developed to link them to more tangible data, this research is still in development. For most studies, they would be listed as intangibles.

Culture and Climate

Organization culture is a very important factor for leadership development. Various programs attempt to strengthen, solidify, or adjust the culture. The culture in some organizations is distinct and defined, but it can be a challenge to measure precisely.

Some organizations use culture instruments to collect data on this measure before and after a program to measure improvement. The scores on these instruments represent important data that may be connected directly to the intervention. In practice it is challenging to convert culture data to monetary value; therefore, culture change is sometimes listed as an intangible measure.

Some organizations conduct climate surveys, which reflect work climate changes such as communication, openness, trust, and quality of feedback. Closely related to organizational commitment and culture, climate surveys are very general and often focus on a range of workplace issues and environmental enablers and inhibitors. Climate surveys conducted before and after a leadership development program is implemented may reflect the extent to which the program has changed these measures.

Diversity

Diversity continues to be important as organizations strive to develop and nurture a diverse workforce. Leadership initiatives influence the diversity mix of the organization, and various data are available to measure the impact of focusing on diversity. The diversity mix is a measure showing employee categories along diversity definitions such as race, creed, color, national origin, age, religion, and sex. This diversity mix shows the makeup of the team at any given time and is not a measure that can be credibly converted to monetary value.

The payoff of having a diverse group influences several other measures, including absenteeism, turnover, discrimination complaints, morale, and sometimes productivity and quality. Many diversity perception instruments are available to measure the attitudes of employees toward diversity issues; they are often administered before and after diversity projects. In addition, some organizations collect input on diversity issues in an annual feedback survey. All of these measures are important and reveal progress on an important issue, but these are difficult to convert directly to monetary value and are usually listed as intangibles.

Stress Reduction

Leadership development programs can reduce work-related stress by preparing employees to identify and confront stress factors to improve job performance, accomplish more in a workday, and relieve tension and anxiety. The subsequent reduction in stress may be directly linked to the intervention. Although excessive stress may be directly linked to other, easy-to-convert data, such as productivity, absenteeism, and medical claims, it is usually listed as an intangible benefit that is difficult to convert to monetary values.

FINAL THOUGHTS

This chapter discussed four key issues in calculating the leadership development contribution. The first and one of the most critical is the concept of isolating the leadership development program, which determines the extent to which the improvement was caused by the program. The second issue involves converting data to monetary values. Regardless of the type of data, there are a number of strategies that can be extremely helpful in translating the data to monetary values to use in ROI formulas. The third aspect is the cost of the program. Calculating the return on investment is the fourth factor of data analysis; however, there are several credible methods to calculate the return. Finally, the intangibles close out this section on data analysis. Data collection and analysis have little use without conveying the results to the right audience in the right way. The next chapter will highlight how to communicate the results.

REFERENCE

Phillips, P.P., and J.J. Phillips. 2015. *Making Human Capital Analytics Work: Measuring the ROI of Human Capital Processes and Outcomes*. New York: McGraw-Hill.

6

Reporting Results to Appropriate Audiences

A leadership development program was implemented to improve quality and speed of service. When the project was concluded the team measured the results, which were a mixed bag. The quality of service had improved, but the speed of service had not; in fact, it was slower than before. To share their findings, the team tried to get on the executive calendar to share results in person; the meeting was to take place six weeks later. Knowing that there were findings that needed to be communicated immediately, the team generated a report, which included major findings and charts and graphs, and was distributed to the executive team via email. Unfortunately, the report was overlooked in the sea of emails received by the executive team. It wasn't until the face-to-face meeting that the executive team saw the mixed results, and with a lot of questions raised, the tone of the meeting was tense and uncomfortable. The leadership development team leader remarked to her team afterward, "If I had to do it again, I would have escalated the need to communicate these findings in a different way."

The issues raised by this scenario represent common challenges of communicating findings. And having worked in hundreds of organizations on evaluation (with our combined experience), we have seen a wide variety of challenges in communicating results. Everything from reports with personal agendas, to dealing with stakeholders who don't know their data and evaluation needs, to groups who seemingly hide their findings under a rock. This real example helps to illustrate the nature and challenge of communication and evaluation in today's workplace.

What and when is the best way to convey results? What is the purpose for the communication? Who is the intended audience? This chapter is about the final step in the ROI process, and will address these questions and more. This chapter will highlight the dos and don'ts of communicating evaluation findings, describe a best practice report formula that can be repeatedly used to sustain momentum and change, and outline key ingredients for a communication plan.

GUIDELINES FOR COMMUNICATING RESULTS

Communicating results effectively is a systematic process with specific rules and steps. Here are seven guidelines.

Communicate Timely

Project results should usually be communicated as soon as they are known and are packaged for presentation. As in the opening story, the timing of the results was a critical factor in the project. Not sharing the results in a timely fashion can lead to a missed opportunity for well-timed improvement. Several questions about timing must be addressed:

- Is the audience prepared for the information when considering the content and other events?
- Are they expecting it?
- When is the best time to have the maximum impact on the audience?

Customize Your Communication to a Specific Audience

The communication will be more efficient when it is designed for a specific group. The message can be specifically tailored to the interests, needs, and expectations of the group. The length, content, detail, and slant will vary with the audience. Table 6-1 shows the specific audience groups with the most common reasons for communicating results.

TABLE 6-1. Common Target Audiences

Primary Target Audience	Reason for Communication
Client	To secure approval for the project
All managers	To gain support for leadership development
Participants	To secure agreement with the issues, to create the desire to be involved, and to improve the results and quality of data
Top executives	To enhance the credibility of the leadership development team
Immediate managers	To reinforce the processes, build support for the program
Leadership development team	To drive action for improvement
Facilitators	To prepare participants for the program
Human resources	To show the complete results of the program
Evaluation team	To underscore the importance of measuring results
All employees	To demonstrate accountability for expenditures
Prospective clients	To market future programs

The most important target audience is probably the client, and this often involves senior management because they need information to approve funding. The entire management group may also need to be informed about project results in a general way. Management's support for, and involvement in, leadership development is important to the success of the effort. The department's credibility is another key issue. Communicating project results to management can help establish this credibility.

The importance of communicating with a participant's immediate manager is probably obvious. In some cases, these managers need to support and allow employees to be involved in programs. An adequate return on investment improves their commitment to leadership development while enhancing the leadership development team's credibility with them.

Participants also need feedback on the overall success of their efforts. This target audience is often overlooked under the assumption that participants do not need to know about the overall success of the program.

The leadership development team members should receive information about program results, and depending on the team's reporting relationships, perhaps include HR too. For small teams, the individual conducting the evaluation may be the same person who coordinated the effort. For larger departments the evaluation may be a separate function. In either case, the team needs detailed information on the program's effectiveness so that adjustments can be made if the project is repeated.

Carefully Select Your Mode of Communication

For a specific group, one medium may be more effective than others. Face-to-face meetings may be better with some groups than special reports. A brief summary to senior management will likely be more effective than a full-blown evaluation report. The selection of an appropriate medium will help improve the effectiveness of the process. Table 6-2 illustrates options for communicating results.

TABLE 6-2. Options for Communicating Results

Detailed Reports	Brief Reports	Electronic Reporting	Mass Publications
Impact study	Executive summary	Website	Announcements
Case study (internal)	Slide overview	Email	Bulletins
Case study (external)	One-page summary	Blog	Newsletters
Major articles	Brochure	Video	Brief articles

Remain Neutral in Your Communication

The challenge for the evaluator is to remain neutral and unbiased. Let the results inform as to whether the program hit the mark. Facts are separated from fiction, and data-driven statements replace opinions. Some target audiences may view communication from the leadership development team with skepticism and may look for biased information and opinions. Boastful statements will sometimes turn off individuals, and most of the content of the communication will be lost. Observable, believable facts carry more weight than extreme claims.

Include Testimonials in Your Report

Testimonials are more effective if they are from individuals with audience credibility. Perceptions are strongly influenced by others, particularly by those who are admired or respected. Testimonials about leadership program results, when solicited from individuals who are generally respected in the organization, can have a strong impact on the effectiveness of the message. Consultants can usually be collected from participants at each level: reaction, learning, application, and impact.

Be Consistent in the Way You Communicate

Look for ways to include evaluation reporting, using the timing and forums of other organization reports. The content of the communication should be consistent with organization practices. A special communication at an unusual time may create more work than it's worth. When a particular group, such as senior management, regularly receives communication, the information should continue even if the results are not what were desired. If selected results are omitted, it might leave the impression that only good results are reported.

Do Drive Improvement From Your Communication

Information is collected at different points during the process, and providing feedback to involved groups enables them to take action and make adjustments if needed. Thus, the quality and timeliness of communication are critical to making improvements. Even after the evaluation is completed, communication is necessary to make sure the target audience fully understands the results achieved, and how the results may be enhanced in future programs or in the current program, if it is still operational. Communication is key to making important adjustments at all phases of the project.

THE CAUTIONS OF COMMUNICATING RESULTS

Communications can go astray or miss the mark. Several cautions should be observed, early and often, in the process. Here are four critical ones.

Don't Hide Your Results

The least desired communication action is doing nothing. Communicating results is almost as important as producing results. Getting results without communicating them is like planting a flower and not watering it. By not sharing the findings from your project, the organization can miss out on a key opportunity to make adjustments and bring about the change that is desired.

Don't Overlook the Political Aspects of Communication

Communication is one of those issues that can cause major problems. Because the results of a program may be closely linked to political issues within an organization, communicating the results can upset some individuals while pleasing others. If certain individuals do not receive the information, or if it is delivered inconsistently between groups, problems can quickly surface. The information must not only be understood, but issues relating to fairness, quality, and political correctness make it crucial that the communication be constructed and delivered effectively to all key individuals.

Don't Skimp on the Recommendations

Recommendations are probably one of the most critical issues and yet, it seems it is often a last minute thought or skipped altogether. Recommendations are the main conduit to change. The best recommendations include specific action-oriented steps that come from the conclusions of the evaluation study and then are discussed with key stakeholders for buy-in and ownership. The point is to collaborate with stakeholders on this section so that the results and the action that is needed are internalized.

Don't Ignore the Audience's Opinion

Opinions are difficult to change, and a negative opinion toward a program or a team may not change with the mere presentation of facts. However, the presentation of facts alone may strengthen the opinions held by those who already support the program. The presentation of the results reinforces their position and provides them with a defense in discussions with others. A project team with a high level of credibility and respect may have a relatively easy time communicating results. Low credibility can create problems when one is trying to be persuasive.

THE COMPLETE REPORT

The type of report to be issued depends on the degree of detail in the information presented to the various target audiences. Brief summaries of project results with appropriate charts may be sufficient for some communication efforts. In other situations, particularly those involving major projects requiring extensive funding, a detailed evaluation report is crucial. A complete and comprehensive impact study report is usually necessary at least in the early use of the ROI Methodology. This report can then be used as the basis for more streamlined information aimed at specific audiences and using various media. The report formula outlined below is one we use repeatedly to convey results in an effective manner. It has all the necessary ingredients to communicate outcomes in the best possible way.

- General Information
  - Background: What were the needs that precipitated the program? Why was this program selected?

- Objectives of study: What are the goals and targets for this program? What are the intended results?
- Methodology for Impact Study
  - Levels of evaluation: Describe the evaluation framework to set the stage for showing the results.
  - ROI process: Briefly describe the 10-step process that was used.
  - Collecting data: What methods were selected to collect data and why? Also, when were data collected?
  - Isolating the effects of the program: What method was used to isolate the effects of the intervention and why?
  - Converting data to monetary values: What methods were used to convert data to money?
- Data Analysis: How were data analyzed? What methods were used?
- Costs: Itemize the costs of the intervention.
- Results: General Information
- Response profile: Include demographics of the population that responded or participated in the evaluation. If a questionnaire was used, what was the return rate and the anticipated return rate?
- Results: Reaction and Planned Action
  - Data sources
  - Data summary
  - Key issues
- Results: Learning
  - Data sources
  - Data summary
  - Key issues
- Results: Application and Implementation
  - Data sources
  - Data summary
  - Key issues
- Results: Impact
  - Data sources
  - Data summary
  - Key issues
- Results: ROI calculation and what it means
- Results: Intangible Measures
- Barriers and Enablers: This section of the report can be a powerful mechanism to lead into conclusions and recommendations. What obstacles were experienced that kept the organization from experiencing the kind of results they wanted? If there were barriers noted, then this should turn into some action items for the organization.

- Conclusions: Summarize key findings from the data.
- Recommendations: Based on the conclusions, what type of action needs to take place? What are stakeholders willing to do?

While the impact study report is an effective, professional way to present ROI data, several cautions are in order. Since this report documents the success of a program involving other individuals, credit for the success must go completely to those involved—the organization members who participated in the program and their immediate leaders. Their performance generated the success.

The methodology should be clearly explained, along with the assumptions made in the analysis. The reader should easily see how the values were developed and how specific steps were followed to make the process more conservative, credible, and accurate. Detailed statistical analyses should be placed in an appendix.

USING MEETINGS

If used properly, meetings are fertile ground for the communication of program results. All organizations hold a variety of meetings, and some may provide the proper context to convey program results. Along the chain of command, staff meetings are held to review progress, discuss current problems, and distribute information. These meetings can be an excellent forum for discussing the results achieved in a program that relates to the group's activities. Program results can be sent to executives for use in a staff meeting, or a member of the evaluation team can attend the meeting to make the presentation.

Regular meetings with management groups are a common practice. Typically, discussions will focus on items that might be of help to work units. The discussion of a program and its results can be integrated into the regular meeting format. A few organizations have initiated the use of periodic meetings for all key stakeholders, where a project leader reviews progress and discusses next steps. A few highlights from interim program results can be helpful in building interest, commitment, and support for the program.

Presentation of Results to Senior Management

Perhaps one of the most challenging and stressful types of communication is presenting an impact study to the senior management team, which also serves as the client for a project. The challenge is convincing this highly skeptical and critical group that outstanding results have been achieved (assuming they have) in a very reasonable timeframe, addressing the salient points, and making sure the managers understand the process. Two potential reactions can create problems. First, if the results are very impressive, making the managers accept the data may be difficult. On the other extreme, if the data are negative, ensuring that managers don't overreact to the results and look for someone to blame is important. Several guidelines can help ensure that this process is planned and executed properly. A case study will help to see the results.

THE JOAN KRAVITZ STORY: PRESENTING THE RESULTS OF AN ROI STUDY TO SENIOR MANAGEMENT

Joan Kravitz was a little nervous as she faced the executive audience. She had been there a couple of times for other briefings, but never with this particular issue. As she scanned the room she saw the senior executives who were interested in her project, and more importantly the success of the project. She was confident she knew the material and had a clear agenda. She had practiced this briefing with her own team, who gave her very candid feedback.

Joan's project was an ROI study on the company's executive leadership development program conducted by a very prestigious business school. It was very expensive and had been conducted for leaders in the company for five years. Although the program was supported by the executives, pushing it to record levels of funding, the top executives had offered an interesting challenge and request. They wanted to see the impact that this program was having on the organization and if possible, the financial ROI. Fortunately, Joan received this request in enough time to implement changes into the program to keep it focused on results and have the participants committed to showing the value of their individual and team projects. She had discovered some very interesting and intriguing data. There were some bumps along the way, but there was still a good story to tell and she was very proud of it.

As Joan scanned the audience, she knew the perspectives of the different audience members. The CEO was not there today but the rest of the senior team was present. She was disappointed, because the CEO was the champion of her project. However, an urgent schedule change prohibited him from being there, so she had to schedule a private session with him later to cover the agenda. The chief financial officer (CFO) seemed to support the program, but he was really concerned about budgets, costs, and the value of every project, including this project. The operations executive VP saw the program as helpful, but was still concerned about business value. The VP of design and engineering did not support the program and rarely nominated participants for it. The VP of marketing was a solid supporter of the program. The executive vice president of HR was a very strong supporter and was actively involved in various parts of it. The remaining members of the group were largely neutral about the program.

Joan knew that there were two major issues she had to address. She needed to show the results and secure approval for some changes in the program, but she also needed to show the methodology she was using. Yes, they all thought they knew ROI, but not the way she was presenting it. Although this particular process used the same formula the CFO used for capital investment, it was the way in which the data were collected that made it so interesting and credible. Conservative processes were used, which should agree with this group, but she had to explain them in only 30 minutes. She was also a little afraid that if they liked this analysis process they would want to use it for all projects. So, they needed to understand that it should only be used very selectively. All of these things were racing through her mind as she opened the presentation.

The Presentation

"Good morning colleagues," Joan began, "Thank you for coming to see the value of a program that you have supported for several years. We all know the Advanced Leadership Program, which has enjoyed a five-year history with this company, with more than 200 participants. We have some results to show you from the group that participated last year. While these results are very intriguing and impressive, they do point to some important changes we need to make and I want to secure your approval for these changes."

As Joan began to relax and get comfortable with her presentation, she saw an engaged audience—no grumpy expressions or frowns so far. Joan quickly described the program and revealed the methods she used to show the value.

"Our method of choice to evaluate this program is the ROI Methodology adopted by 5,000 organizations," she said. "It is the most used evaluation system in the world and it is ideal for measuring this type of program because it captures reaction to the program, learning about the program content, application of the content, business impact, ROI, and intangibles. It operates with a system of logical process and uses some very conservative standards that you will find to be very credible and convincing. Here are two standards as applied to this study. First, the entire cost of the program was used in the calculation, including the executive time away from work. Second, on the benefit side, for individual projects, we claimed only one year of monetary value. If an executive changes behavior and implements changes for the team, there will be multiple years of benefits. For the team projects that are being implemented throughout the organization, a three-year payoff was used, which is very conservative. These time frames were endorsed by finance and accounting. These two standards, which are number nine and 10 on the list in front of you, are only two of the 12 standards we followed in conducting this study."

Joan quickly noticed that the executives were glancing at the standards while also trying to pay attention to her. This was what she wanted. She had captured their interest with those two assumptions, and they were beginning to look at some of the others. However, she had only allocated about two minutes for this issue because she had much more to present.

Reaction and Learning

"As I present the results, please feel free to ask questions at any time," Joan said. "We will keep this very interactive, but I promise to keep it within 30 minutes. The first two levels of results, reaction and learning, are presented first. While these may not be of much interest to you, we knew that the project could go astray if the participants didn't see value in them. Also, if they didn't really learn anything about themselves, their team, or their own competencies, then there wouldn't be any subsequent actions, behavior change, or impact. Fortunately, we have very positive reaction and learning results."

Joan took two minutes to cover Level 1 (reaction) and Level 2 (learning), and quickly moved into Level 3 (application).

Application

"Application describes the extent to which these executives are changing the way they work, changing their behavior from a leadership perspective," Joan continued. "I'm sure that you are more interested in this." She spent three minutes describing the table with the application data. "At this point it is appropriate to examine the barriers and enablers—the important issues that inhibit or enhance application. Here are the barriers for these executives to use this program. As you can see, they are not very strong, but it is good to know what they are. If this program had significant barriers we would want to work on them quickly."

Joan had now been speaking for 10 minutes and would focus on impact and ROI for the remainder of the presentation. Up to this point, to her surprise, there were no questions. She had thought this group would be engaged, but she knew the next section would get them involved.

Business Impact

"In terms of business impact, we examined three sets of data," Joan explained. "The first was the individual projects that the participants took on, centered on an important business measure in their particular unit. They made improvements to these measures using action plans. Your report includes a copy of an action plan and sample copies of completed ones. This chart shows a sampling of individual projects, highlighting the specific measures selected and the amount of money the improvements represent, because participants actually converted the improvements to money. These improvements, which were monitored six months after the action plans were initiated, were impressive. The chart also shows the basis for this conversion and addresses another important issue: isolating the effects of this program."

This is where Joan started to have some anxieties, because she was concerned about the executive reaction to this issue.

"As you know, when any improvement is made there are multiple factors that can drive it," she began. "The executives selected measures that are often influenced by various factors and sometimes we implement programs that are aimed at those improvements. So we must sort out the impact of this program from other influences. The best method for accomplishing this is comparing an experimental group against a control group, where one group of executives is involved in this program and another is not. As you can imagine, this won't work here because they all have different measures from different business units. So we instead rely on the executives to provide this information. These data are still very credible because it's coming from the individuals who have achieved the results, so we don't think there is any reason why they would give more results to this program than some other influence.

"This information was collected in a very nonthreatening, unbiased way," continued Joan. "We had them list any other factors that could have improved the results and then provide the percent of improvement that should be attributed to this program. Because this is an estimate—and we don't like estimates—we asked them another question: 'What is your confidence on the allocation you just provided on a scale of 0 to 100 percent?' This served as our error adjustment. For example, if someone was 80 percent confident on an allocation to the program, that reflects 20 percent error, so we would remove the 20 percent. This is achieved by multiplying by the 80 percent. Let me take you through an example."

Joan described one particular participant and followed the data through the chart to show the value. In the example, an executive had reported an improvement with three other factors causing it. He allocated 25 percent to the leadership program and was 70 percent confident with that. In that case 17.5 percent (25 percent x 70 percent) was allocated to the program.

As expected, this table attracted a lot of interest and many questions. Joan spent some time responding to those in a very confident manner.

The CFO asked, "If I want to see this particular measure, pointing to a particular individual, I could go to that business unit and find the measure and track what has changed."

"Yes," responded Joan. "You can see the actual unit value of that measure and we can provide the business unit if you would like. We did not use specific names on the chart because we did not want this to appear to be performance evaluation. This should be process improvement; if the program doesn't work we need to fix it and not necessarily go after the participant. So, we can provide the business units if you want to do that kind of audit."

"There is really no need to do that, I was just curious," responded the CFO.

"Please remember that the groups took on a team project and this particular group of people had four projects," Joan continued. "Three of those projects have been implemented and the other has not, at least at this point. So we don't count any value for the fourth project. For the three projects implemented, we used a three-year pay-off. These projects represented needed changes in the organization. Let me quickly describe the three projects."

Joan methodically described these projects, showing their monetary value, the assumptions that were made, and the isolation issue. This took about five minutes but attracted interest and questions from the executives.

Joan presented a summary of the money from individual and team projects to show the money saved or generated because of the leadership program. She reminded the audience that the amount claimed was connected to the leadership program, isolated from other influences.

Next, she presented the cost. Joan had previously reviewed the cost categories with finance and accounting and they agreed with her. In fact, her finance and accounting representative had joined her at the meeting. After showing the detailed cost table, with a quick cost summary discussion, Joan noted that all costs were included. She turned to Brenda, her finance and accounting representative, and asked for her assessment of the categories of cost that were included. Brenda confirmed that all costs seemed to be covered, and some items were included that may not be necessary. For example, the time away from work probably should not be included because these executives got their jobs done anyway. Joan added, "We wanted to be consistent and credible, so we have included all costs." She quickly looked at the CFO and could see that he was really intrigued and pleased with this part of the presentation.

ROI

Finally, Joan showed the ROI calculation, presented in two ways. The first ROI assessment, based on individual projects alone, generated an ROI of 48 percent.

"We have a standard that if someone doesn't provide you data then you assume it had no value," said Joan. "Of the 30 people in this session, six did not provide data, perhaps for good reason. Because the data were not there, we included zero for them. This is Guiding Principle 6.

"When the team projects are included, the number is staggering: 831 percent ROI," she continued. "Please remember, the data on these projects have been approved by the executives involved in the program. Only the portion of the project that is connected directly to the program is used in the calculation, recognizing that other factors could have influenced these particular data sets. So this is a huge value add from the program."

Intangibles

Joan then moved on to the intangibles. She had asked the participants the extent to which this program was influencing certain measures that are largely intangibles; key measures were listed in a chart in the report. This attracted some interest from the executives as Joan described how the table was constructed. The CFO asked about connecting these measures to monetary values.

"They have not been converted to money in our organization," Joan replied, "but some organizations have and we recommend that we pursue more of those types of conversions. The current trend is to convert more of the classic intangibles to money. This would be a good time to focus on this task."

The CFO agreed.

Conclusion and Recommendations

Joan quickly concluded with a summary and some recommendations based on comments from participants. The team project seemed to be a bit cumbersome and generated a lot of frustration with the participants. They suggested that the individual project should be enough. They pointed out that since this program had been operating for some time, many of the really challenging and necessary projects had already been addressed. So, while new ones could be generated, it could be an optional part of the process.

Joan recommended to the group that the team project become optional.

However, after some discussion, the executives concluded that the projects should remain part of the process, with administrative support provided to help the executives with their projects. Joan added that some support had always been provided and was accounted for in the project cost, but having more available support would certainly be helpful.

This decision underscored the support for the program and the results that Joan had presented. She concluded the conversation by asking if there were any other major programs that should be evaluated at this level, but cautioned that this level of evaluation takes resources for the team to conduct the study, plus the cost of having it reviewed by an external expert. The executives identified two other projects they wanted to see evaluated at this level.

The chief financial officer said that it was a good presentation and he appreciated the effort. Joan was pleased and the HR executive was elated. "This was exactly what we need to be doing, Joan," she said. "You have done an amazing job."

Reflection

Walking back to her office, Joan was relieved. She felt good about her presentation and the support from executives. She was very pleased that she was able to show the results of an important, but soft, program in a tangible, credible way. The presentation was challenging but not too difficult. She had methodically followed these guidelines:

Purpose of the Meeting

- Create awareness and understanding of ROI.
- Build support for the ROI Methodology.
- Communicate results of the study.
- Drive improvement from results.
- Cultivate effective use of the ROI Methodology.

Use These Ground Rules

- Do not distribute the impact study until the end of the meeting.
- Be precise and to the point.
- Avoid jargon and unfamiliar terms.
- Spend less time on the lower levels of evaluation data.
- Present the data with a strategy in mind.

Follow This Presentation Sequence

- Describe the program and explain why it is being evaluated.
- Present the methodology process.
- Present the reaction, learning, and application data.
- List the barriers and enablers to success.
- Address the business impact.
- Present the costs and ROI.
- Show the intangibles.
- Review the credibility of the data.
- Summarize the conclusions.
- Present the recommendations.

ROUTINE COMMUNICATION TOOLS

To reach a wide audience, internal, routine publications may be used. Whether a newsletter, magazine, newspaper, or electronic messaging, these media usually reach all employees or stakeholders. The content can have a significant impact if communicated appropriately. The scope should be limited to general-interest articles, announcements, and interviews.

Results communicated through these types of media must be important enough to arouse general interest. For example, a story with the headline "New Leadership Development Program Increases Profits" will catch the attention of many readers because they probably know about the program and can appreciate the relevance of the results. Reports on the accomplishments of a small group of organization members may not generate interest if the audience cannot relate to the accomplishments.

For many projects, results are not achieved until weeks or even months after the program is completed. Reinforcement is needed from many sources. Communicating results to a general audience may lead to motivation to continue the program or introduce similar ones in the future.

Stories about those involved in a program and the results they have achieved can help create a favorable image. Employees see that the organization is investing resources to improve performance and prepare for the future. This type of story provides information about a program that may otherwise be unknown, and sometimes creates a desire for others to participate. Public recognition of program participants who deliver exceptional performance can enhance confidence and drive them to excel.

ROUTINE FEEDBACK ON PROGRESS

A primary reason for collecting reaction and learning data is to provide feedback so that adjustments can be made throughout the program. For most programs, data are routinely collected and quickly communicated to a variety of groups. A feedback action plan designed to provide information to several audiences using a variety of media may be an option. These feedback sessions may point out specific actions that need to be taken. This process becomes complex and must be managed in a very proactive manner. The following steps are recommended for providing feedback and managing the overall process. Many of the steps and concepts are based on the recommendations of Peter Block in his landmark book *Flawless Consulting*.

- **Communicate quickly.** Whether the news is good or bad, it should be passed on to individuals involved in the project as soon as possible. The recommended time for providing feedback is usually a matter of days and certainly no longer than a week or two after the results become known.
- **Simplify the data.** Condense the data into an easily understandable, concise presentation. This is not the appropriate situation for detailed explanations and analysis.
- **Examine the role of the leadership team and the client in the feedback process.** The leadership team can wear many hats in the process. On the other hand, sometimes the client plays roles that the team is used to filling. These respective functions must be examined in terms of reactions to the data and the recommended actions.
- **Use negative data in a constructive way.** Some of the data will show that things are not going so well, and the fault may rest with the project leader or the client. In this case, the story basically changes from "let's look at the success we've achieved," to "now we know which areas to change."

- **Use positive data in a cautious way.** Positive data can be misleading, and if they are communicated too enthusiastically, they may create expectations that exceed what finally materializes. Positive data should be presented in a guarded way, allowing the response to be fully in the hands of the client.
- **Choose the language of the meeting and the communication carefully.** The language used should be descriptive, focused, specific, short, and simple. Language that is too judgmental, full of jargon, stereotypical, lengthy, or complex should be avoided.
- **Ask the client for reactions to the data.** After all, the client is the number one customer, and it is most important that the client be pleased with the project.
- **Ask the client for recommendations.** The client may have some good suggestions for what needs to be changed to keep a project on track, or to put it back on track should it derail.
- **Use support and confrontation carefully.** These two actions are not mutually exclusive. At times, support and confrontation are both needed for a particular group. The client may need support and yet be confronted for lack of improvement or sponsorship. The project team may be confronted regarding the problem areas that have developed, but may need support too.
- **Act on the data.** The different alternatives and possibilities should be weighed carefully to arrive at necessary adjustments.
- **Secure agreement from all key stakeholders.** It is essential to ensure that everyone is willing to make suggested changes.
- **Keep the feedback process short.** We discourage allowing the process to become bogged down in long, drawn-out meetings or lengthy documents. If this occurs, stakeholders will avoid the process instead of being willing participants.

Following these steps will help move the project forward and generate useful feedback, often ensuring that adjustments are supported and can be executed.

THE COMMUNICATION PLAN

Any activity must be carefully planned to achieve maximum results. This is a critical part of communicating the results of the program. The actual planning of the communication is important to ensure that each audience receives the proper information at the right time and that necessary actions are taken. Several issues are crucial in planning the communication of results:

- What will be communicated?
- When will the data be communicated?
- How will the information be communicated?
- Where will the information be communicated?
- Who will communicate the information?

- Who is the target audience?
- What are the specific actions required or desired?

The communication plan is usually developed when the program is approved. This plan details how specific information is developed and communicated to various groups and the expected actions. In addition, this plan details how the overall results will be communicated, the timeframe for communication, and the appropriate groups to receive the information. The leadership development team leader, key managers, and stakeholders need to agree on the degree of detail in the plan.

FINAL THOUGHTS

The final step in the ROI Methodology, communication of results, is a crucial step in the overall evaluation process. If this step is not executed adequately, the full impact of the results will not be recognized, and the study may amount to a waste of time. The chapter began with general dos and don'ts for communicating results; these can serve as a guide for any significant communication effort. The various target audiences were then discussed, with the most commonly used media for communicating project results. The next chapter will discuss how to sustain the momentum of evaluation and overcome barriers to using the methodology.

REFERENCE

Block, P. 2011. *Flawless Consulting: A Guide to Getting Your Expertise Used*, 3rd ed. San Francisco: Pfeiffer.

Implementing and Sustaining ROI

E ven the best-designed process, model, or technique is worthless unless it is effectively and efficiently integrated into the organization. Change is not permanent for many reasons. One reason is resistance. As it relates to ROI, some of this resistance is based on fear and misunderstanding. Some is real, based on actual barriers and obstacles. Although the ROI process presented in this book is a step-by-step, methodical, and simplistic procedure, it can fail if it is not integrated properly, fully accepted, and supported by those who must make it work within the organization. This chapter focuses on some of the most effective means of overcoming resistance to implementing the ROI process in an organization.

THE IMPORTANCE OF SUSTAINING THE USE OF ROI

With any new process or change, there is resistance. Resistance may be especially great when implementing a process as complex as ROI. To implement ROI and sustain it as an important accountability tool, the resistance must be minimized or removed. Here are four reasons to have a plan.

Resistance is always present. Resistance to change is a constant. Sometimes, there are good reasons for resistance, but often it exists for the wrong reasons. It is important to sort out both kinds of resistance and try to dispel the myths. When legitimate barriers are the basis for resistance, the challenge is to minimize or remove them completely.

Implementation is key. As with any process, effective implementation is key to its success. This occurs when the new technique, tool, or process is integrated into the routine framework. Without effective implementation, even the best process will fail. A process that is never removed from the shelf will never be understood, supported, or improved. Clear-cut steps must be in place for designing a comprehensive implementation process that will overcome resistance.

Implementation requires consistency. Consistency is an important consideration as the ROI process is implemented. With consistency comes accuracy and reliability. The only way to make sure consistency is achieved is to follow clearly defined processes and procedures each time the ROI Methodology is used. Proper, effective implementation will ensure that this occurs.

Implementation requires efficiency. Cost control and efficiency will be significant considerations in any major undertaking, and the ROI Methodology is no exception. During implementation, tasks must be completed efficiently and effectively. Doing so will help ensure that process costs are kept to a minimum, that time is used economically, and that the process remains affordable.

IMPLEMENTING THE PROCESS: OVERCOMING RESISTANCE

Resistance shows up in varied ways—in the form of comments, remarks, actions, or behaviors. The following is a list of representative comments that indicate open resistance to the ROI process:

- It costs too much.
- It takes too much time.
- Who is asking for this?
- This is not in my job description.
- I did not have input on this.
- I do not understand this.
- What happens when the results are negative?
- How can we be consistent with this?
- The ROI looks too subjective.
- Our managers will not support this.
- ROI is too narrowly focused.
- This is not practical.

Each comment signals an issue that must be resolved or addressed in some way. A few are based on realistic barriers, whereas others are based on myths that must be dispelled. Sometimes, resistance to the process reflects underlying concerns. For example, owners of leadership programs may fear losing control of their programs, and others may feel vulnerable to whatever action may follow if the program is not successful. Still others may be concerned about any process that brings change or requires additional effort.

Leadership development practitioners may resist the ROI process and openly make comments similar to those listed above. It may take evidence of tangible and intangible benefits to convince team members that it is in their best interest to make the project a success. Although most clients want to see the results of the program, they may have concerns about the information they are asked to provide and about whether their personal performance is being judged while the project is undergoing evaluation. Participants may express the same fears.

The challenge is to implement the methodology systematically and consistently so that it becomes normal business behavior and part of a routine and standard process built into projects. The implementation necessary to overcome resistance covers a variety of areas. Figure 7-1 shows the actions outlined in this chapter that are presented as building blocks to overcoming resistance. They are all necessary to build the proper base or framework to dispel myths and remove or minimize barriers. The remainder of this chapter presents specific strategies and techniques devoted to each building block identified in Figure 7-1. They apply equally to the leadership development team and the client organization, and no attempt is made to separate the two.

FIGURE 7-1. Building Blocks for Overcoming Resistance

| Monitoring Progress; Reporting Results |
| Removing Obstacles |
| Preparing the Management Team |
| Initiating the Projects |
| Preparing the Staff; Skill Development |
| Revising Policies, Procedures, and Practices |
| Establishing Goals and Plans for the Transition |
| Developing Roles and Responsibilities |
| Assessing the Climate for Achieving Results |

ASSESSING THE CLIMATE

As a first step toward implementation, some organizations assess the current climate for achieving results. One way to do this is to develop a survey to determine the current perspectives of the leadership development team and other stakeholders. A special instrument is available for this at the ROI Institute (www.roiinstitute.net). Another way is to conduct interviews with key stakeholders to determine their willingness to follow the program through to ROI. With an awareness of the current status, the leadership development team can plan for significant changes and pinpoint particular issues that need support as the ROI process is implemented.

DEVELOPING ROLES AND RESPONSIBILITIES

Defining and detailing specific roles and responsibilities for different groups and individuals addresses many of the resistance factors and helps pave a smooth path for implementation.

Identifying a Champion

As an early step in the process, one or more individuals should be designated as the internal leader or champion for the ROI Methodology. As in most change efforts, someone must take responsibility for ensuring that the process is implemented successfully. This leader serves as a champion for ROI and is usually the one who understands the process best and sees vast potential for its contribution. More important, this leader is willing to teach others and will work to sustain sponsorship.

Develop the ROI Leader

The ROI leader is usually a member of the leadership development team who has the responsibility for evaluation. For large organizations, the ROI leader may be part of HR or learning and development. This person holds a full-time position in larger program teams or a part-time position in smaller teams. Client organizations may also have an ROI leader who pursues the ROI Methodology from the client's perspective. The typical job title for a full-time ROI leader is manager or director of analytics or measurement and evaluation. Some organizations assign this responsibility to a team and empower it to lead the ROI effort.

In preparation for this assignment, individuals usually receive special training that builds specific skills and knowledge of the ROI process. The role of the implementation leader is quite broad and serves many specialized duties. In some organizations, the implementation leader can take on many roles, ranging from diagnostician to problem solver to communicator.

Leading the ROI process is a difficult and challenging assignment that requires unique skills. Fortunately, programs are available that teach these skills. For example, one such program is designed to certify individuals who will be assuming leadership roles in the implementation of the ROI Methodology. For more detail, see www.roiinstitute.net. This certification is built around 10 specific skill sets linked to successful ROI implementation, focusing on the critical areas of data collection, isolating the effects of the project, converting data to monetary value, presenting evaluation data, and building capability. This process is quite comprehensive but may be necessary to build the skills needed for taking on this challenging assignment.

Establishing a Task Force

Making the ROI Methodology work well may require the use of a task force. A task force usually comprises a group of individuals from different parts of the project or client team who are willing to develop the ROI Methodology and implement it in the organization. The selection of the task force may involve volunteers, or participation may be mandatory depending on specific job responsibilities. The task force should represent the cross section necessary for accomplishing stated goals. Task forces have the additional advantage of bringing more people into the process and developing more ownership of and support for the ROI Methodology. The task force must be large enough to cover the key areas but not so large that it becomes too cumbersome to function. Six to 12 members is a good size.

Assigning Responsibilities

Determining specific responsibilities is critical because confusion can arise when individuals are unclear about their specific assignments in the ROI process. Responsibilities apply to two areas. The first is the measurement and evaluation responsibility of the entire leadership development team. Everyone involved in the program will have some responsibility for measurement and evaluation. These responsibilities may include providing input on designing instruments, planning specific evaluations, analyzing data, and interpreting the results. Typical responsibilities include:

- ensuring that the initial analysis or diagnosis for the project includes specific business impact measures
- developing specific application and business impact objectives for the project
- keeping the organization or team members focused on application and impact objectives
- communicating rationale and reasons for evaluation
- assisting in follow-up activities to capture application and business impact data
- providing assistance for data collection, data analysis, and reporting.

Although involving each member of the leadership development team in all these activities may not be appropriate, each individual should have at least one responsibility as part of his routine job duties. This assignment of responsibility keeps the ROI Methodology from being disjointed and separated during projects. More important, it brings accountability to those directly involved in implementation.

The assignment of responsibilities for evaluation requires attention throughout the evaluation process. Although the team must be assigned specific responsibilities during an evaluation, requiring others to serve in support functions to help with data collection is not unusual. These responsibilities are defined when a particular evaluation strategy is developed and approved.

ESTABLISHING GOALS AND PLANS

Establishing goals, targets, and objectives is critical to the implementation, particularly when several evaluations are planned. The establishment of goals can include detailed planning documents for the overall process and for individual ROI projects.

Setting Evaluation Targets

Establishing specific targets for evaluation levels is an important way to make progress with measurement and evaluation. As emphasized throughout this book, not every program should be evaluated to the ROI level. Knowing in advance to which level the program will be evaluated helps in planning which measures will be needed and how detailed the evaluation must be at each level. Table 7-1 presents an example of targets set for evaluation at each level from one of the largest financial services companies in the world. The setting of targets should be completed early in the process with the full support of the entire team. If practical and feasible, the targets should also have the approval of key managers—particularly the senior management team.

TABLE 7-1. Evaluation Targets in a Large Organization

Level	Target
Level 1, Reaction	100%
Level 2, Learning	80%
Level 3, Application and Implementation	40%
Level 4, Business Impact	25%
Level 5, ROI	10%

Developing a Plan for Implementation

An important part of implementation is establishing a timetable for the complete implementation of the ROI process. This document becomes a master plan for completion of the different elements presented earlier. Beginning with forming a team and concluding with meeting the targets previously described, this schedule is a project plan for transitioning from the present situation to the desired future situation. Items on the schedule include developing specific ROI projects, building staff skills, developing policy, and teaching managers the process. Figure 7-2 is an example of an implementation plan. The more detailed the document, the more useful it becomes. The project plan is a living, long-range document that should be reviewed frequently and adjusted as necessary. More important, those engaged in work on the ROI Methodology should always be familiar with it.

REVISING OR DEVELOPING GUIDELINES AND PROCEDURES

Another part of planning is revising or developing the organization's policy or guidelines on measurement and evaluation. The guidelines document contains information developed specifically for the measurement and evaluation process. It is developed with input from the leadership development team and key managers or stakeholders. Sometimes, these guidelines are addressed during internal workshops designed to build measurement and evaluation skills. This statement addresses critical matters that will influence the effectiveness of the measurement and evaluation process. These

FIGURE 7-2. ROI Implementation Plan for a Large Petroleum Company

	J	F	M	A	M	J	J	A	S	O	N	D	J	F	M	A	M	J	J	A	S	O	N
Team formed	█																						
Responsibilities defined		█																					
Policy developed			█	█																			
Targets set		█	█																				
Workshops developed				█	█	█	█																
ROI Project (A)						█	█	█	█														
ROI Project (B)									█	█	█	█											
ROI Project (C)												█	█	█	█								
ROI Project (D)														█	█	█	█	█	█	█			
Project teams trained									█														
Managers trained																█	█	█	█				
Support tools developed			█	█	█																		
Guidelines developed		█	█			█																	

may include adopting the five-level framework presented in this book, requiring Level 3 and 4 objectives for some or all programs, and defining responsibilities for the leadership development team.

Guidelines are important because they provide structure and direction for the team and others who work closely with the ROI Methodology. These individuals keep the process clearly focused, and enable the group to establish goals for evaluation. Guidelines also provide an opportunity to communicate basic requirements and fundamentals of performance and accountability. More than anything, they serve as learning tools to teach others, especially when they are developed in a collaborative way. If guidelines are developed in isolation, the team and management will be denied the sense of their ownership, making them neither effective nor useful.

Procedures for measurement and evaluation are important for showing how to use the tools and techniques, guide the design process, provide consistency in the ROI process, ensure that appropriate methods are used, and place the proper emphasis on each of the areas. The procedures are more technical than the guidelines and often include detailed steps showing how the process is undertaken and developed. They often include specific forms, instruments, and tools necessary to facilitate the process.

PREPARING THE TEAM

Leadership development team members may resist the ROI Methodology. They often see evaluation as an unnecessary intrusion into their responsibilities that absorbs precious time and stifles creative freedom. The cartoon character Pogo perhaps characterized it best when he said, "We have met the enemy, and he is us." Several issues must be addressed when preparing the leadership development team for ROI implementation.

Involving the Leadership Development Team

For each key issue or major decision involving ROI implementation, the leadership development team should be involved in the process. As evaluation guidelines are prepared and procedures are developed, team input is essential. Resistance is more difficult if the team helped design and develop the ROI process. Convene meetings, brainstorming sessions, and task forces to involve the team in every phase of developing the framework and supporting documents for ROI.

Using ROI as a Learning and Process Improvement Tool

One reason the leadership development team may resist the ROI process is that the program's effectiveness will be fully exposed, putting the reputation of the team on the line. They may have a fear of failure. To overcome this, the ROI Methodology should be clearly positioned as a tool for learning and process improvement, not a tool for evaluating project team performance (at least not during the early years of project implementation). Team members will not be interested in developing a process that may reflect unfavorably on their performance.

Evaluators can learn as much from failures as from success. If the program is not working, it is best to find out quickly so that issues can be understood firsthand, not from others. If the program is ineffective and not producing the desired results, the failure will eventually be known to clients and the management group (if they are not aware of it already). A lack of results will make managers less supportive of immediate and future projects. If the weaknesses are identified and adjustments made quickly, not only can more effective projects be developed, but also the credibility of and respect for project implementation can be enhanced.

Teaching the Team

The leadership development team usually has inadequate skills in measurement and evaluation, and will need to develop some expertise. Measurement and evaluation are not always a formal part of the team's or evaluator's job preparation. Consequently, the leadership development team leader must learn ROI Methodology and its systematic steps; the evaluator must learn to develop an evaluation strategy and specific plan, to collect and analyze data from the evaluation, and to interpret results from data analysis.

INITIATING ROI STUDIES

The first tangible evidence of the value of using the ROI Methodology may be seen at the initiation of the first leadership development program for which an ROI calculation is planned. Because of this, it is important to identify appropriate programs and keep them on track.

Selecting the Initial Project

It is critical that appropriate leadership development programs be selected for ROI analysis. Only certain types of projects qualify for comprehensive, detailed analysis. The characteristics of programs that are suitable for analysis were presented in chapter 3.

Using these or similar criteria, the leadership development leader must select the appropriate programs to consider for ROI evaluation. Ideally, sponsors should agree with or approve the criteria.

Developing the Planning Documents

Perhaps the two most useful ROI documents are the data collection plan and the ROI analysis plan. The data collection plan shows what data will be collected, the methods used, the sources, the timing, and the assignment of responsibilities. The ROI analysis plan shows how specific analyses will be conducted, including how to isolate the effects of the project and how to convert data to monetary values. Each evaluator should know how to develop these plans. Please refer to chapter 4 for more detail on these documents.

Status meetings should be conducted to report progress and discuss critical issues with appropriate team members. These meetings keep the leadership development team focused on the critical issues, generate the best ideas for addressing problems and barriers, and build a knowledge base for better implementation of future evaluations. In essence, the meetings serve three major purposes: reporting progress, learning, and planning.

PREPARING THE CLIENTS AND EXECUTIVES

Perhaps no group is more important to the ROI process than the management team that must allocate resources for leadership development and support its implementation. In addition, the management team often provides input to and assistance for the ROI process. Preparing, training, and developing the management team should be carefully planned and executed.

One effective approach for preparing executives and managers for the ROI process is to conduct a briefing on ROI. Varying in duration from one hour to half a day, a practical briefing such as this can provide critical information and enhance support for ROI use. Managers leave these briefings with greater appreciation of ROI and its potential impact on projects, and with a clearer understanding of their role in the process. More important, they often renew their commitment to react to and use the data collected by the ROI Methodology.

A strong, dynamic relationship between the leadership development team and key managers is essential for successful implementation of the ROI Methodology. There must be a productive partnership that requires each party to understand the concerns, problems, and opportunities of the other. The development of a beneficial relationship is a long-term process that must be deliberately planned for and initiated by key leadership development team members. The decision to commit resources and support to an intervention may be based on the effectiveness of this relationship.

REMOVING OBSTACLES

As the ROI Methodology is implemented, there will inevitably be obstacles to its progress. The obstacles are based on concerns discussed in this chapter, some of which may be valid, others of which may be based on unrealistic fears or misunderstandings.

Dispelling Myths

As part of the implementation, attempts should be made to dispel the myths and remove or minimize the barriers or obstacles. Much of the controversy regarding ROI stems from misunderstandings about what the process can and cannot do and how it can or should be implemented in an organization. After years of experience with ROI, and having noted reactions during hundreds of interventions and workshops, observers recognize many misunderstandings about ROI, including:

- ROI is too complex for most users.
- ROI is expensive and consumes too many critical resources.
- If senior management does not require ROI, there is no need to pursue it.
- ROI is a passing fad.
- ROI is only one type of data.
- ROI is not future-oriented; it only reflects past performance.
- ROI is rarely used by organizations.
- The ROI Methodology cannot be easily replicated.
- ROI is not a credible process; it is too subjective.
- ROI cannot be used with soft projects.
- Isolating the influence of other factors is not always possible.
- ROI is only appropriate for large organizations.
- No standards exist for the ROI Methodology.

Delivering Bad News

One of the most difficult obstacles to overcome is receiving inadequate, insufficient, or disappointing news. Addressing a bad-news situation is an issue for most project leaders and other stakeholders involved in the evaluation. The time to think about bad news is early in the process, but without losing sight of its value. In essence, bad news means that things can change, they need to change, and the situation can improve. The team and others need to be convinced that good news can be found in a bad-news situation. Here is some advice to follow when delivering bad news:

- Never fail to recognize the power to learn and improve with a negative study.
- Look for red flags along the way.
- Lower outcome expectations with key stakeholders along the way.
- Look for data everywhere.

- Never alter the standards.
- Remain objective throughout the process.
- Prepare the team for the bad news.
- Consider different scenarios.
- Find out what went wrong.
- Adjust the story line to: "Now we have data that show how to make this program more successful." In an odd way, this puts a positive spin on data that are less than positive.

Using the Data

It is unfortunately too often the case that programs are evaluated and significant data are collected, but no action is taken with the data. Failure to use data is a tremendous obstacle because the team has a tendency to move on to the next project or issue and get on with other priorities. Table 7-2 shows how the different levels of data can be used to improve projects. It is critical that the data be used—the data were essentially the justification for undertaking the project evaluation in the first place. Failure to use the data may mean that the entire evaluation was a waste. As the table illustrates, many reasons exist for collecting the data and using them after collection. These can become action items for the team to ensure that changes and adjustments are made. In addition, the client or sponsor must act to ensure that the uses of data are appropriately addressed.

TABLE 7-2. Use of Evaluation Data

Use of Evaluation Data	Appropriate Level of Data				
	1	2	3	4	5
Adjust program design	✔	✔			
Improve implementation			✔	✔	
Influence application and program impact			✔	✔	
Improve management support for the program			✔	✔	
Improve stakeholder satisfaction			✔	✔	✔
Recognize and reward participants		✔	✔	✔	
Justify or enhance budget				✔	✔
Reduce costs		✔	✔	✔	✔
Market programs in the future	✔		✔	✔	✔

MONITORING PROGRESS

A final element of the implementation process is monitoring the overall progress made and communicating that progress. Although often overlooked, an effective communication plan can help keep the implementation on target and can let others know what the ROI Methodology is accomplishing for the leadership development team and the client. Elements of a communication plan were discussed in chapter 6.

The initial schedule for implementation of ROI is based on key events or milestones. Routine progress reports should be developed to communicate the status of these events or milestones. Reports are usually developed at six-month intervals but may be more frequent for short-term projects. Two target audiences, the leadership development team and senior managers, are critical for progress reporting. All leadership development team members should be kept informed of the progress, and senior managers should know the extent to which ROI is being implemented and how it is working within the organization.

FINAL THOUGHTS

Even the best model or process will die if it is not used and sustained. This chapter explored the implementation of the ROI process and ways to sustain its use. If not approached in a systematic, logical, and planned way, the ROI process will not be an integral part of the leadership development evaluation efforts, and accountability will suffer. This chapter presented the different elements that must be considered and issues that must be addressed to ensure that implementation is smooth and uneventful. Smooth implementation is the most effective means of overcoming resistance to ROI. The result provides a complete integration of ROI as a mainstream component of major projects.

The first part of this book outlined the relevant steps necessary to use the ROI Methodology with leadership development programs. In the next part we share cases illustrating how the ROI process was applied to different leadership development programs.

Part II

Evaluation in Action

Case Studies Describing the Evaluation of Leadership Development Programs

8

Measuring ROI in Leadership for Performance for Store Managers

Fashion Stores Incorporated

Jack J. Phillips and Patti P. Phillips

This case was prepared to serve as a basis for discussion rather than an illustration of either effective or ineffective administrative and management practices. Names, dates, places, and data have been disguised at the request of the author or organization.

Abstract

This large fashion retailer with popular brands is planning for growth and profitability. The store managers were identified as the most critical talent in the organization. The leadership development program was carefully designed for more than 4,000 store managers, with an upfront needs assessment and initial alignment. It is designed to drive key performance measures within the stores using a combination of learning portals, coaches, 360-degree feedback, and a two-day classroom session.

BACKGROUND

Fashion Stores, Inc. (FSI) is a large international retailer with four major brands. The retailer operates stores in more than 50 countries with more than 100,000 employees. Store managers, who are considered to be the critical talent in the organization, manage the stores. The retailer has plans for tremendous growth, with a goal to have stores in more than 100 countries and to be the most profitable retail store chain. While all employees are considered to be important talent, the store managers are considered critical for achieving these two goals. To make this growth and profitability a reality, FSI wants to invest in leadership development for store managers. Moving beyond the current manager training program, sales training, and other types of learning and development opportunities offered to this group, this new program is aimed at developing leaders who can develop high-performance teams that will drive superior results for the stores.

The Analysis

Meeting the needs of the executives to develop this program required the leadership development team to focus on two important areas. The first is to determine the specific competencies necessary for high-performance teams and to ensure that those competencies are needed in the stores. The second important area of the process is to ensure that this program directly aligns with very specific business metrics.

The first part of the analysis included a review of the literature on leadership development for high-performance teams to determine some of the common threads between high-performance workplaces. Next, through interviews with the senior executives and regional store executives, the competencies were further tuned and customized to the company's situation and culture. In addition, a dozen store managers participated in a focus group to understand how these competencies fit into the structure and culture of the stores. The discussion also focused on the extent to which the current store managers currently possessed those competencies. This led to further adjustments, and 10 competencies and skills of high-performance teams were determined to be directly related to this culture and type of business:

1. Identifying opportunities for improvements
2. Addressing challenges and road blocks
3. Building trust and confidence
4. Setting clear goals and expectations
5. Managing conflicts and differences
6. Recognizing and rewarding team members
7. Improving average performers
8. Fostering open and clear communications
9. Providing feedback and support
10. Action planning, reflecting, and adjusting

With these competencies identified, the next phase was to determine the best way to deliver the program and achieve business alignment.

Program Design

As with most retail organizations, taking managers away from their work for an extensive period of time was nearly impossible. Presently, the learning and development team and the leadership development team were using a variety of different types of technology-based learning methods. After reviewing the effectiveness of the different learning delivery methods, and considering the cost and convenience, a learning design was developed that would include e-learning modules, the use of a learning portal, classroom learning, coaching support, and the use of 360-degree feedback—all focused on achieving business impact. Figure 8-1 shows the program design.

FIGURE 8-1. Program Design: Leadership for Performance

	Awareness and Alignment	Learning, Engagement, and Practice	Application, Impact, and Reporting
	Technology Based	Classroom Two Days	On the Job

30 min e-learning	• Awareness
	• Decision to improve
		• Expectations and commitment
		• 360-degree feedback
		• 10 skills of high-performance teams
		• Skill videos
		• Realistic practice
		• Engagement and reflection
		• Skill-impact linkage
		• Planning
		  – Business impact
		  – Behaviors or action
			• Connect with manager and coach

30 min e-learning	• Program design • Process flow		• Implement actions • Make adjustments
30 min e-learning	• Customization • Learning styles • Cultural adjustment		• Review videos • Use tools • Use portal
30 min e-learning survey	• 360-degree feedback • Use • Rules		• Impact capture • Analysis • Documentation
30 min e-learning	• Alignment • Business impact measures • Making the connection		• Reporting • Sharing

The program begins with five 30-minute e-learning modules that participants complete before attending the program. The first module focuses on the awareness of the process, the need to improve results, and how the program is designed to increase store performance, which usually attracts the interest of the store managers. The next module focuses on the program design and how it will flow through the different module segments and components. The third module indicates how the program is customized to their needs, designed around various learning styles, and adapted to cultural differences. This is connected to HR data using a process that matches the individual's learning style, as well as the culture of the store and country. The fourth e-learning module presents the 360-degree feedback process, which describes its purpose, use, and particular rules and conditions. Participants will take the survey shortly after this module is completed. Finally the last, and perhaps most critical, is the fifth e-learning module, which covers the alignment process. It starts with the business impact measures in the store by asking each store manager to select at least two measures that would need to improve using the competencies in the program. This begins with the end in mind, with the end defined as business performance improvement.

With these modules complete, participants are scheduled to attend a two-day workshop near their store. These workshops are offered in major cities, or in countries and regions where fewer stores are located.

The two-day workshop is relevant, engaging, and reflective. The workshop starts with expectations and commitments and moves into a review of the 360-degree feedback. From that, the individuals identify actions where improvement is needed. The 10 skills for high-performance teams are explored in detail. Videos, developed for the skill sets, are very powerful and used to reinforce each skill. Individuals then participate in realistic practice sessions focusing on a particular problem area or opportunity as defined by the business measure. The skill practices involve conversations with employees who can make a difference in the particular measure. The learning is engaging with much time for reflection on what actions are needed. The linkage between the high-performance skills and business impact are also discussed, and the two-day workshop ends with developing at least two action plans. Figure 8-2 shows a typical action plan that is used for this particular project.

The program is not complete at the end of the two-day workshop—five more components of the program are now put in place to be managed on the job. The first is the appointment for the individuals to reconnect with their manager about the measures selected for improvement, give feedback on the program, and secure manager support going forward. There is also an appointment to connect with a coach that was selected by the store manager (the participant). The coach is prepared to assist them along the way, providing guidance and support as needed to make the process work. The second component is to implement actions and make adjustments when necessary. After discussing the issues with the manager and coach, there may be some adjustments in both the business measure and the specific actions necessary to improve the measures.

The third component of the project's application is using the videos and tools provided in the learning portal. This includes reviewing the videos, checklists, and job aids that might be helpful in working with the team using the competencies. A fourth component, which is a very important part of the process, is to record the impact improvement, conduct an analysis, isolate the effects of the program from other influences, and calculate the monetary value of each process. The information and tools for this were provided in the workshop and are available to them online and from store databases. The summary information was recorded on each action plan. Finally, the last component is to report results to the leadership development team. This information is then shared with the rest of the group.

The program components, shown in Table 8-1, represent a tremendous amount of variety, all designed to enhance learning, encourage engagement, facilitate application, and drive business impact. Technology use is significant, with much of the program operating virtually. E-learning is an important part of this program, with five

FIGURE 8-2. Action Plan Template

Action Plan

Participant: _____ Manager: _____ Program Manager: _____

Objective: Increase sales with existing clients by 20 percent Evaluation Period: January to March

Improvement Measure: Monthly Sales Current Performance: $56,000/mo. Target Performance: $67,000

Action Steps		Analysis
Meet with key clients to discuss issues, concerns, opportunities.	Jan. 31	A. What is the unit of measure? Monthly sales, existing clients
Review customer feedback data—look for trends and patterns.	Feb. 1	B. What is the value (cost) of one unit? 25% profit margin
Counsel with "at-risk" clients to correct problems and explore opportunities.	Feb. 2	C. How did you arrive at this value? Standard value
Develop business plan for high-potential clients.	Feb. 5	D. How much did the measure change during the evaluation period (monthly value)? $13,000
Provide recognition to clients with long tenure.	Routinely	E. What other factors could have contributed to this improvement? Changes in market, new promotion
Schedule appreciation dinner for key clients.	Feb. 15	F. What percent of this change was actually caused by this program? 30%
Encourage marketing to delegate more responsibilities.	Feb. 20	G. What level of confidence do you place on the above information? (100% = Certainty and 0% = No confidence) 60%
Follow up with each discussion and discuss improvement and plan other action.	Routinely	
Monitor improvement, provide support when appropriate.	March 15	
Intangible benefits: Client satisfaction, loyalty		Comments: Excellent, hard-hitting program

117

modules serving as the prelude to the classroom. The classroom is supplemented with a coach, support, and tools that are available virtually. The learning portal provides a variety of tools, templates, process checklists, and the videos used in the workshop— all of which are aimed at reinforcing, explaining, and enhancing performance as the managers use the competencies and drive store performance. In addition, the program has the flexibility of being adapted to different learning styles and can be adjusted culturally to the different countries where the program is conducted.

TABLE 8-1. Program Components

1.	E-learning
2.	Learning portal
3.	360-degree assessment
4.	Classroom involvement and engagement
5.	Practice in real situations
6.	Learning, reflection, and action
7.	Cultural adjustment
8.	Learning styles
9.	Realistic videos
10.	Coaching support

The leadership development team was in charge of this project from the very beginning. They engaged with external vendors for needs assessment, the program design, and a separate production company for the videos. Finally, an external firm was involved in the evaluation.

THE EVALUATION APPROACH

Eventually, this program will be available to 4,000 managers. Although it is required, if managers are convinced that they have the necessary skill sets, they have the option to skip the classroom portion, but they still have to take on the part of the process that involves application and impact. It is anticipated that very few, if any, will opt out of this process because they will understand the need for the program and realize that it is aimed at improving store performance.

To understand how well the program is working and to see if adjustments are made, the organizers targeted about 100 people for the initial evaluation, with representatives from one workshop in each of the four largest markets in the company—the United States, South America, Asia, and Europe. An early workshop will be offered in those areas if possible, and it is anticipated that approximately 25 participants will attend each workshop. However, attendance numbers may be higher or lower depending on availability and the concentration of managers in the area.

Because of the cost of the program and its link to the success of the business and strategic objectives, the management team would like the evaluation to include both the impact and the ROI. The leadership development team engaged the services of the global leader in ROI evaluation to provide oversight, guidance, support, and advice for the evaluation. Its role was planning the evaluation, data collection and analysis, and presentation to the senior executives. In addition, the ROI expert worked hand-in-hand with the leadership development team to develop this level of evaluation capability internally for future projects.

Data Collection
Figure 8-3 shows the data collection plan for this program. The plan starts with the objectives and defines the measures, data collection method and source, timing, and responsibilities. This is a classic plan for ROI analysis.

ROI Analysis Plan
Figure 8-4 presents the ROI analysis plan for this project, and represents a very common approach to this type of analysis. It begins with the business impact measures that will be influenced by the program. Each participant selects at least two measures to improve, using the competencies and skills for high-performance teams. The method of isolation is the participant's estimate. A comparison group would be best; however, experimental versus control group comparison is not possible because participants may have selected different measures. With participant estimates, the data are collected in a nonthreatening, nonbiased way, and there are adjustments for error in their estimates. The method used to convert data to money is using standard items (presented later) provided to participants in the two-day workshop or through experts.

RESULTS
A total of 93 participants attended the workshop and applied the competencies. A variety of data collection methods were used, including questionnaires, action planning, and observation to provide the results organized by different levels.

Level 1 (Reaction) Results
Table 8-2 shows how participants reacted to the program. This was done one month after the workshop to give individuals an opportunity to clarify their reactions and provide responses. The group's average reaction was meeting or exceeding expectations (four out of five on a five-point scale). A total of 89 responded to this

FIGURE 8-3. Data Collection Plan

Program/Project: _____ Responsibility: _____ Date: _____

Level	Broad Program Objective(s)	Measures	Data Collection Method/Instruments	Data Sources	Timing	Responsibilities
1	**SATISFACTION/PLANNED ACTION** Participants will rate the following reactions: • The program was important to my success • My coach was helpful • Content is relevant • The technology was effective • I will use the content with my team • The classroom session was valuable • I would recommend this program to others • The program is easy to follow • The action plan was valuable	4 out of 5 on a 5-point scale	Questionnaire	Participants	2 to 4 months from start of program (some items collected one month after end of workshop)	Leadership development team
2	**LEARNING** Demonstrate successful use of the following skill sets: • Identifying opportunities for improvement • Addressing challenges and road blocks • Building trust and confidence • Setting clear goals and expectations • Managing conflicts and differences • Providing feedback and support • Recognizing and rewarding team members • Improving average performers • Fostering open and clear communication • Action planning, reflecting, and adjusting	3 out of 4 on a 4-point scale	Observation	Facilitator	At the end of the workshop	Facilitator

Level	Broad Program Objective(s)	Measures	Data Collection Method/Instruments	Data Sources	Timing	Responsibilities
	Participants will know how to: • Increase effectiveness as a leader • Build high-performance teams • Build self-assessed learning change	4 out of 5 on a 5-point scale	Questionnaire	Facilitator	At the end of the workshop	Facilitator
3	APPLICATION/IMPLEMENTATION Participants will: • Complete the action plan within 4 months • Use the coach • Use the learning portal • Apply the 10 leadership skills • Use the 10 skills frequently • Will achieve success with the 10 skills	• Checklist • 4 out of 5 on a 5-point scale	Questionnaire Action Plan	Participants	2 months	Leadership development team
4	BUSINESS IMPACT Participants will make improvements in at least two of the following measures: • Increased sales with existing customers • New customers • Staff turnover • Store profit margin • Inventory shrinkage • Product returns • Store expenses • Customer complaints • Staff sick leave • Other:		Action plan	Participants	4 months after workshop	Leadership development team
5	ROI 20%	Comments:				

FIGURE 8-4. Sample ROI Analysis Plan

ROI ANALYSIS PLAN
Program/Project: _____

Purpose of this evaluation: _____
Responsibility: _____   Date: _____

Data Items (Usually Level 4)	Methods for Isolating the Effects of the Program/Process	Methods of Converting Data to Monetary Values	Cost Categories	Intangible Benefits	Communication Targets for Final Report	Other Influences/ Issues During Application	Comments
At least two measures selected by participant	Participant's estimate	Standard values or expert input	• Initial analysis and assessment • Development of solutions • Implementation and application • Salaries and benefits for LD team • Salaries and benefits for participants' time • Salaries and benefits for coaches' time • Program materials • Hardware and software • Travel, lodging, and meals • Use of facilities • Administrative support and overhead • Evaluation and reporting	• Job engagement • Career satisfaction • Net promoter score • Image • Reputation • Brand	• Top executives • Regional store managers • HR team • Participants • Leadership development team • Prospective participants		

questionnaire, representing a 96 percent response rate. The technology effectiveness question (question four) had a lower than expected result. There were a few technology glitches that got in the way and some managers had difficulty following the program's different modules and processes. Otherwise, the reaction to the program was quite good, with "intent to use" being the star measure.

TABLE 8-2. Reaction Results

The program was important to my success.	4.2
My coach was helpful.	3.7
Content is relevant.	4.1
The technology was effective.	3.9
I will use the content with my team.	4.7
The classroom session was valuable.	4.4
I would recommend this program to others.	4.3
The program was easy to follow.	3.9
The action plan was valuable.	4.3

*Using a 5-point scale

Level 2 (Learning) Results

The first measure of learning was the observation of the skill practices. Because they had repeated practices if the skills were unsatisfactory, all participants scored satisfactory, as reported by the facilitators. Additional learning results were connected, as displayed in Figure 8-3, with the individuals rating the extent to which the program changed their knowledge and use of skills. This was completed during the one-month follow up after the workshop. In addition, they were asked two knowledge questions regarding being a more effective leader and knowing how to build high-performance teams. In both cases, the results exceeded expectations. A total of 89 responded.

TABLE 8-3. Learning Results

I know more about my effectiveness as a leader.	4.7
I know how to build a high-performance team.	4.5
10 skill self-assessment on learning change.	4.1

*Using a 5-point scale

Level 3 (Application) Results

Application results were collected two months after the workshop. It begins with the percent of individuals completing action plans (86 percent), which is a very high number considering the detail involved in the actual planning process. The percent using coaching was a little less than expected (72 percent), as well as those using the learning portal (54 percent). Although there were no objectives set for portal use or coach use, it was expected that almost all the participants would use both. Pre- and post-feedback showed gains, although the skill sets were already there for many participants. The pre-feedback score of 3.82 is close to where it needs to be for success (four out of five). On the post-assessment, the results moved to 4.6 for total skill assessment. For extent of use, on a five-point scale, this result just barely met the objective (4.2), and was lower for frequency and success with use (3.8 and 3.9, respectively). The most valuable skill was improving the average performer, the least valuable skill was managing conflicts and differences, and the most difficult skill was fostering open and clear communications. These results were what would be expected for this kind of process.

Barriers and Enablers

Table 8-4 shows the barriers and enablers to use. As expected, there were not many barriers. The greatest barrier was not enough time, and this was anticipated given the time constraints for the e-learning and virtual modules. The other noted barriers were minor, ranging from technology to lack of support, although lack of support was in the acceptable range. Overall, barriers were not a problem.

Also, as expected, the enablers were present with many of the participants. This is encouraging because there was high use of the skill and follow-through on the action plans. The greatest enabler was the content, which was relevant for the managers. Following this was regional manager support. It was anticipated that the coach would be rated higher, but the learning portal was rated a little higher than expected. The 360-degree feedback did not seem to be much of an enabler to manager success.

TABLE 8-4. Barriers and Enablers

Barriers to Use	Percent responding	Enablers to Success	Percent responding
1. Not enough time to do it properly	14%	1. Great content	72%
2. Technology problems	11%	2. Regional manager support	85%
3. Lack of support from regional manager	7%	3. Convenient to participate/use	58%
4. Program was too complicated	6%	4. Effective design	45%
5. Doesn't fit the culture	5%	5. Videos were helpful	32%
6. Too difficult to use the skills	3%	6. Coaching was effective	19%
7. Other	7%	7. Learning portal	18%
		8. Other	14%

Level 4 (Impact) Results

Table 8-5 shows the impact results in terms of the particular measures chosen by the participants. Each participant was asked to select at least two measures to improve using the competencies in the program. As expected, the number one measure was increasing sales in existing customers—taking extra effort to up-sell, cross-sell, and entice existing customers to come in the store more often and provide excellent service to make them buy more (38 percent of the managers selected this measure). The next most often selected measure was acquiring new customers. FSI provided mechanisms to reach out to individuals who are not current clients and that was important for the managers who selected that particular measure for improvement (27 percent). Not surprisingly, staff turnover came in third with 24 percent, although turnover at FSI is lower than typical retail stores.

Increasing the store profit margin was the next measure (20 percent), which was improved by controlling expenses, limiting waste, and avoiding price discounting or the need to give discounts to compensate problems. Inventory shrinkage was another important measure for consideration with 18 percent. Product returns were reduced and 15 percent selected this measure. Returns occur when customers aren't fully satisfied with the product they have purchased or the product has not lived up to expectations. Good customer service can reduce returns. Controlling costs and reducing customer complaints were the next two measures (15 percent and 12 percent, respectively). Cost control is related to store profit margin and was not that difficult to tackle. Recognizing that there are fewer complaints at the store—and the goal was to have zero complaints—a few of the managers took on complaints as an opportunity for reduction.

Finally, some managers addressed the sick leave measure (11 percent). The store pays employees when they are on sick leave unless it becomes excessive. However, some employees were taking too many sick days, which was a costly and disruptive process. There were several other miscellaneous measures that were either unique to a particular store or an unusual problem that was not one of the main measures. A few ambitious managers selected more than two measures and one manager selected four measures for improvement.

TABLE 8-5. Impact Results

Business Measures Selected	Percent Selecting
Increased sales with existing customers	38%
New customers	27%
Staff turnover	24%
Store profit margin	20%
Inventory shrinkage	18%
Product returns	15%
Store expenses	15%
Customer complaints	12%
Staff sick leave	11%
Other	28%
Each manager was required to select at least two measures. A total of 176 usable measures were selected. A few managers selected three measures. One participant selected four measures. n = 85	

Isolating the Effects of the Program

To have a credible analysis, initial steps had to be taken to isolate the effects of the program from other influences. Given the sales and marketing metrics that were used, there are many other factors that affect these measures, which often leaves a program like this with only a minor part of improvement. While several processes were considered, such as setting up a control group or using simple trend-line analysis, the team settled on using estimates from the participants.

The estimates would be collected on the action-planning document with explanation in the classroom as to what was involved and how important the issue was to the final analysis. In addition, the estimate was adjusted for error using a confidence estimate. Research has shown that estimates from credible people are accurate and conservative.

Converting Data to Money

To determine the monetary benefits, each individual data item has to be converted to money for use. This has to be profit-added, costs reduced, or costs avoided. The measures that are driven in this program are shown in Table 8-6 with the monetary value. These monetary values were provided to the participants in the program, so it took almost no effort on their part to locate and use them in their action plan.

TABLE 8-6. Converting Data to Money

Data Item	Value
Sales to existing customers	23% margin
New account	$745
Staff turnover	50% of annual salary
Store profit margin	All is value add
Inventory shrinkage	All is value add
Product returns	5% of average sale
Store expenses	All is value add
Customer complaints	$550 per complaint
Sick leave	$150 per day

For the first measure, sales to existing customers, the store operating profit margin is the value add, which is averaging 23 percent. For new accounts the marketing analytics section calculated the value based on the profit from the customer over the lifetime of the customer. This number appears to be low, but is accepted by executives. In essence, if the customer stays active with the company for an average of five years, the company will make $745 in profit during that time.

The staff turnover figure comes from external studies in the cost of turnover for the retail industry—it totals 50 percent of annual pay and this number is accepted within the company as a credible, conservative number. This figure includes all recruiting, selection, and onboarding, as well as the disruption cost of the exit.

The store profit margin is already converted to money and any increases in value are benefits. The operations department used 5 percent of the average sale to calculate inventory shrinkage cost. The cost is based on the assumption that the items may be damaged and cannot be resold, the items always need to be restocked, and sometimes there is an alteration or adjustment made.

Store expenses are direct cost reductions, and are value added directly into the calculation. Customer complaints come from the customer relations division in marketing, where complaints are investigated locally, regionally, and globally if needed. The group uses a model that estimates it costs the company $550 per complaint. This assumes the time to deal with the complaint, the cost of making the customer happy (which sometimes includes waiving part or all of the charge), and the ill will caused by the complaint.

The human resources department provided a standard value of $150 lost for each day that a person uses a sick day. Although sick days are allowed, ideally, they only want them to be taken when a person is really sick. Some employees abuse this, and the company wants to prevent excessive sick leave days.

Monetary Benefits

When the changes in impact measures, identified in Table 8-5, are adjusted for the effect of the program and converted to monetary values using the data in Table 8-6, the monetary benefits are developed. The amount of improvement is different from one store manager to another—96 people completed the workshop and every manager's task was to improve at least two measures. Ideally, approximately 192 measures would be influenced by this program. Unfortunately, for a variety of reasons not fully known by the team, 11 out of the 96 store managers did not provide an action plan after completing the two-day workshop. Although it would be helpful to find out what happened to these individuals, in terms of the analysis, there is a very specific rule for addressing missing data. Guiding Principle 6 indicates that missing data get a zero in the process. Thus, the total benefits are adjusted based on the 85 individuals who provided data, but the cost will be based on all 96 store managers. Table 8-7 shows a one-page sample of 12 pages of data showing the improvements connected to this program. This table represents only 14 measures, illustrates the variety of data represented in the program, and shows how the adjustments are made.

Next, the first year value of this measure is developed using the data conversion numbers in Table 8-6. Although there could be some argument to suggest that this is a long-term program and that benefits should be considered for a longer period, only the first year of benefits are calculated. This means that after the impact has occurred, when the action plans were delivered, the amount is extrapolated for the entire year. Some may suggest that this is not credible because the data might not continue at that level for the entire first year. However, when considering that the vast majority of the store managers will still be in their jobs the second, third, and perhaps, even a fourth year, there should be some benefit from this program as long as they are in that job. Because it is possible to take the prework, attend the two-day workshop, and work the virtual process in the weeks after the live session, this could be considered a two-year solution. But, to be conservative, Guiding Principle 9 is applied and only one year of benefits are considered for a short-term solution. Table 8-7 shows the monetary value for one year.

TABLE 8-7. Business Impact Data

Participant	Annualized Improvement ($Values)	Measures	Other Factors	Contribution Estimate From Program	Confidence Estimate	Adjusted $ Value
1	39,000	Sales-Existing	3	30%	60%	7,020
2	17,880	New Accounts	2	50%	85%	7,599
3	90,000	Turnover	2	40%	70%	25,200
4	50,200	Sales-Existing	3	35%	70%	12,299
5	12,000	Product Returns	1	40%	60%	2,880
6	26,870	New Accounts	2	30%	80%	6,449
7	1,800	Sick Leave	0	100%	90%	1,620
8	28,000	Store Expense	0	100%	80%	22,400
9	18,300	Inventory	1	50%	80%	7,320
10	6,600	Customer Complaints	1	40%	70%	1,848
11	68,000	Turnover	2	30%	70%	14,280
12	55,600	Store Profit	4	25%	85%	11,815
13	46,250	Sales-Existing	2	40%	80%	14,800
14	43,550	Store Expenses	1	60%	80%	20,904
					Total this group	$156,439

The contribution factor is the allocation to this program, as the store manager gave a particular percent of the improvement directly to the Leadership for Performance program. The next column is the confidence, which reflects the error in the allocation. Following the process, particularly with Guiding Principle 7, the three values are multiplied to provide an adjusted value. When these are calculated for all 85 participants, including both measures, the total is 170 measures improved, at least by some amount, with a few minor exceptions, as some people suggested that the measure did not improve or could not properly estimate the improvement connected to this program. However, some managers provided three measures and one manager provided four measures. With all of these totaled, the improvement is based on 176 measures and valued to be $1,341,970.

The Costs

Table 8-8 shows the costs allocated to this program. Some costs were prorated just to this sample size. For example, the needs assessment cost was estimated to be approximately $15,000. That amount involves all of the upfront analysis necessary to decide on the specific need for this program. The most significant cost was the development. Some content was purchased from a major supplier for leadership development, an outside production company produced the videos, and other content was developed under contract with freelancers or by the L&D team. In total, the development and production costs for the workshops and videos totaled $478,000.

The content for the learning portal was developed for approximately $60,000. The learning portal was already operational, but its development costs ($45,000) were allocated entirely to this program. The development of each e-learning module represented about $12,000, totaling $60,000. These costs were prorated over the 4,000 managers to develop a cost per participant. The total costs allocated to this sample of 96 represent the cost per participant multiplied by 96. Table 8-8 shows the prorated costs for these items.

The coach's time was allocated at a half day per participant, because not all of the participants used their coach and others used the coach for more than half a day total. For the participants, the costs were calculated by their time for the two days, the time away from work for the e-learning modules, and the other virtual activities (this totaled three days of time). Most store managers also required a travel expense. And a very nominal amount was included for the use of their devices to access the virtual materials and the e-learning modules. Although some would question whether that should even be included, a very nominal amount (6 percent) was included for the workshops to be completely transparent in all costs.

In addition, there was an overhead cost for the total learning development team, including the L&D leadership not directly involved in the program. This was at $400 per day or $800 for the program, totaling $3,200 for the four programs. The cost of the evaluation, which included the planning, data instrument design, data collection, analysis report writing, and briefings, was $40,000. The total cost of the briefings with travel was $25,000. When all of the costs are included, the total as indicated in Table 8-8 is $576,865.

TABLE 8-8. Program Cost Summary

Needs assessment (prorated over all sessions) 15,000/4,000 = 3.75 x 96	360
Program development and production costs (prorated over all sessions) 478,000/4,000 = 119.50 x 96	11,472
Content development for learning (prorated over all sessions) 60,000/4,000 = 15 x 96	1,440
Learning portal (prorated over all sessions) 45,000/4,000 = 11.25 x 96	1,080
E-learning programs (prorated over all sessions) 60,000/4,000 = 15 x 96	1,440
Devices used by participants	670
Program materials 120 x 96	11,520
Travel and lodging (participants) 982 x 96	94,272
Facilitation and coordination 19,000 x 4	76,000
Facilities and refreshments 8 days at 250	2,000
Participants' salaries, plus benefits 2,674.62 x 96	256,763
Coaches' salaries, plus benefits 538 x 96	51,648
Overhead	3,200
ROI evaluation 40,000 + 25,000	65,000
Total	**$576,865**

ROI Calculation

When the total monetary benefits from Table 8-8 are compared with the total fully loaded costs from Table 8-8 the calculations are as follows:

$$BCR = \frac{\$1,341,970}{\$576,865} = 2.33$$

$$\text{ROI} = \frac{\$1,341,970 - \$576,865}{\$576,865} \times 100 = 133\%$$

This is a very impressive ROI that greatly exceeds the objective of 20 percent. For every dollar invested in this program, the dollar is returned plus another $1.33 in monetary benefits.

Intangible Benefits

The following intangibles were connected with this project:

- job engagement
- career satisfaction
- net promoter score
- image
- reputation
- brand.

The participants were asked to indicate the extent to which these intangibles were influenced by this program. In order to be included on this list, at least 10 percent of participants had to identify the influence as at least three out of five on a five-point scale.

These intangibles represent an important data set for executives. If they were converted to monetary value, there would be even more value from this program and a higher ROI.

Credibility of the Data

When leadership development is connected to the business in a program like this, there are always questions about the credibility of data. Here is what makes these data credible:

1. The business impact, which drives the ROI, represented actual store measures. They can be identified directly to the store, tracked, and validated if necessary.
2. The participants selected the measures that were important to them with input from their immediate manager.
3. Store managers had a desire to improve the measure and took ownership in this program as they connected the skills of developing high-performance teams to those important measures.
4. For participants who did not provide data, (12 individuals in this case), there was an assumption that they received no value from the program. In reality, some of these individuals changed stores, either through promotion or transfer, and actually added value despite not completing the project. The conservative approach is to use zero for them.

5. Only one year of improvement was recognized in the calculation. In reality, the significant behavior change, which was validated with the data collection at Level 3, should provide some value for the second, third, and even fourth year. However, to be conservative, only the first year was used.

6. All of the costs were included, including time away from work. Some of these costs are debatable, but to be credible, every cost category was included.

7. Using participant estimates to isolate the effects of the program was not the most favored approach, but it is credible. The estimation was collected in a very nonthreatening, unbiased way, and was adjusted for error. This credible method is backed by much research as a conservative approach representing an understatement of the actual results.

8. A balanced profile of financial and nonfinancial, quantitative and qualitative data was presented. This provided executives with a great data set to make decisions about the future implementation.

COMMUNICATION OF RESULTS

With the results in hand, the data was communicated to the groups according to the communication plan. First, a live briefing was conducted with top executives and those responsible for the implementation of the program. Because of the dispersion of the groups in the study, this briefing was held at four locations in North America, Europe, South America, and Asia. In addition, briefings were conducted with regional executives during normal meetings and with the HR team. A three-page summary was sent to all store managers. The participants received a summary of the results shortly after they submitted them, as well as a summary of the changes made as a result of the program.

Based on the briefings with the executive team, the following adjustments were made:

● Improvements were made to the technology to make it easier and more reliable.
● The role of the participant's manager was strengthened to make sure that proper measures are selected and any needed support is provided.
● The role of the coach was diminished.
● Some efforts were taken to strengthen the link between the 360-degree feedback and the rest of the program. There was concern that the 360-degree feedback was not tightly integrated into the program.

LESSONS LEARNED

In this program several important lessons were learned:

- The power of connecting this program directly to business was phenomenal. The store managers saw this as a way to improve store performance, which was something they wanted and needed to do.
- The concept of developing a high-performance work team was intriguing to these individuals and was partially responsible for the good results that followed.
- The program design, using a mix of learning approaches, delivery mechanisms, and customization options, made it a workable project across cultures and countries.

QUESTIONS FOR DISCUSSION

1. Critique the credibility of this study.
2. Do you think these results are CEO and CFO friendly? Explain.
3. Could there be alternative ways to isolate the effects of the program? Explain.
4. Would it have been better if all store managers addressed the same measure? Explain.
5. Why are leadership development directors reluctant to connect leadership development to business, as illustrated in this case?

ABOUT THE AUTHORS

Jack J. Phillips, PhD, is chairman of the ROI Institute, the leading provider of services for measurement, evaluation, metrics, and analytics. A world-renowned expert on measurement and evaluation, Phillips provides consulting services for more than half of the Fortune 100 companies and workshops for major conference providers worldwide. A former bank president, Phillips has served as head of HR for three organizations, including a Fortune 500 company for eight years. Author of the first book on training evaluation in the United States, Phillips has authored or edited more than 75 books in evaluation, metrics, and analytics. He is the developer of the ROI Methodology, the most used evaluation system in the world. His work has been featured in the *Wall Street Journal, Bloomberg Businessweek,* and *Fortune,* and on CNN. He can be reached by email at jack@roiinstitute.net.

Patti P. Phillips, PhD, is president and CEO of the ROI Institute, the leading source of ROI competency building, implementation support, networking, and research. A renowned expert in measurement and evaluation, she helps organizations implement the ROI Methodology in more than 60 countries. She serves as principal research fellow for The Conference Board, where she co-authored the research reports *Human Capital Analytics: A Primer* (2012) and *Human Capital Analytics @ Work Volume 1* (2014). Patti serves on the faculty of the UN System Staff College in Turin, Italy, and the University of Southern Mississippi's human capital development doctoral program. She can be reached at patti@roiinstitute.net.

9

Measuring ROI in a Supervisory Leadership Development Program

IAMGOLD

Lisa Parker and Caroline Hubble

This case was prepared to serve as a basis for discussion rather than an illustration of either effective or ineffective administrative and management practices.

Abstract

In response to its first employee engagement survey, IAMGOLD Corporation designed and implemented the comprehensive Supervisory Leadership Development Program (SLDP). The objective is to build a leadership pipeline while developing supervisory capabilities to engage, empower, and support employees. The program is highly visible, linked to key business objectives, and requires substantial resources for the design and implementation, which covers a three-year timeline. These factors and a need to measure program success and improvement opportunities led to an evaluation study using the ROI Methodology. The evaluation study found that the SLDP favorably affected IAMGOLD's key business measures and a positive ROI was realized. Other intangible benefits not converted to monetary value included improving supervisory effectiveness, which ultimately affected employee engagement.

BACKGROUND

IAMGOLD Corporation is a midtier Canadian gold-mining company engaged internationally in mining and the exploration of gold. IAMGOLD has operations in North America, South America, and West Africa. The foundation of the company's culture is empowering people and extraordinary performance. They believe in engaging, empowering, and supporting employees to build a company in which the pursuit of excellence and an industry-leading vision of accountable mining exist in harmony.

With that in mind, the SLDP was created in alignment with the organization's leadership model, which encompasses 15 capabilities. The specific objectives of the program include:

- Clarify the role and expectations of the supervisory role at IAMGOLD.
- Develop a soft-skill set necessary for workforce development, improvement, and engagement.
- Develop skills to drive employee performance.
- Build awareness of the critical skills and aspects that support effective and successful leaders.
- Explore the knowledge and skills needed to manage conflict effectively.
- Fill in the gaps in mining knowledge.
- Explore the knowledge and skills associated with IAMGOLD's financial practices and processes.
- Develop an action plan to outline ways in which participants would apply the knowledge and skills from the SLDP in the workplace.

To ensure success of the program, IAMGOLD's chief operating officer and senior vice president of human resources co-sponsored the program, and from the onset there was buy-in from the individual mine site leadership teams.

In order to effectively cover the content highlighted within the needs analysis and meet the program's objectives, the design, development, and implementation of the SLDP was managed at the corporate level. However, sustainability to run the program at the site level was built into the project. The program's design included implementation over a three-year period as outlined below.

Year One

Year one includes three modules that provide foundational information focused on alignment to the business and building supervisory skills.

- **Module 1:** The Role of the Supervisor. Focus areas include key role accountabilities, diversity leadership capabilities, and coaching.
- **Module 2:** Mining 101. Focus areas include the mining cycle, underground mining, mineral processing and open-pit mining, and gold production.
- **Module 3:** Supervisory Skills. Focus areas include goal setting, accountability, planning, coaching, and delegation.

Year Two

Year two of the program connects the SLDP to IAMGOLD's business objectives, including highlighting specific measures that can be influenced by successful supervisory performance and potentially lead to improvement in employee engagement.

- **Module 4:** Production Efficiency. Focus areas include production efficiencies, key performance indicators (KPIs), production dashboards, a strong emphasis on health and safety, and continuous improvement.
- **Module 5:** Achieving Results. Focus areas include planning, communication, problem solving, time management, meeting management, and managing up and across.

Year Three

Year three continues to connect the SLDP to the business, and includes highlighting skills and knowledge areas needed to be a successful supervisor at IAMGOLD.

- **Module 6:** Managing Conflict. Focus areas include difficult conversations, diversity and respect, conflict resolution management, and managing up and down.
- **Module 7:** Finance 101. Focus areas include cost analysis, cost control, and understanding decisions from cost perspective.
- **Module 8:** Empowering and Developing People. Focus areas include empowerment, coaching for development, motivation, leading teams, and change management.

Following the full implementation in early 2015, the program will then be self-sustainable as a two-year program run independently by each operations site with corporate oversight.

At the time of this case study, the program had been implemented through module 5 (end of year two) within four locations: two in North America and one each in South America and West Africa. The target audience was front-line supervisors who supervise workers, but other participants included those supervisors with no direct reports and managers of the front-line supervisors. Senior management from each site also participated in the program in order to provide top-down support.

It is important to note that many of the supervisors in West Africa and South America lack formal education and many even have literacy problems. Consequently, the SLDP is experiential in nature and offers creative, engaging activities for learners to explore and arrive at new meanings. Transfer of learning is built into the program, and each activity seamlessly links to the next segment of learning. The program is delivered in three languages to meet the specific linguistic needs of each site.

EVALUATION REQUIREMENT

IAMGOLD's comprehensive SLDP program is highly visible, linked to key business objectives, and requires substantial resources. These critical factors, along with the need to identify program successes and improvement opportunities, led to the implementation of an evaluation study to Level 5 (ROI) using the ROI Methodology. In addition to determining the extent to which the program was increasing supervisory capabilities and positively affecting key IAMGOLD business measures, the evaluation was positioned to help identify opportunities for improvement for further implementation throughout the organization. In order to meet this need, the study was designed to report findings at two points: end of year one (post module three) and end of year two (post module five).

EVALUATION METHODOLOGY

IAMGOLD's SLDP is a comprehensive program that is highly visible and linked to key business objectives. With these factors in mind, a robust evaluation was planned to identify:
- satisfaction of the program by the IAMGOLD participants
- knowledge and skills gained through participation in SLDP modules
- success with the application of knowledge and skills in the participants' workplace
- barriers and enablers to the application of knowledge and skills
- business impact and return on investment of the SLDP.

The identification provided insight into what was working well with the program and opportunities for improvement. Furthermore, evaluation results helped communicate the program's value to increase adoption once it becomes fully integrated into the organization.

The ROI Methodology serves as the structure for designing, planning, and implementing the evaluation study. This approach reports a balanced set of measures, follows a step-by-step process, and adheres to a set of guiding principles as shown in Table 9-1. These elements ensure a thorough and credible process for communicating the impact of the SLDP to key stakeholders.

TABLE 9-1. Guiding Principles

1. When conducting a higher-level evaluation, collect data at lower levels.	7. Adjust estimates of improvement for potential errors of estimation.
2. When planning a higher-level evaluation, the previous level of evaluation is not required to be comprehensive.	8. Avoid using extreme data items and unsupported claims when calculating ROI.
3. When collecting and analyzing data, use only the most credible sources.	9. Use only the first year of annual benefits in ROI analysis of short-term solutions.
4. When analyzing data, choose the most conservative alternative for calculations.	10. Fully load all costs of a solution, project, or program when analyzing ROI.
5. Use at least one method to isolate the effects of a program.	11. Intangible measures are defined as measures that are purposely not converted to monetary values.
6. If no improvement data are available for a population or from a specific source, assume that little or no improvement has occurred.	12. Communicate the results of the ROI Methodology to all key stakeholders.

The ROI Methodology approach begins with a fundamental framework by which evaluation data are categorized. It is based on the five-level framework described by Jack Phillips and serves as a categorization of data representing measures that capture program success from the participant, system, and economic perspectives. Table 9-2 presents the definition of each level of evaluation data. When combined with intangible data, these five levels tell the complete story of the SLDP's success.

TABLE 9-2. Evaluation Framework

Level	Measurement Focus
1. Reaction, Satisfaction, and Planned Action	Measures participant reaction to the program and planned action.
2. Learning	Measures changes in knowledge, skills, and attitudes.
3. Application and Implementation	Measures changes in on-the-job behavior.
4. Impact	Measures changes in business impact measures.
5. ROI	Compares the monetary benefits with the costs.

Since SLDP is very comprehensive with many activities, the evaluation required careful planning. As highlighted in Figure 9-1, the different evaluation activities were aligned to the specific program modules and activities. Detailed data collection and ROI analysis plans were developed for each module. Figure 9-2 provides a sample of one of the data collection plans.

FIGURE 9-1. SLDP and Evaluation Alignment Plan

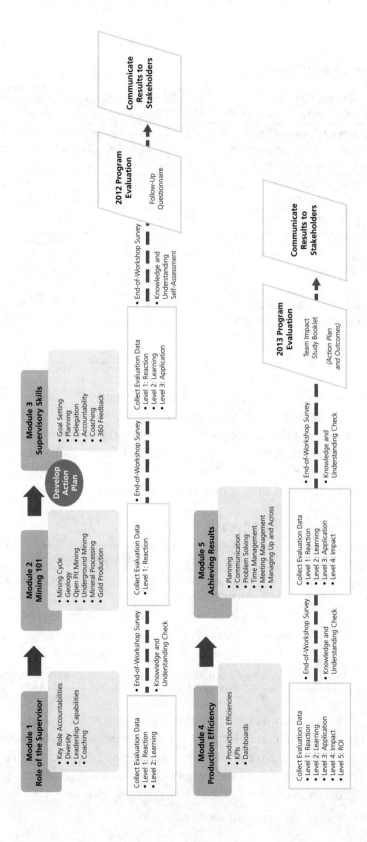

FIGURE 9-2. SLDP Data Collection Plan

Level	Broad Program Objective(s)	Measures	Data Collection Method/Instruments	Data Sources	Timing	Responsibilities
1	REACTION AND PLANNED ACTION Achieve a positive reaction on relevance to my work, important to my job, necessity, and practicality	• At least 4 out of 5 on a 5-point scale	• Feedback Survey	• Participants	• End of Workshop	• Facilitator
2	LEARNING AND CONFIDENCE Improve knowledge of production efficiencies, KPIs, and dashboards	• Pre- and post-improvements of at least 50%	• Self-Assessment Tool	• Participants	• End of Workshop	• Facilitator
3	APPLICATION AND IMPLEMENTATION Use all of the skill sets in the SLDP program to achieve business improvement	• At least 4 out of 5 on a 5-point scale • Checklist on action plan	• Questionnaire • Action Plans	• Participants	• 3 months after the workshop	• Talent management team/ROI Institute
4	BUSINESS IMPACT Improve two business measures of production/efficiency/safety	• Standard measures in the mine	• Action Plans	• Participants	• 3 months after the workshop	• Talent management/ROI Institute
5	ROI 30%	Baseline Data: Available as standard measures in the mine. Comments: ROI objective was set by the senior executive team.				

In order to collect the necessary data, various data collection tools were used. The end-of-workshop feedback questionnaire and the knowledge and understanding self-assessment tool collected data from all participants who completed the modules. The follow-up questionnaire collected additional reaction and learning data as well as application and business impact data. A 360-degree assessment tool was used to identify the extent to which supervisors were performing capabilities associated with IAM-GOLD's Supervisory Leadership Model. The team impact study booklet was used to collect and report improvements in key business measures aligned to IAMGOLD's key drivers.

For any program, once the participants apply what they learned on the job, improvement in performance and outcomes should occur. While the program and the improvements may appear to be linked, there may have been other factors that contributed to the improved outcomes. Because of this, the essential step of isolating the effects of the program was built into the evaluation process. This enabled the evaluation to identify the specific contributions of the SLDP and use this data to calculate the ROI as well as communicate the evaluation results.

The estimation process was the technique used for isolating the effects of the SLDP, and the participants were identified as the most credible source for estimating the contribution of the program to the outcomes of the study. Since the evaluation practice requires that estimates err on the conservative side, the participants were also asked to provide their level of confidence in the estimates provided. By multiplying the estimated percent improvement by the confidence factor, the lower-end range is reported.

To determine the ROI, two additional steps were taken. First the program's benefits were converted to monetary value using standard values within IAMGOLD and participant estimates. Then the fully loaded costs of the SLDP needed to be identified. Tabulating the costs involved identifying all the related costs of the program, such as direct program costs per participant (program development, material, implementation, and evaluation costs), participants' time, and other costs. Lastly, the ROI was determined by comparing the program benefits with the investment made in the program using the following formula:

$$ROI = \frac{\text{Net Benefits}}{\text{Program Costs}} \times 100$$

EVALUATION RESULTS

This case study only reports the findings based on the evaluation through module five (end of year two).

Level 1, Reaction

The various tools used to collect data for the program indicated positive reactions from participants. Overall, the reaction results were favorable, with the participants reporting that the content was relevant to their role and important to their success. They also believed that the program was a good investment of their time and would recommend it to others.

By the end of the session, both Level 1 (reaction) and Level 2 (learning) data were collected. Level 1 data were collected from 100 percent of participants in all sessions. In addition, an end-of-year follow-up questionnaire was used to collect additional evaluation data, including some questions that were focused on collecting additional reaction data. During this data collection effort, the reaction results were favorable. More specifically, of the 93 follow-up questionnaire respondents, 82 (or 88 percent) reported that the coaching aspect of the program provided at least moderate value.

Level 2, Learning

The primary tools used to assess participants' learning were the knowledge and understanding assessment pre- and post-questionnaires. Data were collected from 100 percent of participants in all sessions, except for module 2 (Mining 101), which was facilitated by a third-party entity. The results showed that the participants reported an increase in knowledge and understanding following the completion of the modules. These findings validated that the modules ensured participants acquired the necessary knowledge.

Level 3, Application

As part of the evaluation process, it was important to know the extent to which the participants were using what they learned on the job. This information illustrated the program's chain of impact, because it cannot be assumed that just because participants reacted favorably and learned new information, there was successful on-the-job application. Key post–module three findings regarding on-the-job application are highlighted below:

- 92.12 percent reported (agree or strongly agree) that they had an opportunity to use what they learned.
- 94.69 percent reported that they actually used the content and 84.44 percent reported successfully using the content.
- 73.39 percent reported using job aids, and 79.36 percent completed their action plans.

145

Furthermore, 78 respondents reported applying, on average, 61.47 percent of the first three modules' content. They reported on the various ways that they were applying the content, such as providing coaching and effective feedback when working with their staff, increasing their communication skills and processes, and improving their own awareness and skills. They also reported completing the intersession activities with plans to continue to use the associated skills. Lastly, they reported experiencing improvement in the 15 leadership capabilities associated with IAMGOLD's leadership model.

For both modules four and five, the participants reported that they at least moderately applied the content and planned to continue to use their new skills to improve IAMGOLD's key performance indicators.

Another critical part of the Level 3 application results includes identifying what supported (enablers) and what deterred (barriers) the participants from applying what they learned in the program. These findings are important because they can assist in identifying and reinforcing actions that foster the use of the knowledge and skills. Additionally, if barriers are identified, steps can be taken to mitigate the factors that deter or prevent application on the job. For the SLDP, the participants identified various enablers and some barriers to the application of program's content on the job. One noted enabler related to the fact that the program addressed a need for developing supervisors. Time to apply was noted as a barrier by many. Table 9-3 provides a summary of the most commonly noted enablers and barriers for this program.

TABLE 9-3. Enablers and Barriers to Application of the SLDP

Enablers to Application	Barriers to Application
• My team needed it	• I did not have enough time
• There was a need for the SLDP at my site	• My priorities changed
• A positive expectation was created prior to my attendance at the SLDP	• My manager did not support it
• I felt an obligation to use what I learned	• No opportunity to use it

Level 4, Business Impact

One of the primary objectives of the evaluation effort was to identify the business impact due to participating in the program and using the acquired knowledge and skills. In the follow-up questionnaire, respondents reported improvement regarding specific business measures. The highest improvement ratings were for safety, quality of work, and job satisfaction. The lowest improvement ratings were for innovation, reduced costs, and work unit efficiencies, and 24 respondents identified other measures improved such as communication, employee satisfaction, and improved operations.

Postmodule five, more comprehensive data were collected via the team impact study booklet in order to determine specific impact and ROI findings. To effectively manage the data collection process and time investment for gathering this information, a random selection of 170 frontline supervisors (approximately 30 percent of participants) were asked to complete the team impact study. Following the completion of module four, these participants were instructed to select two KPIs that required improvement, documented the initial results, and developed an action plan to improve results based on applying what they had learned from the program to date. Then postmodule five, approximately three months later, they were asked to document the actual results and improvements with the help of specific questions included in the study booklet. They were asked to identify the improvement item, outcome, cost savings information, and any added benefits realized by their team. Additionally, to help with isolating the effects of the program, the following two questions were included:

1. To what extent is the improvement attributed to the use of your new skills gained in modules one through five? 1 (0 percent or no extent), 2 (40 percent), 3 (60 percent or moderate extent), 4 (80 percent), and 5 (100 percent or very significant extent)

2. How confident are you that the SLDP was the main contributing factor for the improvements? Scale: 1 (0 percent or not confident), 2 (40 percent), 3 (60 percent or moderately confident), 4 (80 percent), and 5 (100 percent or very confident)

Of the 170 frontline supervisors involved in the data collection effort, 167 (98 percent) returned their study booklet and 85 (50 percent) provided useable data for Level 4 and Level 5 analysis.

Results were isolated to the SLDP by using the participants' estimates regarding the improvement in business measures (for example, cost savings, productivity, time savings, quality, and so on) and the monetary value of the improvement (estimated percent of improvement multiplied by the percent of improvement attributable to the program multiplied by the percent of confidence in the estimates).

In addition to the data provided by the participants, the evaluation team worked with the continuous improvement and business performance measurement teams within IAMGOLD to secure additional business improvement data, assist with converting data to monetary value, and validate the findings. Once all the data were obtained, a detailed analysis occurred.

From the 85 sets of usable data provided, the benefits reported by the frontline supervisors were aligned to one or more of IAMGOLD's key operation drivers, as well as other specific business impact outcomes including:

- improvements in mine or mill and equipment productivity
- efficiencies related to inspections
- decreases in fuel consumption

- improvements in work or service hours
- improvements related to health and safety
- decreases in downtime
- improvements related to the number of samples from mine geology.

For the tangible benefits that aligned to mine or mill availability, mine operations, and mine development, the specific improvement and monetary value was determined. Standard methods, the participants' estimates, and calculations provided by experts were used for the calculations. Lastly, the estimation process was implemented whereby the attribution percentage and confidence in estimate (as a percent) were factored into the improvement. The outcome of these steps was the SLDP's three-month monetary benefit of $2,490,083.

In addition to the ROI Methodology's 12 guiding principles, other guidelines and assumptions were followed when determining the program's impact and monetary benefits.

- The measurement period was standardized and estimated improvements remained consistent throughout the measurement period.
- Only the unit having the smallest impact was considered when the unit was not specified and reported.
- Duplicate impacts were not counted more than once.
- Results of impact at the individual level (such as improvement achieved by one employee, one truck, one drill, and so on) were combined to complete the sum of the team impact.
- When using the average margin figure for determining the monetary value of extra tons, it was assumed that the figure applied for the full year at the respective sites.
- Specific formulas applicable to each site were used to determine the value of the extra tons.

Level 5, ROI

In order to develop the ROI, the program's benefits were compared with the fully loaded costs. The program benefits were calculated, as discussed in the previous section. In addition to determining the three-month monetary benefit of the program, the annual benefit of the program was also determined. The results of both of these are captured in Table 9-4.

TABLE 9-4. Total SLDP Program Benefits

Site	A) Program Benefit (based on 3 months)	B) Annual Benefit (A x 4)
Abitibi	$212,129	$848,516
Abitibi (one-time benefit)	$11,200	N/A
Essakane	$861,458	$3,445,832
Niobec	$982,302	$3,929,208
Rosebel	$422,994	$1,691,976
Total	$2,490,083	$9,915,532

The next step involved calculating the fully loaded cost of the program. For the SLDP, a per-participant cost was already determined based on direct program costs. Additional costs per participant were calculated based on the time involved while participating in the program and other costs, such as site-level coordination and facilitation costs. To determine the participants' time in the program, salary data from all four sites were compiled, and an average hourly rate was determined. This figure was then multiplied by the number of participant hours per module. Table 9-5 provides a summary of both the predetermined per participant costs and then additional identified costs.

TABLE 9-5. Total SLDP Program Costs per Participant

Category	Details		Costs
Direct Program Costs per Participant Includes program development, materials, implementation, and evaluation costs	Module 1		a) $4,200
	Module 2		
	Module 3		
	Module 4		b) $3,000
	Module 5		
	Module 6		c) $1,800
	Module 7		
	Module 8		
Participant's Time	Module 1-3	37.5 hrs x $34.27 (average salary + benefits)	d) $1,285
	Module 4-5	30 hrs x $34.27 (average salary + benefits)	e) $1,028
	Module 6-8	37.5 hrs x $34.27 (average salary + benefits)	f) $1,285
	Total per Participant Direct Costs		g) $12,598
Other Program Costs Site level costs and on-site facilitation costs	x amount per participant		h) $500
	Total Cost per Participant		i) $13,098

Lastly, the ROI was determined from two perspectives. First, the ROI based on the participants' time in the program through module five was calculated. Since the results discussed in this report only reflect impact based on the completion of modules one through five, it was important to determine the ROI from this perspective. The following was identified to calculate the ROI:

- Program benefits (three months) = $2,490,083
- Program cost: $1,702,210
  - Participants involved in post–module five evaluation: 170
  - Cost per participant through module five (a + b + d + e + f): $10,013
- Net program benefits (program benefits – program costs): $787,873

$$ROI = \frac{\$787,873}{\$1,702,210} = 0.46 \times 100 = 46 \text{ percent}$$

The second ROI calculation was determined by considering the annual benefits of the program (current realized benefits annualized) and the costs associated with the participants completing all eight modules of the program. This provides insight into the annual benefit of the program. To determine the ROI from this perspective, the following was determined:

- Program benefits (annual benefit) = $9,915,532
- Program cost: $2,226,660
  - Participants involved in post–module five evaluation: 170
  - Cost per participant through module eight: $13,098
- Net program benefits (program benefits – program costs): $7,688,872

$$ROI = \frac{\$7,688,872}{\$2,226,660} = 3.45 \times 100 = 345 \text{ percent}$$

As both ROI findings reflect, the cost of investing in the SLDP was outweighed by the benefit received. This finding, along with the other results discussed throughout the report, illustrates the value of the SLDP to IAMGOLD.

INTANGIBLE BENEFITS

In addition to the above ROI findings, the SLDP also contributed to a variety of other noted business measurement improvements. Although these measures were not converted to monetary value, they are an important part of the program's outcomes. One noted intangible benefit was the improvement in employee engagement. In 2013 IAMGOLD conducted a second global employee engagement survey that resulted in a four-point increase in overall engagement. Noteworthy were significant improvements in the categories of learning and development, communication, leadership, and respect. Other benefits realized were employee coaching improvement, cross-shift effectiveness, problem solving, procurement efficiency, health and safety declaration, team-work, managing conflict, team effectiveness, communication, and leadership.

COMMUNICATION STRATEGY

The team impact study results were communicated in detail with the co-sponsors of the program. Following this, a presentation was made at the operations leadership team meeting, which included the general managers of each of the four sites. The results were very well received, with various people publicly crediting the program for site-level results. This success was shared with employees through a monthly president's message and was also posted on the company intranet.

In addition, IAMGOLD applied for and won a gold Canadian Award for Training Excellence (CATE) from the Canadian Society of Training & Development. The assessment panel gave the program a 100 percent in evaluation as a result of the extensive evaluation plan and team impact study.

LESSONS LEARNED

From a program perspective, the findings from this evaluation highlight the importance of top-down leadership development. With this in mind, IAMGOLD is now pursuing the development of a Manager Leadership Development Program (MLDP). With regard to the evaluation efforts, this study reinforced the importance of understanding the participants of a program and their specific needs. Had the program owners not built in mechanisms to support the participants' multicultural and multiple language needs and education, the program's success may not have been realized. Furthermore, the evaluation effort to collect the needed data from the participants would not have been as successful.

Another key lesson is in regard to knowledge transfer. While all indicators are such that the program is a success, there is still a lot of value left to gain through the application of learning on the job. Therefore IAMGOLD is taking steps to ensure the effective sustainability of the program in its third and final year. The sites will name a sponsor with the operations to co-lead with HR efforts at each site. Corporate created a role to assist sites with integration and sustainability efforts. As the MLDP is implemented, pieces of the SLDP will also be redesigned for the general employee population (such as what it means for an employee to be coached).

QUESTIONS FOR DISCUSSION

1. This case study only represents the evaluation of the program's ROI through module five. What evaluation steps would you take to evaluate the program after its completion, post year three?

2. How would the fact that the program is going to be self-sustained at the individual sites factor into your evaluation strategy?

3. The program and the evaluation included a need to address many cultures and languages, as well as literacy challenges in some countries. In this study, most evaluation tools were online, but classroom sessions and pre- and post-session meetings were set up to help ensure that the program and evaluation efforts were implemented successfully. What steps would you take to accommodate multicultural, language, and literacy challenges?

4. For this study, a select group of frontline supervisors (who were part of the target audience) were invited to complete the team impact study booklet. Do you agree with only a select group being asked to complete this activity? Should other participating groups (such as supervisors with no direct reports, managers) be invited to complete the booklet? If so, why? If not, why not?

5. As referenced in the steps to determine the program's monetary benefits, guidelines and assumptions were noted in addition to the ROI Methodology's 12 guiding principles. Why are they important to reference in a study?

6. What considerations should you incorporate based on your organization's structure, culture, and business practices that ensure alignment and credibility of your findings?

7. Given that there are many initiatives in organizations that focus on continuous improvement, it can be very challenging to gain agreement for the ROI results credited to a learning program such as this. What steps could you take up front to ensure buy-in and support for any evaluation results reported?

ABOUT THE AUTHORS

Lisa Parker is the senior manager, talent management & organizational effectiveness with IAMGOLD Corporation. She is currently leading global talent management initiatives for IAMGOLD on three continents and in three languages. Lisa has held leadership roles in corporate learning and organization development for more than 15 years. She has led the establishment of learning cultures and talent management frameworks in medium to large organizations in five industries, both public and private. Her experiences in pharmaceutical R&D and manufacturing, municipal government, wholesale commercial distribution, agricultural risk management, and now mining have provided her with a unique blend of skills and perspectives. Lisa holds a degree in biology, a diploma in adult learning, and four professional certifications: certified training and development professional, human capital strategist, strategic workforce planner, and certified ROI professional. She is fluent in French and English, and is working on Spanish as her third language. She also sits on the Advisory Committee (MiHR) for Labour Market Intelligence for the Canadian Minerals and Metals Sector (LMI Committee).

Caroline Hubble is the director of research and consulting services with the ROI Institute. She manages complex program evaluation projects, and designs and facilitates various courses on the ROI Methodology. She has significant experience conducting research and evaluation studies in areas such as leadership development, process improvement, and not-for-profit and community-related initiatives. Additionally, she provides expert coaching to individuals working toward ROI Certification. Caroline's professional background includes working in financial services, market research, and not-for-profit professional development industries. She holds a BA in psychology from Rollins College and a master's of science in organizational development from Avila University. She is a certified ROI practitioner and received ATD's Certified Professional in Learning and Performance credential in 2006. Her publications include *ASTD Handbook of Measuring and Evaluating Training,* chapter 4 (ASTD 2010), *Measuring ROI in Learning & Development: Case Studies From Global Organizations*, chapter 4 (co-authored) (ASTD 2012), and "Offering Money for School Pays Off" (co-authored) *Chief Learning Officer Magazine* (2012). She can be reached at caroline@roiinstitute.net.

REFERENCES

HayGroup. 2012. *IAMGOLD Supervisory Leadership Capability Model Composite Report: Composite—Supervisors.* HayGroup.

IAMGOLD. Excel workbook. ROI_to Institute_JZ_20140506.

IAMGOLD. 2012a. Careers. IAMGOLD Corporation. www.iamgold.com/files/careers /default.html.

IAMGOLD. 2012b. Home. IAMGOLD Corporation. www.iamgold.com.

Phillips, J.J. 1997. *Handbook of Training Evaluation and Measurement Methods.* 3rd edition. Boston: Butterworth-Heinemann.

Phillips, J.J. 2003. *Return on Investment in Training and Performance Improvement Programs.* 2nd edition. Boston: Butterworth-Heinemann.

Phillips, P.P., and J.J. Phillips. 2008. *ROI Fundamentals: Why and When to Measure Return on Investment.* San Francisco, CA: Pfeiffer.

Supervisory Leadership Development Program (SLDP). 2013. Presentation at the GM Meeting. November 13.

10

Measuring ROI in Fundamentals of Business Leadership

Global Manufacturing Company

Amy Happ and Kirk Smith

Abstract

In early 2010, Global Manufacturing Company (GMC), a leading manufacturer of advanced materials, recognized gaps in leadership skills and partnered with Advantexe Learning Solutions (Advantexe) to create a customized training engagement program, Fundamentals of Business Leadership (FBL). Advantexe conducted an ROI impact study using the ROI Methodology. This case study explores the results of that analysis.

BACKGROUND

In late 2009, GMC identified the need to develop the leadership and management competencies of executives, managers of managers, managers of people, and high-potential managers within the organization. These individuals are critical in achieving the short- and long-term business objectives of the company. To determine the specific needs and objectives, Advantexe interviewed key personnel within GMC.

Advantexe and GMC identified the following high-level goals and customized the FBL program for GMC:

1. Review with managers the need to ensure that objectives are linked to the company product differentiation strategy and the business' strategic initiatives (identified by general managers each year). Emphasize that the action plans managers create from objectives must also be aligned and tracked throughout the year. As market conditions or other changes take place, help managers understand how to evaluate when adjustments are needed and how to communicate those changes.

2. Teach managers how to have developmental coaching dialogues with their direct reports. There is a lack of coaching and feedback from managers, but with the new corporate initiative around talent management, developmental coaching will become more important and essential.
3. Review with managers the basics of providing performance coaching, feedback, and how to conduct a performance improvement dialogue. These dialogues can create tension and conflict, and managers need tools to conduct them productively to address performance issues as soon as they occur.

Program Design

The Fundamentals of Business Leadership program is one of Advantexe's three flagship classroom learning engagements. Advantexe currently delivers this classroom program to four major clients. Each one is specifically customized. Much of the content is the same across the various clients, while some is only delivered to certain clients who have a specific need for it. The program duration is typically three days in the classroom, and the flow for GMC is outlined in Figure 10-1.

FIGURE 10-1. Program Flow

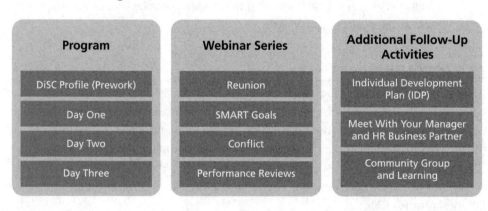

After the three-day classroom program there is a one-month break before coming back together in a virtual setting. Participants are encouraged to finalize an action plan by the time the class reconvenes.

The first reunion webinar involves participants sharing a success story of how they have applied a new leadership skill or new learning on the job. This is followed by webinars every two weeks on additional topics.

Over the course of these webinars, participants complete their own individual development plan (IDP). The goal is for each participant to have a completed IDP by the end of the final webinar, and to have set up a meeting with their manager and HR business partner to review the plan.

When designing the Fundamentals of Business Leadership program for GMC, the first audience was a group of approximately 30 functional managers with a mix of direct reports of either managers or line employees—all functional managers work closely with general business managers within this matrixed organization. After this initial pilot delivery, an audience of approximately 100 managers went through the program.

Advantexe conducted the initial, five-day pilot session. After the pilot was completed, the session length was reduced to three days, with some of the content delivered via virtual classroom following the live engagement. It was estimated that the program would be delivered five times, and it has since been delivered eight times, as its popularity expanded and new managers were hired. Figures 10-2 and 10-3 display the final three-day agenda and schedule.

FIGURE 10-2. Three-Day Agenda

Day One	Day Two	Day Three
Welcome and Introductions (30 minutes)	Welcome Back and Review of Day One (30 minutes)	Welcome Back and Review of Day Two (30 minutes)
Framework of Business Leadership (30 minutes)	Communication Skills (60 minutes)	Motivating Others (45 minutes)
Horizontal Leadership (60 minutes)	Introduction to the Simulation and Objective Setting (30 minutes)	BREAK
BREAK		Simulation Round Three (60 minutes)
Overview of Strategy (75 minutes)	BREAK	Simulation Debrief (60 minutes)
LUNCH	Simulation Round One (60 minutes)	LUNCH
Overview of Financial Statements (60 minutes)	LUNCH	Developing Others (30 minutes)
BREAK	Simulation Debrief (60 minutes)	Delegation (30 minutes)
DiSC Personality Styles (120 minutes)	BREAK	BREAK
Leadership Styles (90 minutes)	Developmental and Performance Improvement Coaching (75 minutes)	Influence (90 minutes)
	Simulation Round Two (60 minutes)	Action Planning (30 minutes)
	Simulation Debrief (60 minutes)	

FIGURE 10-3. Program Schedule

2010	2011	2012
July 27-29	January 18-20	June 19-21
August 3-5	June 7-9	October 9-11
October 12-14	August 9-11	

PLANNING FOR EVALUATION

When the program began, Advantexe worked with GMC to design an evaluation data collection instrument that was distributed at the completion of each program via SurveyMonkey. The evaluation at that time included Level 1 (reaction) only.

Due to a low response rate, in 2012 they decided to return to a paper survey. The same questions were asked on a paper form that was handed out and completed at the end of the program. This increased the response rate to approximately 100 percent.

In fall 2012, when Advantexe approached GMC about conducting an ROI analysis on the program, an additional questionnaire was developed for the two programs in order to gather Level 2 (learning), 3 (application), 4 (impact), and 5 (ROI) data from the program participants.

One of the most important actions was the creation of a questionnaire that was delivered to past participants from the June and October 2012 programs to gather Level 2, 3, 4, and 5 data. Advantexe created that questionnaire and administered it in January 2013.

To conduct the evaluation, Advantexe followed the ROI Methodology as shown in Figure 10-4.

FIGURE 10-4. ROI Methodology Process Model

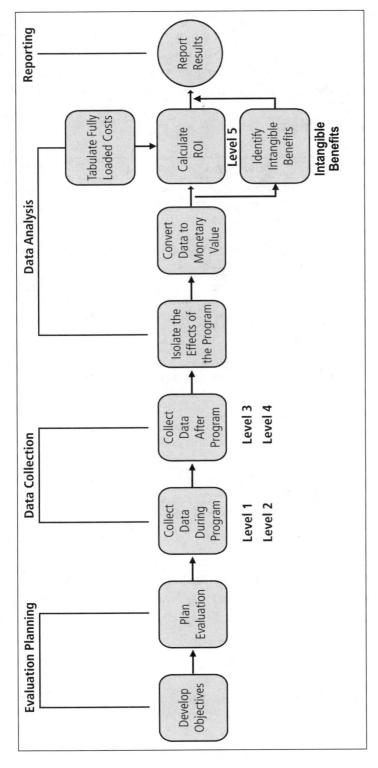

An effective ROI study flows from the objectives of the particular project being evaluated. For leadership development programs, it is important to clearly indicate the objectives at different levels. Table 10-1 shows the detailed objectives associated with this project, which were developed using the Phillips Business Alignment Model. The objectives reflect the four classic levels of evaluation, plus a fifth level for ROI.

TABLE 10-1. Objectives

Level	Objectives	Measure
Level 1: Reaction	Participants rate ability to immediately apply content and make improvements back on the job. Participants would recommend the program to other managers within the company.	4 out of 5 on 5-point scale 4.5 out of 5 on 5-point scale
Level 2: Learning	Participants report increased awareness, knowledge, and skills as a result of the program. Participants demonstrate ability to apply learning in classroom exercises (role play and simulation).	50% increase in knowledge, awareness, and skills across all categories 80% of class is learning and applying new skills in class
Level 3: Application	Participants apply new leadership behaviors with team members back on the job.	80% of class is applying new skills at level 4 on 5-point scale
Level 4: Impact	Participants identify at least one business measure of impact.	Various measures
Level 5: ROI	Monetary benefits outweigh the costs.	ROI is at least 25%

Figure 10-5, the completed data collection plan for this project, shows the objectives as well as the techniques and strategies used to collect data for this project.

FIGURE 10-5. Data Collection Plan

Level	Broad Program Objective(s)	Measures	Data Collection Method/ Instruments	Data Sources	Timing	Responsibilities
1	**SATISFACTION/PLANNED ACTION** • Participants rate ability to immediately apply content and make improvements back on the job	• 4 out of 5 on 5-point scale	• Post-program evaluation, questions 3a, 3b (already collected)	• Participant	• End class	• Project Manager/ Program Support
	• Participants would recommend the program to other managers within the company	• 4.5 out of 5 on 5-point scale	• Post-program evaluation question 3e (already collected)	• Participant	• End class	
2	**LEARNING** • Participants report increased awareness, knowledge, and skills as a result of the program	• 50% increase in knowledge, awareness, and skills across all categories	• Self-assessment questionnaire (to be developed) "As a result of the program, rate your level of improvement in skill or knowledge in each of the following areas" 10% to 100%	• Participant	• End class	• Project Manager/ Program Support
	• Participants demonstrate ability to apply learning in classroom exercises (role play and simulation)	• 80% of class is learning and applying new skills in class	• Facilitator assessment of class based on observation during role plays, simulation, and class discussions	• Project Manager/ Program Support	• During class	

Level	Broad Program Objective(s)	Measures	Data Collection Method/ Instruments	Data Sources	Timing	Responsibilities
3	**APPLICATION/IMPLEMENTATION** • Participants apply new leadership behaviors with team members back on the job	• 80% of class is applying new skills at level 4 on 5-point scale	• Self-assessment questionnaire (to be developed) "To what extent are you applying skills…" (including barriers and enablers)	• Participant	• 30 days post class	• Project Manager/ Program Support
4	**BUSINESS IMPACT** • Participants identify at least one business measure of impact	• Various measures	• Questionnaire	• Participant	• 30 days post class	• Project Manager/ Program Support
5	**ROI** 25%	Comments:				

Figure 10-6 shows the completed ROI analysis plan for this project. This document addresses the key issues needed for a credible analysis of the data and includes the following:

1. Data items: The data items were determined by the participants.
2. Isolating the effects of the program: Participant estimation was used to isolate the effects of the program on the data. Although there are more credible methods, such as control groups and trend analysis, these methods were not appropriate for the situation. The estimates may be subjective, but they are made by individuals who know the data best, have developed them, and have adjusted them for error in the estimate.
3. Converting data to monetary values: Because of the varied measures selected by the participants, the monetary value was also estimated by the participants and adjusted for the error of the estimate.
4. Cost categories: The standard cost categories include the typical costs for a leadership development program.
5. Communication targets: Several audiences representing key stakeholder groups—participants, senior executives, and prospective participants—were included for program results and as a marketing tool for Advantexe. Other influences and issues are also detailed in this plan.

Figure 10-6. ROI Analysis Plan

Data Items (Usually Level 4)	Methods for Isolating the Effects of the Program/ Process	Methods of Converting Data to Monetary Values	Cost Categories	Intangible Benefits	Communication Targets for Final Report	Other Influences/ Issues During Application	Comments
Varies by participant	Participant estimate	Participant estimate	• Needs assessment and interviews • Program customization (initial and per program) • Prorated pilot program delivery • Prorated revisions • Facilitation fees • Per person fee • Project management • Printed materials • Equipment (rental or use) • Facilities (need to get from GMC) • Travel, lodging, and meals (get from GMC and do one local and one in Houston including Advantexe) • Participant salaries and benefits for three days • Evaluation	• Improved communication • Increase in select employee engagement scores	• Participants • Senior executives (including head of HR) • Prospective participants • PR for own company	• Program is at end of roll-out phase, so other colleagues and their managers have likely been through the program and applying leadership behaviors • Additional Six Sigma and process improvement projects under way	• Need to achieve buy-in from client • Need to get high response rate from participants • Some metrics may be difficult to monetize without access to client's data or systems

EVALUATION RESULTS

Level 1 (Reaction) Results

Many questions were asked in the post-program evaluation for Level 1, yet only a few key questions are chosen as targets to analyze and report. The target was exceeded for the three selected questions.

Other questions in the Level 1 evaluation included reaction measures important to improving the facilitation, content, and materials. The strongest scores were reported around facilitation, and the lowest score was around the timeframe. This feedback was consistent with the program, as the three days and webinars contain a lot of content. This validates the program's need for a strong facilitator who can maintain a good pace without sacrificing rich classroom discussion. After review of all the content, it was decided that no extraneous content could be removed without reducing the impact of the program.

FIGURE 10-7. Reaction Results

Question	Target	Result
3a. I will be able to immediately apply what I learned in my day-to-day work.	4.0	4.30
3b. I will be able to make improvements in performing my responsibilities within the next 90 days.	4.0	4.32
3e. I would recommend this program to managers within Global Manufacturing Company.	4.5	4.60

Level 2 (Learning) Results

Changes in knowledge, skills, and attitudes, as a result of the program, were estimated by participants through a post-program survey. In addition, managers of the participants were surveyed and asked the same questions. Over the course of the program, participants engaged in several classroom discussions, role-playing exercises, and a computer-based simulation. During this time the facilitator observed the participants to ensure that each one was engaged, as well as understanding the new knowledge. The results are shown in Figure 10-8.

FIGURE 10-8. Learning Results

Question	Target	Participant Result	Manager Result
As a result of your attendance at the Fundamentals of Business Leadership program and subsequent webinars, please rate your level of improvement in skill or knowledge around business leadership. (0% = no improvement; 100% = significant improvement.)	50%	Average/Mean: 53% Median: 60% Mode: 70%	Average/Mean: 48% Median: 50% Mode: 30%

Mean: average of a list of numbers

Median: the middle value of a list of numbers; when there is an even number of values in a list it is the middle two values added together and divided by two

Mode: the number that occurs most frequently in a list of values

The participants' average (53 percent) slightly exceeded the goal of a 50 percent increase in skills and knowledge. The managers were in relative agreement, with a slightly lower result of 48 percent. Of interest are the median and mode results: Many participants listed their number as 70 percent, whereas managers more often listed 30 percent. This is a large discrepancy that results in a similar average. This prompted a Level 3 analysis to see if participants reported applying skills that managers were not observing.

Level 3 (Application) Results

A follow-up questionnaire was sent seven months after the program for June participants and three months after the program for October participants. This was determined to be sufficient time for participants to begin application, as assessed through several questions. The first listed each skill or knowledge area covered in the program and asked participants and their managers to rate the level of application. Figure 10-9 shows a comparison of participant and manager responses.

FIGURE 10-9. Application Results

Content	Target	Participant Result	Manager Result
1. Horizontal Leadership	Often	Often (64%)	Often
2. DiSC Personality Styles	Often	Mod/Often (48%)	Moderate
3. Leadership Styles	Often	Often (50%)	**Moderate**
4. Feedback Model (situation, behavior, impact, next steps)	Often	Moderate (27%)	Moderate
5. Active Listening	Often	Often (73%)	Often
6. Cultural and Generational Differences	Often	Moderate (43%)	Often
7. SMART Cascading Objectives/ Goals	Often	Little (36%)	Little
8. Developmental Coaching	Often	Moderate (30%)	Moderate
9. Performance Improvement Coaching	Often	Moderate (25%)	Little/Moderate
10. Motivation	Often	Often (55%)	Moderate/Often
11. Delegation	Often	Moderate (30%)	Moderate
12. Influence	Often	Often (55%)	**Moderate**
13. Conflict	Often	Little/Mod (36%)	Little/Moderate
14. Performance Reviews	Often	Little (25%)	Little

This question refers to the extent to which you are applying the knowledge, skill, and/or information acquired during the Fundamentals of Business Leadership program and webinars. Please indicate your level of application in each of the areas using the below scale. (Not at All, Little, Moderate, Often, All the Time)

The target was to have 80 percent of participants rate the content in each area at "4–Often" on the five-point scale of 1–Not at All, 2–Little, 3–Moderate, 4–Often, and 5–All the Time. Only six of the 14 areas scored "Often" by the majority of participants. No category received an 80 percent participants rating of "Often" or "All the Time." The highest rating was 73 percent for active listening. Cultural and generational differences had a 43 percent rating for the top two categories. Nearly 50 percent of the topic areas were rated at the "Often" level, which would align with 50 percent improvement in the Level 2 question.

The results show that participants are applying the skills and knowledge from the program—just not at the targeted levels, which may have been overly ambitious. Further analysis revealed that the three areas that received the "Little" rating (SMART goals, conflict, performance reviews) were topics covered via webinar. These results led Advantexe to conclude that the classroom is likely a better way to ensure application of leadership skills, because no other topic received that rating.

One area of concern was noted regarding the Level 3 responses in comparing the participant ratings with those of the managers. The responses were similar, except for leadership styles and influence, which are highlighted in bold. For leadership styles, this result is likely because participants are applying this skill with their teams and direct reports, and managers are not in the position to observe their behavior change. Influence is a skill applied in interactions with their superiors, so managers perceive that participants are using this skill less than participants report. The results are shown in Figure 10-10.

Figure 10-10. Manager Comparison

Question	Participant		Manager	
On a scale of 0% (not at all) to 100% (all the time), what percent of your total work time requires the above knowledge and skills?	Average: Median: Mode:	63% 70% 70%	Average: Median: Mode:	65% 70% 70%
On a scale of 0% (not at all) to 100% (extremely critical), how critical is applying the content of this program to your job success?	Average: Median: Mode:	67% 70% 80%	Average: Median: Mode:	73% 80% 90%
What percent of new knowledge and skills learned from this training do you estimate you have directly applied to your job?	Average: Median: Mode:	51% 50% 30%	Average: Median: Mode:	51% 50% 30%

Mean: average of a list of numbers

Median: the middle value of a list of numbers; when there is an even number of values in a list it is the middle two values added together and divided by two

Mode: the number that occurs most frequently in a list of values

These numbers are consistent with other questions regarding the amount of skills and knowledge gained, as well as almost half of the content areas receiving "Often" or higher for application. Participants noted that they are directly applying 51 percent, which was the same as the managers' response. The only difference is that managers rate the skills as slightly more critical than the participants.

Continuing to identify the application of skills and knowledge, participants were then asked to identify up to four specific, program-related actions they will undertake, or have already undertaken, as a result of the program.

1.   Action 1: 44 participants (100 percent)
2.   Action 2: 40 participants (91 percent)
3.   Action 3: 34 participants (77 percent)
4.   Action 4: 25 participants (57 percent)

The managers were also asked to report the actions they observed the participants taking. The actions submitted by the participants and managers covered several content areas. Of note is that the top five participant responses by popularity were all rated as "Often" when asked to what extent they were applying skills. It is also interesting that feedback received a high score, as it was included in the actions of at least 10 participants, but this area received only a "Moderate" score in the application questionnaire. The responses of the managers moderately aligned with those of the participants, as shown in Figure 10-11.

FIGURE 10-11. Application Categories

Category	#Part	#Mgr	Category	#Part	#Mgr
Active Listening	6 (9)	—	Horizontal Leadership	13 (2)	2 (4)
Coaching	9 (6)	3 (3)	IDPs	12 (3)	2 (4)
Communication	7 (8)	1 (5)	Influence	3 (10)	1 (5)
Conflict	8 (7)	—	Leadership Styles	3 (10)	—
Cultural and Generational Differences	2 (11)	—	Meetings	15 (1)	6 (1)
Delegation	7 (8)	—	Motivation	11 (4)	3 (3)
DiSC	15 (1)	3 (3)	SMART	6 (9)	2 (4)
Feedback	10 (5)	4 (2)			

Barriers

Examining the barriers to application of skills and knowledge learned in the program and webinars highlighted some of the reasons why there was less change in some areas than targeted. The most often cited response was "no opportunity to use" followed by "systems and processes do not support application." A further look at the comments revealed that several participants did not have direct reports. These individuals were encouraged to attend the program because the same skills could be applied in the matrixed environment of GMC and on projects. This lack of direct reports likely contributed to the lower application levels for feedback model, developmental coaching, and performance improvement coaching. Figure 10-12 displays the barriers.

Managers cited insufficient knowledge and confidence more frequently than participants, indicating they may perceive the lack of application is more highly correlated to the participants' lack of skill and confidence than organizational or cultural factors cited by participants.

Figure 10-12. Barriers

Barrier	Participant Result	Manager Result
No opportunity to use the skills	18 / 41%	4 / 31%
Systems and processes do not support application of knowledge/skills	12 / 27%	3 / 23%
Lack of confidence to apply knowledge/skills	6 / 14%	3 / 23%
Insufficient knowledge and understanding	4 / 9%	4 / 31%
Lack of management support	3 / 7%	3 / 23%
Lack of support from colleagues and peers	0 / 0%	3 / 23%

Enablers

Enabling factors supported the application of skills and knowledge learned in the classroom and from webinars. The enabler most often cited by participants was opportunity to use skills, followed by sufficient knowledge and understanding of the content.

Managers, similar to the prior question around barriers, cited most of the areas equally, whereas participants had a wider range of distribution in their responses, shown in Figure 10-13.

Figure 10-13. Enablers

Enabler	Participant Result	Manager Result
Opportunity to use skills	34 / 77%	11 / 85%
Sufficient knowledge and understanding	30 / 68%	11 / 85%
Confidence to apply knowledge and skills	25 / 57%	9 / 69%
Management support	23 / 52%	11 / 85%
Support from colleagues and peers	13 / 30%	8 / 62%
Systems and processes support the application of knowledge and skills	5 / 11%	7 / 54%

Level 4 (Impact) Results

Since participants were asked to provide their own leadership actions, they were also asked to select which key performance areas they affected. The results are shown in Figure 10-14.

FIGURE 10-14. Key Performance Areas

The key performance area(s) for the savings or contribution from your actions will be:
(Click more than one if appropriate)

Key Performance Area	Participant Response	Manager Response
Increased personal efficiency, productivity, output	32 / 73% (1)	8 / 62% (2)
Improved communication, information flow	31 / 70% (2)	8 / 62% (2)
Increased department, function, team effectiveness	30 / 68% (3)	7 / 54% (3)
Improved employee, team morale	28 / 64% (4)	10 / 77% (1)
Increased accountability (goal achievement)	24 / 55% (5)	10 / 77% (1)
Increased managerial effectiveness	19 / 43% (6)	8 / 62% (2)
Increased buy-in to strategy and goals	19 / 43% (6)	8 / 62% (2)
Increased employee job satisfaction	17 / 39% (7)	4 / 31% (4)
Reduction in errors	15 / 34% (8)	2 / 15% (5)
Improved quality of products or services (output)	15 / 34% (8)	2 / 15% (5)
Increased direct report efficiency, productivity, output	13 / 30% (9)	4 / 31% (4)
Reduction in customer complaints	10 / 23% (10)	1 / 8% (6)
Increased sales	10 / 23% (10)	4 / 31% (4)
Reduced absenteeism	3 / 7% (11)	0 / 0% (7)

Participants and managers were similar in the overall order of their rankings. And the results link to the leadership actions in which personal productivity, communication, and team meetings and effectiveness are high in the list. Lower on the list are improvement in quality, reduction in customer complaints, or improved sales, which were rarely mentioned in participant's actions.

To complete the ROI study, participants were asked to estimate the monetary impact of their leadership actions along with the percentage of that impact they attribute to the FBL program and their confidence in these estimates. When combined, the results are the monetary benefits of the program used to calculate ROI. The detailed results are in Figure 10-15.

FIGURE 10-15. Monetary Benefits (Isolated and Adjusted)

Participant USD estimate	% attributable to program	Confidence in estimates	Result
$1.00	10%	80%	$0.08
$10,000.00	70%	80%	$5,600.00
$20,000.00	10%	50%	$1,000.00
$250,000.00	30%	80%	$60,000.00
$50,000.00	50%	30%	$7,500.00
$280,000.00	40%	50%	$56,000.00
$1.00	50%	50%	$0.25
$250,000.00	40%	80%	$80,000.00
$50,000.00	10%	30%	$1,500.00
$ –	40%	80%	$ –
$100,000.00	20%	10%	$2,000.00
$20,000.00	60%	30%	$3,600.00
$18,000.00	30%	70%	$3,780.00
$900,000.00	70%	20%	$126,000.00
$ –	20%	60%	$ –
$20,000.00	50%	30%	$3,000.00
$20,000.00	40%	70%	$5,600.00
$341,000.00	60%	60%	$122,760.00
$13,000.00	60%	50%	$3,900.00
$750,000.00	50%	70%	$262,500.00
$ –	20%	20%	$ –
$50,000.00	40%	90%	$18,000.00
$1,000.00	10%	70%	$70.00
$5,000.00	50%	40%	$1,000.00
$50,000.00	30%	90%	$13,500.00
$6,000.00	70%	80%	$3,360.00
$5,200.00	20%	30%	$312.00
$90,000.00	30%	80%	$21,600.00
$ –	30%	100%	$ –
$2,000,000.00	40%	50%	$400,000.00
$100,000.00	90%	90%	$81,000.00
$100,000.00	10%	10%	$1,000.00
$20,000.00	40%	70%	$5,600.00

Participant USD estimate	% attributable to program	Confidence in estimates	Result
$10,000.00	40%	80%	$3,200.00
$ –	80%	80%	$ –
$178,436.00	40%	70%	$49,962.08
$15,000.00	70%	70%	$7,350.00
$100,000.00	50%	100%	$50,000.00
$ –	20%	50%	$ –
$200,000.00	30%	60%	$36,000.00
$1,000.00	50%	30%	$150.00
$250,000.00	70%	70%	$122,500.00
$10,000.00	50%	70%	$3,500.00
$ –	20%	70%	$ –
$6,283,638.00	Average 41%	Average 60%	$1,562,844.41

General Comments

Participants and managers were then asked to provide any additional comments; some meaningful thoughts are shown below:

- I believe the leadership module was very good and tailored to GMC. I have been through several leadership courses in the past, and some of the material was just a refresher. However, I did appreciate the ability to work cross functionally through the class with GMC team members from around the globe, and to work on common solutions to problems we all had in common.
- I thought that this program was probably one of the best training programs I have been on at GMC. I believe I am more aware of different leadership techniques and think that this has opened my eyes to a different approach to work. Since the program, I have been able to use some of my training in my current role, and I look forward to using it further as my career at GMC develops. I would be interested in having more training in this area and to be assigned a role or responsibility to use this knowledge more actively.
- In an effort to be completely honest, I would say the course was valuable on some levels. But if I were spending my own money, I doubt I would make the investment in the course. I think for me personally, that is because I believe I already did a pretty good job in a number of areas the course covered, so I may not have gained a great deal from the course.

- I think the program could benefit from giving more examples for members of the program that do not have direct reports. It is very geared toward managers with direct reports.
- I personally found the business leadership program to be very helpful in not only solidifying previous notions of what leadership should consist of, but understanding how best to motivate and lead others of differing styles. The role playing and team exercises were particularly helpful as these activities challenged me to execute on potentially difficult scenarios.
- Reducing costs is critical for any manufacturing company to succeed. Proper training and investing in the workforce is paramount to this objective. As GMC grows it needs to improve upon its training practices for the shop workforce as well as its supervisors. Offer seminars and workshops to them, get them informed, and get them more involved. Then true money savings can be calculated.
- Some of this is on me as a manager and on our HR partners, but we need to work the application of FBL tools into the individual's performance objectives. We have done well to align objectives to business results, but not at tying manager and supervisor application of FBL to the performance on those business goals.

Costs

The following items were used to calculate costs:
- program fees (Advantexe facilitator fees, program material fees, printing costs, facilitator expenses)
- other Advantexe costs (prorated pilot changes, customization time, evaluation time)
- GMC participant costs (salaries, travel, lodging, meals)
- facility expenses
- other GMC costs (kickoff speaker time, computer monitor use).
  A summary of the major cost categories is shown in Figure 10-16.

Figure 10-16. Costs

Advantexe Costs

Fees	Program Fees	Classroom and Webinars	$49,000.00
Invoiced	Per Person	Materials, HBR, DiSC	$10,850.00
	Administration	Project Management, Printing, and Expenses	$8,079.70
Design, Evaluation, Other	Upfront Customization	Needs Assessment	$7,200.00
Not invoiced	Pilot Adjustments	Prorated Pilot	$22,450.00
	Customization	Per Program	$7,200.00
	Evaluation		$7,200.00
	Equipment	GoToMeeting, Adobe Connect	$182.33
TOTAL			**$112,162.03**

GMC Costs

Upfront Customization	Interviews		$4,984.62
Participant Salaries	June and October		$85,024.32
Participant Expenses	June and October		$52,430.00
Facility Expenses	Conference Rooms and Meals	June and October	$24,000.00
Other	Monitor Delivery, Kickoff		$817.35
TOTAL			**$167,256.28**

There were 23 participants in the June 19-21 class and 25 at the October 9-11 class. The participant salary sheets have 24 and 26 individuals, likely due to a last minute cancellation and therefore the participant salary was maintained in costs and due to anonymity of data cannot be accurately removed. So participant salaries are slightly overstated.

ROI Calculation

The return on investment for the two FBL classes was 459 percent, as shown by the following calculation.

$$\text{BCR} = \frac{\$1,562,844}{\$279,418} = 5.59$$

$$\text{ROI} = \frac{\$1,562,844 - \$279,418}{\$279,418} \times 100 = 459\%$$

When calculating ROI, a conservative approach is always taken. Given the subjective nature of business leadership actions, the monetary benefits collected have been adjusted downward, while the program costs components have been adjusted upward. This conservative approach builds credibility and makes the result more reliable.

Although the exact value of this program is nearly impossible to quantify, the process used in calculating the ROI is a generally accepted technique for measuring training programs. The participants provided the information voluntarily and their responses remained anonymous. In addition, four adjustments were made to produce more conservative estimates.

- The ROI calculation of 459 percent uses only the 44 responses provided by participants. The four participants who did not answer the questionnaire were not included in the benefits, but were included in the cost component of the formula. In addition, even though there were 48 participants in the classes, the cost component had 50 participants, and due to anonymity of the data, the two who cancelled at the last minute were unable to be removed.
- The questionnaire only asked for monetary benefits in the current calendar year, although there should be continuing benefits in years to come.
- The value of the leadership actions were reduced to reflect the percentage that participants link directly to the program.
- The value is further reduced by the confidence level that the individual places on the estimate.

Intangible Benefits

The financial impact of the FBL program is an important outcome of the evaluation. However, other important outcomes occurred as well. Increased frequency of communication and improved meetings between managers and employees improved employee engagement and commitment.

In addition, GMC engages in a biannual employee survey. The results were monitored and key measures improved over the duration of the program. Other factors influenced the increase in key metrics, including overall employee engagement, yet GMC and Advantexe believe that part of this can be attributed to the Fundamentals of Business Leadership initiative. Figure 10-17 reports the engagement levels as well as the other key metrics for comparison.

FIGURE 10-17. Engagement Levels

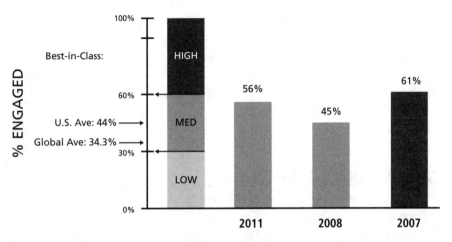

Global Manufacturing Company Engagement Level Comparisons

Global Manufacturing Company Associate Engagement

Global Manufacturing 2011 Engagement Survey

Response Categories

1. Strongly Disagree   4. Agree
2. Disagree   5. Strongly Agree
3. Agree Somewhat, Disagree Somewhat

Category	Valid N	% of Respondents:				Response Distribution (by %)					Avg. Score
			Favorable (Agree + Strongly Agree)	Neutral (Agree Somewhat, Disagree Somewhat)	Unfavorable (Disagree + Strongly Disagree)	5	4	3	2	1	
Employee Commitment	912	2011	85	12	3	44	41	12	2	1	4.2
	868	2008	79	16	5	30	49	17	3	2	4.0
Employee Retention	912	2011	69	21	10	30	39	21	7	3	3.9
	867	2008	65	23	12	24	41	23	8	4	3.7
Education & Development	907	2011	58	27	15	16	42	27	11	5	3.5
	865	2008	56	30	14	14	42	30	10	5	3.5
Work Environment	907	2011	55	30	15	13	42	30	10	4	3.5
	864	2008	51	32	17	12	39	32	11	6	3.4
Innovation & Risk Taking	904	2011	62	29	9	15	47	29	7	2	3.7
	865	2008	57	32	11	13	44	32	9	3	3.6
Communications	899	2011	64	24	12	20	43	24	8	4	3.7
	871	2008	58	27	15	16	42	26	11	5	3.5
Associate Engagement	919	2011	56	44							
	878	2008	45	55							

Associate engagement is defined as those associates who "Strongly Agree" or "Agree" to all engagement items that were included in the survey (see the engagement category in the "Detail Scores" for a full list of the engagement items.)

2011 = Current Year
2008 = Previous Administration
Percentages may not total 100 due to rounding

COMMUNICATION STRATEGY

As the provider of the program, Advantexe's communication strategy was different than it would have been if GMC had conducted its own internal evaluation. Advantexe communicated the results to stakeholders within GMC, as well as other potential clients by incorporating it into their marketing collateral.

Within GMC, Advantexe also wanted the participants to see the results so they could get a sense of how valuable it had been to not only themselves, but to their fellow participants and the organization. Because of the high visibility and importance of this program within GMC, Advantexe also presented the results to senior executives. Internally, GMC used these results as a tool to recruit future participants in the program.

QUESTIONS FOR DISCUSSION

1. What are the advantages and disadvantages of participants selecting their own impact measures?
2. In this study, participants are estimating the amount of improvement instead of locating the specifics. Is this credible? Explain.
3. Critique the evaluation design and data collection methods.
4. Do you think the data are credible? Why or why not?
5. What are some of the ways this story attempted to be conservative with results?
6. Do you think the evaluators were comprehensive in the costs they included? Why or why not?
7. How can this case study help you in your evaluation practice?

ABOUT THE AUTHORS

Amy Happ is a senior vice president with Advantexe Learning Solutions, leading the business leadership practice. In this position, Amy's primary charge is to work with clients to customize leadership development learning solutions. Amy also facilitates classroom training in topics such as team building, communication skills, and change leadership. Amy is a certified ROI professional (CRP). She can be reached at amy.happ@advantexe.com

Kirk Smith, PhD, is an assistant professor of human resources and leadership at Western Carolina University, where he specializes in teaching research and evaluation methods and leadership. Smith has been affiliated with the ROI Institute as a consultant and facilitator since 2006 and has conducted many ROI impact studies, especially in leadership. He has published several book chapters and journal articles on evaluation, organizational culture, and consulting. Smith can be reached at wksmith@email.wcu.edu.

11

Measuring ROI in a Selection and Onboarding Program for New Leaders

Global Bank Inc.

Patti P. Phillips

Abstract

This case study measures the success of a project that is very common to large organizations. Each year companies hire new MBA graduates and integrate them into the organization in leadership roles. Some of the new prospects are successful and some are not. This is an example of a program that worked extremely well because it was designed to achieve the desired results. It involves changes in recruiting and selection of rotational assignments where the participants add value to the department to which they are assigned. This study shows the impact and financial ROI of this revised program.

BACKGROUND

Global Bank Inc. (GBI) is a large commercial and consumer banking organization with a strong presence in the United States and a significant presence outside the United States. Functionally, Global Bank operates through different divisions, including retail banking, electronic banking, international banking, consumer loans, commercial loans, home mortgages, wealth management, corporate services, and investments. The bank provides services to several regions in the United States as well as globally, with a strong presence in six countries. GBI is experiencing significant growth and is planning for future growth; however, the management team is concerned that the management talent is not deep enough in the organization.

The Situation

Each year, Global Bank recruits from major business schools, hiring more than 100 MBA graduates. Executives had two concerns about the program: there were not enough new MBAs and the turnover among newly hired MBAs seemed too high. The records show that up to 30 percent of new MBA hires left in the first two years, after GBI invested a significant amount of money in their development. GBI had experimented with rotational training programs in the past, but that did not seem to work out well, and the turnover rate was even higher. Management was convinced that the turnover had more to do with the way new hires transitioned into the bank. They concluded that three issues were contributing to the problem:

- The need for a distinct career path.
- A lack of meaningful assignments in rotational areas.
- Placements were not occurring as quickly as they should be.

These three challenges led the global talent management team to develop a new onboarding program for MBA candidates.

The talent management team decided to conduct additional analyses to understand what was causing the high turnover rates and to understand why the previous program was not more successful. They also wanted to understand how a new program could be implemented in a different way so that it would be successful. The ultimate goal is to retain these individuals, assign them to key positions, and have them perform exceptionally.

Although the team felt that these conclusions were correct, HR wanted to make sure they were approaching the right solution. With this in mind, the HR team reviewed exit interview data and made calls to previous MBA hires who had left the company to ask what would have been helpful to improve the program. They also explored what they could have done differently to keep the graduates at Global Bank. These proved to be very fruitful conversations.

Current MBA graduates who were still employed were invited to join focus groups to understand why some of their colleagues had left and to solicit specific actions to lower the turnover rate. This approach, using the nominal group technique, removed the pressure for current MBAs to explain why they might leave—no one wants to admit that leaving the company is something they plan to do. Some analysis was run on the MBA graduates employed by the company to uncover the cause of their success. This was conducted in an attempt to understand whether school, age, gender, marital status, or grades were linked to tenure and career progression. This analysis revealed that grades, age, gender, and marital status made very little difference. However, three schools had significantly higher tenure and career success, which seemed to be based on the MBA curriculum in those schools that was applied to and focused on leadership.

Finally, the selection process itself was reviewed to see whether some adjustments could be made to ensure that the right candidate was selected. This analysis revealed some insight and new assessment possibilities that could predict success. With these analyses complete, the program was developed and proposed.

PROGRAM DESCRIPTION

The new program involved three parts: The first part was recruiting and selection, which had three changes. The second part was the MBA rotational assignment, which had five changes. Finally, the third part was a comprehensive, two-week workshop.

Recruiting/Selection

In the first change, the recruiting team placed an emphasis on the three schools that seemed to generate more success. These particular schools had a higher number of graduates who had progressed in the organization. After interviewing these candidates it appeared that the philosophy of the business schools was to produce graduates who accelerate quickly and take more responsibility in a leadership position.

The second change represented an assessment tool that was customized to GBI and was focused on three important dimensions:

- eagerness to lead a team
- willingness to assume responsibility and accountability quickly
- the values of the candidate compared with the culture of GBI.

This instrument, purchased from a reputable supplier and adjusted for GBI, was used to connect these issues with retention. Low scores on this assessment would normally mean that the candidate would not be employed. However, there could be some overriding exceptions, so at this point it was merely used as an indicator, not an absolute cutoff. Only after more data analysis would it be used as a go or no-go decision maker.

The third change was to focus the interviews on three areas: the culture of the organization, a sense of responsibility and accountability, and the desire to lead teams to success.

Rotational Assignments

The rotational program had five changes. The first focused on the amount of time in the program. Previously, graduates completed the program in two years, with each assignment set for three or six months. Now, those times are negotiated between the participants, a career advisor, and the appropriate departments.

The second change involved the nature of the rotational assignment. With this change, the participant is assigned to fill a current job within a particular department and is expected to rise to the average performance level of that job within two months. For most of the departments, that should not be a difficult task.

The third change was that participants would have to recommend changes to improve the function within their assigned department. They were encouraged to take a fresh look at the process, examine the tasks, and review the systems. Any suggested improvements could be technology driven, procedure driven, or leadership driven, or involve human resources in terms of reward systems, job design, and so on. Recommendations are required in the new program, and showing the monetary value of the improvement using a conservative estimation process is even better.

A fourth change involved the rotational schedule. Participants must now complete at least six rotations, ideally seven or eight. This would be in part determined by the eagerness of the participants to assume the full-time responsibility, and their readiness for a full-time assignment. Thus, participants will not always be rotating through functions that have little need for them, saving the functions with the most growth opportunities near the end of their rotations. This way they can likely translate their assignments into full-time positions.

The final change in this process is that the new candidates must assume a leadership role in their permanent assignment, ideally within a year after employment. The objective of this program is to develop leaders who had business experience before they entered the graduate MBA program. These candidates should be able to rapidly move into leadership roles and up the career ladder.

Formal Training

An important part of this program is a comprehensive two-week workshop that provides the training necessary to succeed at Global Bank. The workshop is taught by external faculty and internal experts, covering 16 modules:

1. Introduction to the MBA Program
2. Company Mission, Vision, Values, and Strategic Objectives
3. Retail Banking
4. Electronic Banking
5. International Banking
6. Corporate Services
7. Consumer Lending
8. Commercial Lending
9. Home Mortgages
10. Wealth Management
11. Investment Services
12. Negotiations
13. Process Improvement
14. Managing Change
15. Performance Management
16. Leadership Development

Because only a few participants have banking experience, this aligns the new MBA recruits to the company and the banking business, while covering key soft-skills topics that are necessary to succeed in the bank.

THE EVALUATION APPROACH

Rationale for ROI

Some conversations with the senior team revealed a desire to see the impact of this program and maybe the financial ROI. The most important measure to track is retention, as these high-potential candidates need to remain with the bank. Second, and just as important, is that they should be successful when they are placed in permanent jobs. Third, they need to meet the performance levels with their rotating assignments. Finally, the participants need to drive improvements throughout the system as they rotate through the program. It was decided to measure this program using the ROI Methodology process, which captures reaction, learning, application, impact, and ROI. This is the most comprehensive evaluation system and is ideally suited for this type of analysis.

The Objectives

The objectives of this program were comprehensive and follow the levels of evaluation. All objectives were developed with input from executives and other stakeholders.

For Level 1 (reaction), the program should be perceived by participants as relevant to their individual needs, important to their own career success, and something they would recommend to others. The managers in the departments where the participants work need to see the program as necessary and important to the company's success.

For Level 2 (learning), before participants can begin their rotational assignments they must learn the basics of banking and the organization during the two-week classroom program. This program includes a variety of exercises and the learning is measured using a combination of self-assessments, quizzes, role plays, and simulations. The objective is to have a minimum of 90 percent of participants successfully complete this program. If participants do not complete the program successfully, they could be removed from the program. This would be examined on a case-by-case basis with the decision based on objective criteria.

As participants proceed through the assignments they must complete a simple quiz about the work in that function. They are briefed ahead of time about the topics, which are all focused on the work of that particular department. This quiz is designed to ensure that participants know the key elements of activity for that department. Those who fail to score at least 80 percent would have an opportunity to try again with verbal questions. If the results are unsatisfactory, the participant will usually have to work in the department for a longer period. Additionally, during every assignment participants complete a self-assessment on how well the program is meeting their learning needs.

For Level 3 (application), the application part of the process focuses on job assignments and individual projects. As participants learn a particular job, they must perform it. Job performance is measured with very specific criteria and success is defined with input from the department manager. The goal is to perform the job at an average performance level within two months. For most of these situations, that goal should not be difficult. The MBA graduates are talented individuals and most of them should achieve this within the first month for a majority of the assignments.

Another application objective focuses on the project and has two parts: A project improvement recommendation must be submitted after three months, and if possible, it should have a monetary value assigned to it. Participants will be given instructions on how to formulate their project, complete it, conduct the analyses, and present it. They will also be asked to present the recommendation in a formal meeting with the department manager and any key employees.

Several objectives are developed at Level 4 (business impact). After the program is fully operational:

1. 80 percent of participants will receive a permanent assignment within one year.
2. A 90 percent retention rate will be achieved after two years.
3. At least 50 percent of participant projects are implemented in the rotational departments representing direct efficiency and effectiveness measures, with a $10,000 average target.

For Level 5 (ROI), the ROI objective is set at 20 percent, keeping it slightly above the minimum required for capital expenditures. This is only a minimum acceptable performance.

Monetary value would come from a reduction in turnover, participant performance in their job, and implementing improvements in the departments. The cost of the program would include administrative costs, the cost for the two weeks of training, and subsidized salaries in the department where the participants work. In those departments, salaries would be subsidized by 20 percent from the global talent team budget to entice department heads to use these participants in their work. The department absorbs the rest of their salary because the participants are performing an actual job. This is an important monetary contribution from the participant.

EVALUATION PLANNING

Data Collection Plan

Figure 11-1 shows the data collection plan for this program, which is quite comprehensive, involving a variety of data collection methods, including questionnaires and data monitoring. The challenge is to collect an appropriate amount of data without significantly burdening the participants to provide too much. At the same time, participants know they are proving themselves and will take these assignments seriously. A major part of the evaluation is the promotion to permanent assignment, followed by retention and the implementation of individual projects.

FIGURE 11-1. Data Collection Plan

Program: MBA Onboarding **Responsibility:** **Date:**

Level	Broad Program Objective(s)	Measures	Data Collection Method/ Instruments	Data Sources	Timing	Responsibilities
1	**REACTION AND PLANNED ACTION** After completing this program, participants will: • Perceive this program as relevant to their individual needs • Perceive this program as important to their own career success • Recommend this program to other participants After participants visit each department, section manager will: • Perceive this program as necessary • Perceive this program to be important to the company's success	• Achieve 4 out of 5 on 5-point rating scale	• Questionnaire	• Participants • Section managers	• After two months and every two months • After each rotation	• Talent development team
2	**LEARNING AND CONFIDENCE** After completing the two-week program on 12 knowledge and skill areas for banking, partipants will: • Demonstrate successful acquisition of knowledge and skills After completing each rotational assignment participants will: • Demonstrate their knowledge of the department's function, processes, and activities	• 90% of participants score successful • 80% Score	• Quizzes • Exercises • Department quiz	• Participants	• At the end of two-week program • After each assigned area	• Talent development team

Level	Broad Program Objective(s)	Measures	Data Collection Method/ Instruments	Data Sources	Timing	Responsibilities
	• Assess the extent to which the visit met their learning needs	• Achieve 4 out of 5 on 5-point scale	• Questionnaire			
3	**APPLICATION/IMPLEMENTATION** During the rotational assignments: • Participants achieve average performance in two months in an existing job in the department • Participants submit a process improvement project to the section manager no later than three months into the assignment. • Participants complete at least four assignments in the program	• Rating of performance 3 out of 5 on 5-point scale	• Rating form • Report submitted	• Section manager • Participants	• After each assignment • Three months into assignment	• Talent development team
4	**BUSINESS IMPACT** After completing the program: • 80% of participants receive a permanent assignment in one year • Annualized turnover rate of MBA graduates will be less than 18% after one year and two years of operation • A least 50% of process improvement projects will be implemented realizing at least $10,000 of direct effectiveness and efficiency measures	• Transfer complete • Voluntary turnover rate • Monetary value of improvement	• Job transfer form • Performance monitoring • Project report summary	• HR records • HR records • Project documents	• Program completion • One year, two years • End of assignment	• Talent development team
5	**ROI** • The project will deliver at least a 20% ROI	Baseline Data: Comments:				

FIGURE 11-2. ROI Analysis Plan

Program/Project: __MBA Onboarding__   Responsibility: _____   Date: _____

Data Items (Usually Level 4)	Methods for Isolating the Effects of the Program/Process	Methods of Converting Data to Monetary Values	Cost Categories	Intangible Benefits	Communication Targets for Final Report	Other Influences/ Issues During Application	Comments
Job Assignment	• Expert Estimation	• Estimation	• Needs Assessment • Design Development • Coordinated Administration • Participant Salaries • Classroom • On-the-job and Classroom Training • Facilities • Evaluation	• Job Satisfaction • Job Engagement • Recruiting Image • Leadership Succession • Operational Efficiency	• Senior Executives • Department Managers • Section Managers • MBA Participants • Talent Development Team • Prospective MBA Students • All Employees		
Voluntary Turnover Rate	• Participant Estimation	• Standard Value					
Project Implementation	• Expert Estimation	Variety: • Standard Values • Expert Input • External Consultants					

The ROI Analysis Plan

Figure 11-2 shows the ROI analysis plan for data analysis techniques and information. For isolating the effects of the program, expert estimates would need to be used. Sometimes the expert is the participant and at other times the expert is the talent management staff. For converting data to monetary values, the turnover reduction is the critical impact. An accepted value taken from previous studies is used where the cost of turnover is 1.5 times the annual salary. For these projects the availability of monetary value will depend on the extent that the participants have already tackled the issue. If they have, then the number is used, subject to credibility tests and potential further analysis.

The costs are fully loaded, including 20 percent of the salaries of the MBA participants while they are on the rotational assignments. A variety of intangibles is perceived to be linked directly to this program. The executives will need this information along with other audiences. Communication of results is a critical part of the plan.

Timing and Sampling

The program was developed and ready to go in January 2013 for MBA graduates recruited for the year. The target was to recruit about 125 MBAs who would be cycled through the program. The largest group would join the company after spring graduation (during May and June). The talent development team decided that the evaluation would be for the first year, but only for the 54 graduates that were recruited in the spring. Essentially, this becomes the sample of graduates that measures impact and ROI.

The graduates participated in a two-week learning program as their first assignment in the organization. Because they were available in May or June, three separate two-week learning sessions were organized for these graduates and all 54 attended.

Although data were collected from the other graduates during the year, the analysis was confined just to these 54, and their performance was traced for one year, or until their first permanent assignments. The tracking would include the participants' performance in the potential assignments. Although the sample size was small, it represents almost half of the graduates for the year and was the appropriate size for the executives who wanted to see the effects of the program as quickly as possible.

Execution

As the new program was implemented, a full-time program director was assigned to be part of the talent development team. Initially, this person was responsible for the design and development of the program using external vendors. Then after implementation, she was responsible for administering the program effectively. This person had a full-time assistant, and the cost of both of these individuals would be included in the overall cost. These two individuals worked through placements in rotational assignments; addressed performance issues; assisted with data collection, coordination, and administration; provided performance feedback; and tackled other issues that surfaced during the program.

Time for Payout

Although this plan required tracking the graduates' performance until the permanent assignment, which would usually be about one year, an important question had to be addressed during the planning process—is this a long-term or short-term solution? Following the guiding principles of the ROI Methodology, if it is a short-term solution, only one year of benefits are used in the analysis. It was clear to the team that this was not a short-term solution because it involves at least a one-year commitment for each individual and much planning, preparation, and cost. Some could argue that the benefits of the program should be monitored for several years (or at least the data should be extrapolated for several years). After some discussion, it was decided to use a two-year payout, which was a very conservative approach. On a practical basis, the team would monitor the turnover for one year and extrapolate it for a second year. The monetary value from the participants' process improvement projects would be extrapolated for two years. This was considered to be ultraconservative, as a case could be made for extrapolating this data for three or four years. The important point is that the decision was made to stick with a two-year analysis before data collection began.

RESULTS

The results are presented in this section, arranged by levels of data, from reaction to ROI. In addition, the intangibles are presented to make a complete set of six types of outcome data sets.

Reaction Data

Table 11-1 shows the reaction data from both the participants and the managers. For the participants, the numbers exceeded the target of an average of four-out-of-five, but for the managers it was slightly less. Although the managers seem to support the program, there was some concern about how necessary and important the program was to company success. This early feedback allowed the talent development team to work with the section managers to continuously explain the importance of the program.

TABLE 11-1. Reaction Data

Participant's Perception	Rating
1. Relevant to Needs	4.3
2. Important to Career	4.4
3. Recommend to Others	4.2
Manager's Perception	
4. Program Is Necessary	3.9
5. Program Is Important to Company Success	3.7
Scale: 1 = Not at All; 2 = A Little; 3 = Moderate Amount; 4 = Much; 5 = Very Much	
N = 54 MBA Participants 100% Response	

Learning Data

Table 11-2 shows the learning data, which have several important parts. Data were collected for the 16 modules of the two-week program. Through a variety of exercises, quizzes, and simulations, evidence was available to the faculty that the participants were completing the program. Of the 54 individuals, only one was unsuccessful, leaving a 98 percent completion rate. The unsuccessful individual was allowed to make up extra time and continue the program.

TABLE 11-2. Learning Data

Learning Component	Successful Completion
Two-Week Workshop	98%
Rotational Assignment Quiz	96%
Rotational Assignment Self-Rating	4.4 of 5
N = 54 MBA Participants 100% Response	

The departmental quiz administered at the end of the rotational assignment tested the participants' knowledge of the activities, processes, and functions of the departments. All but two MBA participants successfully completed the quiz, and those two individuals stayed a little longer in the department and verbally passed the assessment.

At the end of the assignment the participants provided feedback, including the amount to which the assignment met their learning needs. Collectively, they scored a 4.4 out of a five-point scale.

Application Data

Table 11-3 shows the application data. As this table reveals, there were several components to application. The first, and perhaps most important, was the performance rating of the individuals performing an actual job in each rotational assignment. The goal was for the individual to assume the job as quickly as possible and reach an acceptable level of performance within two months. Ninety-six percent, representing 52 out of 54, achieved average performance within that timeframe, with the average time being 1.2 months. The other two were counseled and allowed to spend more time. One of those individuals left the organization. Collectively, 93 percent provided process improvement projects, which represented 50 out of the 54. The individuals who did not provided acceptable reasons for not being able to complete that assignment and they were allowed to continue the program.

TABLE 11-3. Application Data

Application Component	Success
Achieved Average Performance	96%
Average Time to Performance	1.2 months
Submitting Process Improvement Project	92% (50)
N = 54 MBA Participants 100% Response	

Impact Data

Table 11-4 shows the impact data for this program, which involved several issues. The first issue was the time for permanent assignment. The goal is to secure an assignment quickly, with an objective for 80 percent to have a permanent assignment in one year. That objective was exceeded, with 84 percent landing assignments in that time period. The average time to permanent assignment was 13.2 months, indicating that several individuals remained in the program for more than one year. This is acceptable considering that the pressure is on to find a permanent assignment as soon as possible.

TABLE 11-4. Impact Data

Impact Component	Success
Permanent Assignment	
Secure Assignment in One Year	84%
Average Time to Permanent Assignment	13.2 months
Turnover and Retention	
Voluntary Annualized Turnover Rate One Year	4%
Previous Annualized Turnover Rate One Year	22%
Process Improvement Projects	
Process Improvement Projects Submitted 50	93%
Process Improvement Projects Implemented 24	48%
Average Value of Process Improvement Projects	$7,340
Highest Value of Process Improvement Projects	$40,000
Lowest Value of Process Improvement Projects	$1,200
Total Monetary Value	$176,160
Percent Attributed to This Program	81%
Confidence in the Estimation	78%
Adjusted Monetary Benefits	**$111,298**

In regard to turnover, the annualized voluntary turnover rate for this group was 4 percent (two individuals left) in one year, as compared with the previous turnover rate of 22 percent. The team concluded that no external conditions could have lowered this number aside from the new approach of the program. Thus, the difference in these turnover rates would be attributed to the program. Essentially this is a trend analysis, in which the team suggested that the 22 percent turnover trend would have continued if the new program had not been implemented. The difference in the two, which is the 18 percent, is attributed to this program.

Process improvement is the next area for adding value. Fifty participants, representing 93 percent, submitted projects. However, only 24 projects (48 percent) were implemented, which was slightly less than the goal of 50 percent. The average monetary value for these projects was disappointing ($7,340), which is less than the $10,000 goal. The largest value of $40,000 was a surprise to the team. They felt that some individuals' projects would have a much higher cost savings.

Other factors could have caused these projects to be implemented and other factors could have influenced the results. In some cases, the projects would probably have been implemented anyway because they were opportunities that needed to be addressed, or problems that needed solving. Participants were asked, along with the section manager, to estimate the percent of this improvement as related to the program. For many projects, 100 percent of the improvement was allocated to this program, suggesting that this project would probably not have been attempted otherwise and that there were no other variables influencing the savings.

To make it more credible, the individuals were asked to indicate their confidence in the percentage, and the confidence ranged from as low as 60 percent to as high as 100 percent, with an average of 78 percent. When these adjustments are made, the total monetary value, attributed to the program, with adjustments for confidence in the allocation, is $111,298.

Converting Data to Money

Table 11-5 shows the process of converting data to money. The turnover rate conversion was straightforward. First, the number of turnovers was calculated. Basically, 18 percent turnover (10 turnovers), annualized, was prevented by this program. There were two turnovers by the end of the program (4 percent); however, previously it would have been 12 turnovers, so the improvement is 10. The cost of turnover, which is usually a multiple of an annual salary, is readily available in the literature and generally accepted within the talent development team. The team used a value of 1.5 times the annual salary to represent the cost of turnover. This is a conservative amount because when an individual leaves there is a tremendous loss of effort and time into the processes, as well as cost of recruiting and selection. The average MBA salary was priced at $80,000 for this group. It is interesting to note that most of the graduates came from three schools that seemed to have the best record at Global Bank. These were not the highest-ranked MBA schools, but rather those that stressed leadership as an important component, and prepared their MBA students to take leadership roles. Had Global Bank recruited at the top-tier schools, this salary would have been higher. So the cost of a single turnover is determined by $80,000 times 1.5 yields $120,000. By avoiding 10 turnovers, this provided a monetary benefit of $1.2 million.

TABLE 11-5. Converting Data to Money

For Year One	
Turnover Data	
Improvement 22% – 4% = 18%	
Cost of Turnover = 1.5 x Annual Salary	
Annual MBA Salary = $80,000	
Cost Avoided $80,000 x 1.5 x 10 =	$1,200,000
Process Improvement Projects	
From Table 11-4	$111,298
Early Job Assignment	
The Value Is Not Very Credible	N/A
Total Monetary Benefits (First Year)	$1,311,298
For Year Two (Extrapolated)	
Turnover Data	$1,200,000
Process Improvement Projects	$111,298
Total Monetary Benefits (Second Year)	1,311,298
Total Monetary Benefits Two Years	**$2,622,596**

Regarding the process improvement projects, the projects themselves required the individuals to show the monetary value possible with the improvement. Multiple years were included when it was appropriate and most of the projects contained second, third, and in one case even 10 years of revenue stream. From those implemented projects, $111,298 was claimed for the first year, and the same amount was claimed for the second year.

The early job assignment, which is very critical in the new design, had some obvious value. Having a person in a leadership role quickly adds value to the bank, sometimes even preventing an external hiring into the job. Although the number could have been estimated, it was not pursued because the value is not credible enough to include. This left a total monetary value for the first year of $1,311,298. When this is extrapolated for the second year, it leaves $2,622,596 for the total monetary value.

Program Costs

Table 11-6 shows the cost of this program. All the costs for needs assessments and program development were included, although there would be value for this for the next few years. The workshop development, workshop materials, facilitation, and facilities for the workshop were also included. The workshop materials are used beyond the two-week assignment, and included some other reading assignments that were required during rotational assignments. The coordination and administration, which involved two full-time people, were also included. The salaries of participants were indicated completely from the two-week assignment, recognizing that there is no direct value to the organization while they are in the two-week class. Therefore, the total salaries fully loaded using a 40 percent benefit factor realized a total of $232,615. A 40 percent benefit factor is suggesting that the total benefits package represented about 40 percent of the annual pay.

TABLE 11-6. Total Cost of Program

For Year One	
Needs Assessment	$10,000
Program Development	5,000
Workshop Development	20,000
Coordination	93,000
Facilitation of Workshop (3 Groups)	150,000
Facilities, Food, and Refreshments	45,000
Administrative Expense	16,000
Workshop Materials	16,000
Participants (Salaries)	
Two-Week Workshop	232,615
Rotational Assignments (20%) 12 Months	1,209,600
Executive Time (Salaries)	55,000
Evaluation	50,000
	Total $1,902,215
For Year Two (Extrapolated)	
Coordination	16,000
Administration	5,000
MBA Participants Salaries 20%, 1.2 months	120,960
Executive Time	5,500
	Total $147,460
	Two-Year Total $2,049,675

For the rotational assignment, the talent development department assumed 20 percent of their pay, and the visiting department absorbed the remaining 80 percent. When this 20 percent is calculated on a one-year basis, the total is $1,209,600. A salary of $80,000 was used with a 40 percent adjustment for the benefits (80,000 x 54 x 1.4 x 20% = $1,209,600). Executives at different levels were involved in the program, reviewing data, helping to plan, reviewing consequences, having discussions, and serving as mentors. This total time was estimated to be $55,000 by the talent development team. The cost of evaluation was $50,000 as an external firm conducted it. This gave a one-year total cost of $1,902,215.

When the year-two costs were calculated, they are not repeated for those who were placed into assignments. Some costs were still there for any MBA students who were not yet assigned. They represent coordination and administration time and salaries for 1.2 months, the average length of time beyond the 12 months included in the first-year monetary costs. The executive time is now down to $5,500, leaving a total of $147,460 for the second year. The two-year total cost of this program, fully loaded and being ultraconservative, is $2,049,675.

BCR and ROI Calculations

Table 11-7 shows the benefit-cost ratio and the ROI calculations for this program. Using the total benefits for two years and the total costs for two years, the benefit-cost ratio is 1.28 and the ROI is 28 percent, exceeding the minimum acceptable performance of 20 percent. Using two years of costs and benefits is very conservative. If a third-year framework is used, the total costs do not change from the second year because all students are assigned and in their permanent assignment. However, the benefits continue as these individuals remain on the job. If there is still only a 4 percent turnover in the third year, the ROI calculation would be almost 100 percent. This would not only meet the objective, but is an impressive payoff for the program.

TABLE 11-7. BCR and ROI Calculations

$$\text{Benefits} = \$2,622,596$$
$$\text{Costs} = \$2,049,675$$

$$\text{BCR} = \frac{\$2,622,596}{\$2,049,675} = 1.28$$

$$\text{ROI} = \frac{\$2,622,596 - \$2,049,675}{\$2,049,675} \times 100 = 28\%$$

INTANGIBLE BENEFITS

Table 11-8 shows the intangible benefits derived from this program. The most obvious one is the early job assignment. There is no calculation of this benefit, although it should be very substantial. Because it was not converted to money, it is considered to be an intangible. This allows the bank to use the talents of these graduates to fill key jobs sooner. The program is also building a leadership team, efficiently and effectively, which is a major purpose of the team. The individuals were asked on a follow-up questionnaire to indicate the extent to which certain intangible measures are connected to the program. The table lists those intangible benefits in the order of the strength of their connection to this program. They all were rated at least 3.5 out of a five-point scale, with four as an average. The strongest is career satisfaction, and the weakest is recruiting image, which is perhaps more difficult for them to see.

TABLE 11-8. Intangible Benefits

	Rank
Early Job Assignment	
Build Leadership Team	
Job Satisfaction (Career)	1
Job Engagement	2
Leadership Succession	3
Operational Efficiency	4
Recruiting Image	5

At least 3.5 out of 5-point scale

CONCLUSIONS AND RECOMMENDATIONS

From all indications, this is a successful program with few minor adjustments that need to be made. It appears that the analysis has yielded the proper solution—having an early assignment is critical, and having detailed training to build capability, knowledge, and thinking in Global Bank was important. The focus on the rotational assignments to learn the job and achieve success was a critical component that seemed to work extremely well.

The disappointing part is that the process improvement projects had less than expected monetary value, which is an opportunity for improvement. In addition, some work is still needed with the managers and executives who did not have the benefit of this type of program. Many of them came up the hard way, starting at the bottom without an MBA and without the comprehensive focus of the program. It is difficult for them to see how critical this program is to the success of the organization.

The conclusion is to continue to administer the program as planned, with the exception of placing more focus on process improvement. Another module should be added to the two-week program to focus on the work projects in each rotational assignment using data from this study, in which the individual topics and how they are calculated are outlined. The participants are encouraged to examine big-picture items as well as small process improvement opportunities. The goal is to have the benefit of an external view from a highly trained individual to see improvements in the processes. This ultimately may be one of the biggest benefits of this program.

LESSONS LEARNED

Ultimately, the talent development team was very pleased with this program, and there were some lessons learned in the process.

1. **Conduct a very thorough needs assessment to understand what is needed to make this program work.** The principal problem was excessive turnover. The nominal group process seemed to reveal many of the key issues that were causing the participants to leave during the program. This enabled a very focused solution that seemed to work extremely well.

2. **Create expectations and plan the process very appropriately.** Individuals must know that they are being evaluated at each rotational assignment, not because of punitive issues, but just to ensure that they are learning what they need to learn. This created expectations that the MBA graduates met. Regarding the process improvement, the success that was achieved was because of the early planning dedicated to that process. With more planning, it will be much better.

3. **The number of years of benefits is an important issue.** This project was negative for only one year of monetary benefits. But clearly, this is not a one-year, short-term solution. It is a solution that could easily expect to pay off in a three-, four-, or five-year timeframe. Two years were used to keep it extremely conservative, and it may be too conservative. So the lesson learned is to make sure that this is addressed properly, so that it is not too short for the monetary benefits tabulation.

QUESTIONS FOR DISCUSSION

1. Is this study credible? Please explain.
2. Critique the methods used to isolate the effects for the program.
3. Should a monetary benefit be placed on achieving early assignments? Please explain.
4. Should a longer period of time be used for monetary benefits? Please explain.
5. How should this be communicated to the senior executives?

ABOUT THE AUTHOR

Patti P. Phillips, PhD, is president and CEO of the ROI Institute, the leading source of ROI competency building, implementation support, networking, and research. A renowned expert in measurement and evaluation, she helps organizations implement the ROI Methodology in more than 60 countries. She serves as principal research fellow for The Conference Board, where she co-authored the research reports *Human Capital Analytics: A Primer* (2012) and *Human Capital Analytics @ Work Volume 1* (2014). Patti serves on the faculty of the UN System Staff College in Turin, Italy, and the University of Southern Mississippi's human capital development doctoral program. She can be reached at patti@roiinstitute.net.

12

Measuring ROI in Safety Leadership for Construction Project Leaders

Global Engineering and Construction Company

Jack J. Phillips

Abstract

This case study shows the power of a safety leadership program for project safety leaders on construction sites. These are large construction sites and the safety project leader is a full-time safety and health professional. Responding to disappointing safety performance, a thorough needs analysis was conducted, yielding a variety of actions that needed to be taken through the project safety leaders. These managers are responsible for safety for their large projects. They need to take leadership actions to improve a variety of measures. This program involved a two-day workshop with action plans to drive business performance measures. Each participant selected three measures to improve, using the content of the program and the detailed action planning process provided. The results are very impressive, underscoring the benefit of having an action plan built into the program and the power of the program's focus on results.

BACKGROUND

Global Engineering and Construction Company (GEC) designs and builds large commercial projects such as chemical plants, paper mills, and municipal water systems. The company employs 35,000 full-time associates. In addition, another 200 to 1,500 contract workers are involved during each project's peak construction phases. During a typical year, contract workers account for another 100,000 at construction sites. Safety is always a critical matter at GEC and usually commands much management attention.

From a corporate perspective, safety is managed by a safety and health team composed of specialists and managers who report to the director of environment, health, and safety (EHS). Each project has at least one person responsible for safety who functions as a project safety leader.

The Need

During the previous two years, safety performance has deteriorated or remained flat at unacceptable levels. Because of this disappointing and sometimes erratic safety performance, the chief operating officer (COO) asked the EHS director to explore the causes of the unacceptable performance and to offer a remedy. The department reviewed the safety records, safety procedures, and safety administration, searching for common threads of causality. Questionnaires were sent to all the project safety leaders at each site, and a select group of safety leaders were interviewed in an attempt to pinpoint what could be done to improve safety. From this initial needs assessment, the following conclusions were made:

1. There is still a lack of knowledge about the different tools and techniques available for the project safety leaders to use to improve safety performance.
2. There is clear evidence that project safety leaders are not operating on a proactive basis, but merely reacting to events and issues as they happen.
3. Routine safety meetings need more content, better planning, and improved coordination.
4. Project safety leaders need to use available tools for investigation, causation analysis, and corrective action.

With this in mind, the EHS Team recommended a two-day safety leadership workshop for all the project safety leaders. This workshop would focus on the gaps defined in the needs assessment and would provide the motivation, knowledge, skills, and tools to improve safety performance.

The program was designed for project safety leaders, who usually had the title of safety manager, safety engineer, or safety superintendent. The program focused on safety leadership, safety planning, safety inspections and audits, safety meetings, accident investigation, safety policies and procedures, safety standards, and safety problem solving. The objectives for the program are listed in Table 12-1.

TABLE 12-1. Objectives for Safety Management Program

Level	Measurement Focus
1. Reaction	Obtain favorable reaction to program and materials on: • need for program • relevance to project • importance to project success Identify planned actions.
2. Learning	After attending this program, participants should be able to: • Establish safety audits. • Provide feedback and motivate employees. • Investigate accidents. • Solve safety problems.
3. Application and Implementation	• Use knowledge, skills, and tools routinely in appropriate situations. • Complete all steps of action plan.
4. Business Impact	• Improve at least three safety and health measures.
5. Return on Investment	20%

These topics were fully explored in a two-day safety leadership program conducted regularly. Safety leaders (the participants) were expected to improve the safety performance of their individual construction projects. The safety performance measures used in the company were also reviewed and discussed in the workshop. This particular program would be expensive, because it would be necessary for all the project safety leaders to travel, and they would miss two days of work while participating in the program. The COO wanted to make sure that this was the right solution and that it represented a good investment. He asked for success measures that would show how safety performance has improved. Ideally, he wanted to see the ROI for conducting this particular program.

Business Alignment

The program facilitator asked participants to provide limited needs assessment data before attending the program. Participants were asked to review the safety performance of their projects and identify at least three safety measures that, if improved, should enhance safety performance. Each measure selected should be important and have the possibility of being improved using the topics covered in the safety management program. Some possible business impact measures include disabling injury rate, accident severity rate, first aid treatments, OSHA citations, OSHA penalties, property accidents, hazardous material incidents, or near misses. Each participant could have different measures, but it is important to avoid selecting measures that cannot be enhanced through the team's efforts and the content covered in the program.

As the participants register for the program, they are reminded to complete the action plan. This requirement is presented as an integral part of the program, not as an add-on data collection tool, because action planning is necessary to show actual improvements generated from the program.

WHY EVALUATE THIS PROGRAM?

Although the COO had suggested the ROI calculation, the EHS director was convinced that this program would add value and he wanted to show top executives that investments in safety and health had high payoffs. The safety team decided at the outset to collect and present improvement data to the C-suite, so the evaluation and action plan steps were built into the program. This decision was based on three issues:

- This program is designed to add value at the construction-project level and the outcome is expressed in project level measures that are well known and respected by the management team. The evaluation should show the actual monetary value of improvement.
- The application data enable the team to make improvements and adjustments.
- The data also help the team gain respect for the program from the operating executives and project managers.

THE ROI PROCESS

The safety and health team staff used a comprehensive evaluation process to develop the ROI. The ROI Methodology generates six types of data: reaction, learning, application and implementation, business impact, ROI, and intangible measures.

To determine the contribution the program makes to the changes in business impact measures, a technique to isolate the effects of the program was also included in the process. Figure 12-1 shows the ROI process model used. Data collection plans and an ROI analysis plan were developed before data collection actually began. Four levels of data were collected, which represents the first four types of data listed above, and the process also included techniques to convert data to monetary value. The ROI is calculated by comparing the monetary benefits with the cost of the program. The intangible measures, the sixth type of data, are those impact measures not usually converted to monetary value, such as job satisfaction and image. This comprehensive model allows the organization to follow a consistent standardized approach each time it is applied to evaluate safety programs.

FIGURE 12-1. ROI Methodology Process Model

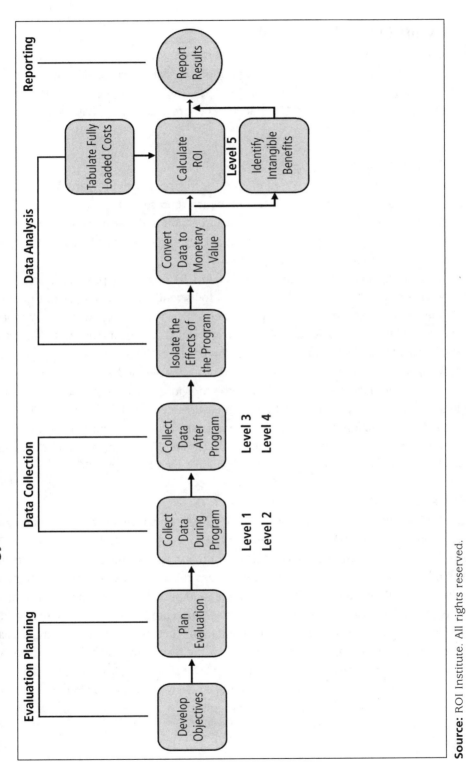

PLANNING FOR EVALUATION

Planning for the evaluation is critical to save time and improve the quality and quantity of data collection. It also provides an opportunity to clarify expectations and responsibilities and shows the client group—in this case, the senior operating team—exactly how this program is evaluated. Two documents are created: the data collection plan and the ROI analysis plan.

Data Collection Plan

Figure 12-2 shows the data collection plan for this program. Program objectives are detailed along the five levels of evaluation, which represent the first five types of data collected. As the figure illustrates, the typical reaction and learning data are collected at the end of the program by the facilitator. Learning objectives focus on the major areas of the program.

Through application objectives, participants focus on two primary broad areas. The first is to use the knowledge, skills, and tools routinely in appropriate situations, and the second is to complete all steps on their action plans. A follow-up questionnaire was selected to measure the use of knowledge, skills, and tools. This was planned for two months after the program. For the second area, action plan data are provided to show the actual improvement in the safety measures planned.

Business impact objectives vary with the individual, as each project safety leader identifies at least three safety and health measures needing improvement. These are detailed on the action plan and serve as the basic principal document for the safety and health team to tabulate the overall improvement. The ROI objective is 20 percent, which was higher than the ROI target for capital expenditures at GEC.

ROI Analysis Plan

The ROI analysis plan, which appears in Figure 12-3, shows how data are analyzed and reported. Safety performance data form the basis for the rest of the analysis. The effects of the program were isolated using estimations from the safety project leader. The method to convert data to monetary values relied on three techniques: standard values (when they are available), expert input, and participant's estimates. Most of the costs of safety measures were readily available. Cost categories represent a fully loaded profile of program costs, including direct and indirect costs; anticipated intangibles are detailed and the communication audiences for the results are outlined. The ROI analysis plan represents the approach to process business impact data to develop the ROI analysis and capture the intangible data. Collectively, these two planning documents outline the approach for evaluating this program.

Figure 12-2. Data Collection Plan

Level	Broad Program Objective(s)	Measures	Data Collection Method/ Instruments	Data Sources	Timing	Responsibilities
1	**REACTION** • Obtain favorable reaction to program and materials on – Need for program – Relevance to project – Importance to project success • Identify planned actions	• Average rating of 4 out of 5 on feedback items • 100% submit planned actions	• Standard questionnaire	• Participant	• End of program	• Facilitator
2	**LEARNING** After attending this session, participants should be able to: • Establish safety audits • Provide feedback and motivate employees • Investigate accidents • Solve safety problems • Follow procedures and standards • Counsel problem employees • Conduct safety meetings	• Achieve an average of 4 on a 5-point scale	• Questionnaire	• Participant	• End of program	• Facilitator

Level	Broad Program Objective(s)	Measures	Data Collection Method/ Instruments	Data Sources	Timing	Responsibilities
3	**APPLICATION/IMPLEMENTATION** • Use knowledge, skills, and tools in appropriate situations • Complete all steps of action plan	• Ratings on questions (4 of 5) • The number of steps completed on action plan	• Questionnaire • Action plan	• Participant • Participant	• Two months after program • Three months after program	• Safety and health team
4	**BUSINESS IMPACT** • Improve three safety and health measures	• Varies	• Action plan	• Participant	• Six months after program	• Safety and health team
5	**ROI** 20%	Comments: Several techniques will be used to secure commitment to provide data on the questionnaire and action plan.				

FIGURE 12-3. ROI Analysis Plan

Program: Safety Management Program Responsibility: _____ Date: _____

Data Items (Usually Level 4)	Methods for Isolating the Effects of the Program/ Process	Methods of Converting Data to Monetary Values	Cost Categories	Intangible Benefits	Communication Targets for Final Report	Other Influences/ Issues During Application	Comments
• Three safety and health measures identified by project safety leader	• Participant estimation	• Standard values • Expert input (Safety team) • Participant estimation	• Needs assessment • Program development • Program materials • Travel and lodging • Facilitation and coordination • Participant salaries plus benefits while in the program • Extra project expenses related to program • Evaluation	• Job engagement • Job satisfaction • Stress • Image • Brand	• Construction project general manager • Participants • Director, environment, health and safety • Corporate safety and health team • Operating executives • Senior VP human resources		

Client Signature: _____ Date: _____

ACTION PLANNING: A KEY TO ROI ANALYSIS

Figure 12-4 shows the sequence of activities as the action planning process is introduced to participants and reinforced throughout the program. The requirement for the action plan is communicated prior to the program along with the request for needs assessment information.

FIGURE 12-4. Sequence of Activities for Action Planning

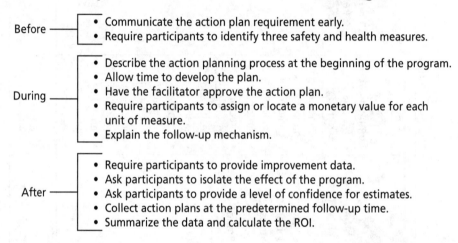

Before
- Communicate the action plan requirement early.
- Require participants to identify three safety and health measures.

During
- Describe the action planning process at the beginning of the program.
- Allow time to develop the plan.
- Have the facilitator approve the action plan.
- Require participants to assign or locate a monetary value for each unit of measure.
- Explain the follow-up mechanism.

After
- Require participants to provide improvement data.
- Ask participants to isolate the effect of the program.
- Ask participants to provide a level of confidence for estimates.
- Collect action plans at the predetermined follow-up time.
- Summarize the data and calculate the ROI.

Teaching and Explaining the Plan

On the first day of the program, the facilitator described the action planning process in a 15-minute discussion. The guidelines for developing action plans were presented using the SMART (specific, measurable, achievable, realistic, and time-based) requirements. The participants were given five blank action plans (three of which they needed to complete). The facilitator also presented examples to illustrate what a complete action plan should look like. This discussion reinforced the need for action plans and the importance of the tool to participants.

Developing the Plan

At the end of the second day, the booklets were completed in a session that lasted about 90 minutes. Participants worked in teams to complete three action plans, which took 20 to 30 minutes each. Figure 12-5 shows a blank action plan. During the session, participants completed the top portion of the action plan; they listed the action steps in the left column and parts A, B, and C in the right column. The remainder of the form was completed during a three-month follow up. A facilitator monitored the session and several operations executives were present. Involving operations executives not only keeps participants focused on the task, it usually leaves executives impressed with the program and the quality of the action planning process.

FIGURE 12-5. Action Plan Form

Name: _____ Facilitator Signature: _____ Follow-Up Date: _____
Objective: _____ Evaluation Period: _____ To: _____
Improvement Measure: _____ Target Performance: _____

Action Steps	Analysis
1. _____	A. What is the unit of measure? _____
2. _____	B. What is the value (cost) of one unit? $ _____
3. _____	C. How did you arrive at this value? _____
4. _____	_____
5. _____	D. How much did the measure change during the evaluation period? (monthly value) _____
6. _____	E. What other factors could have caused the improvement? 1. _____ 2. _____ 3. _____
7. _____	
8. _____	F. What percent of this change was actually caused by this program? _____%
9. _____	G. What level of confidence do you place on the above information? (100%=Certainty and 0%=No Confidence) _____ %
Comments: _____	H. How many months to project completion? _____ %
_____	Other benefits and consequences _____

211

The action plan could focus on any specific steps, as long as the steps are consistent with the program's content and are related to the safety and health improvement measures. The most important part of developing the plan is to convert the measure to a monetary value (B and C). Three approaches were offered to the participants. First, standard values, which are values already known to the project safety leaders, are used if they are available. In this case, standard values were available for most of the EHS measures because the safety and health team had previously assigned a cost to particular measures for use in controlling costs and developing an appreciation for their impact. If a standard value was not available, the participants were encouraged to use expert input, such as from a corporate safety and health team member who may know the value of a particular item. The program facilitator encouraged participants to call the expert and include the given value in the action plan. If a standard value or expert input was not available, participants were asked to estimate the cost or value using the knowledge and resources available to them. It was important to require this value to be developed during the program.

ROI FORECAST WITH REACTION DATA

At the end of the two-day leadership program, participants completed a customized questionnaire to evaluate the safety leadership program. Participants were asked to provide a one-year estimated monetary value of their planned actions, explaining the basis for and placing a confidence level on their estimates. Table 12-2 presents these data. Data were supplied by 19 of the 25 participants. The estimated cost of the program, including participants' salaries for the time devoted to the project, was $120,000.

The monetary values of the planned improvements were extremely high, reflecting the participants' optimism and enthusiasm. As a first step in the analysis, extreme data items were omitted (one of the guiding principles of the ROI Methodology). Data such as millions, unlimited, and $4 million were discarded, and each remaining value was multiplied by the confidence value and totaled. This adjustment is a way to reduce highly subjective estimates.

The resulting tabulations yielded a total improvement of $990,125 (rounded to $990,000). The projected ROI, which was based on the feedback questionnaire, is:

$$\text{ROI} = \frac{\$990,000 - \$120,000}{\$120,000} \times 100 = 725 \text{ percent}$$

Although these projected values are subjective, the results were generated by project safety leaders (participants) who should be aware of what they could accomplish. The follow-up study will determine the true results delivered by the group.

TABLE 12-2. Level 1 Data for ROI Forecast Calculations

Participant No.	Estimated Value ($)	Basis	Confidence Level	Adjusted Value ($)
1	80,000	Reduction in accidents	90%	72,000
2	91,200	OSHA reportable injuries, OSHA Fines	80%	72,960
3	55,000	Accident reduction	90%	49,500
4	10,000	First-aid visits/visits to doctor/DIR	70%	7,000
5	150,000	Reduction in lost-time injuries, OSHA Fines	95%	142,500
6	Millions	Total accident cost	100%	—
7	74,800	Workers' compensation, Injury	80%	59,840
8	7,500	OSHA citations, Accidents	75%	5,625
9	50,000	Reduction in accidents	75%	37,500
10	36,000	Workers' compensation (lost time)	80%	28,800
11	150,000	Reduction in total accident costs	90%	135,000
12	22,000	OSHA fines/accidents	70%	15,400
13	140,000	Accident reductions	80%	112,000
14	4 Million	Total cost of safety	95%	—
15	65,000	Total workers' compensation	50%	32,500
16	Unlimited	Accidents	100%	—
17	20,000	Accidents	95%	19,000
18	45,000	Injuries	90%	40,500
19	200,000	Lost-time injuries	80%	160,000
				Total: $990,125

Collecting this type of data focuses increased attention on project outcomes. This issue becomes clear to participants as they anticipate results and convert them to monetary values. This simple exercise is productive because of the important message it sends to participants—they will understand that specific action is expected, which produces results. The data collection helps participants plan the implementation of what they are learning.

Because a follow-up evaluation of the program is planned, the post-project results will be compared with the ROI forecast. Comparisons of forecast and follow-up data are helpful. If there is a defined relationship between the two, the less expensive forecast may be substituted for the more expensive follow-up in the future.

IMPROVING RESPONSE RATES

Data were collected at Level 1 and 2 (reaction and learning) at the end of the two-day workshop. As expected, the facilitator was able to secure a 100 percent response rate directly from the participants. However, not everyone completed the forecast of results, with only 19 of the 25 providing data. A follow-up questionnaire, which was completed two months after the program, had an impressive response, with 22 out of the 25 providing data.

This response rate was achieved by taking on the following techniques:

1. The questionnaire was reviewed at the workshop, with the expectation that the data would be provided in two months.
2. The questionnaire was positioned as a tool for participants to see the progress they were making.
3. The questionnaire was designed for ease of response, with the expectation that it would take only about 20 minutes to complete.
4. The COO signed the memo to the participants, asking for the data and encouraging them to reflect over what they were actually doing as a result of this program. The participants were promised a summary of the questionnaire results, and were assured that actions would be taken to improve the program as a result of their comments.
5. Two follow-up reminders were provided: an email and a phone call directly from the facilitator.
6. Participants were given a new book on the importance of safety as an incentive for responding—this was an exchange, the questionnaire for the book.

Action plans were collected three months after the program, providing an opportunity for the participants to show the impact of their work. Because of their commitment and ownership of the data, a response rate of 92 percent was achieved. The facilitators also used several techniques similar to those used with the questionnaire to obtain the action plans.

In summary, the data collection was extremely effective with high levels of commitment and participation by the individuals.

RESULTS

The safety and health team reported results in all six data categories developed by the ROI Methodology, beginning with reaction and moving through ROI and the intangibles. Here are the results in each category with additional explanations about how some of the data was processed.

Reaction and Learning

Reaction data, collected at the end of the program using a standard questionnaire, focused on issues such as relevance of and intention to use the content. The delivery and facilitation also are evaluated. Table 12-3 shows a summary of the reaction data with ratings. Learning improvement was measured at the end of the program using self-assessment. Table 12-4 shows the summary of the learning results. Although these measures are subjective, they provide an indication of improvements in learning.

TABLE 12-3. Reaction Measurements

Topic	Rating
Need for the program	4.3
Relevance to construction project	4.5
Importance to project success	4.5
Delivery of the program	4.2
Facilitation of the program	4.2
Planned actions developed	100%

1= Unsatisfactory   5 = Exceptional

TABLE 12-4. Learning Measurements

Topic	Rating
Establish safety audits	4.2
Provide feedback and motivation to employees	4.0
Investigate accidents	4.9
Follow safety procedures and standards	4.2
Counsel problem employees	3.9
Conduct safety meetings	4.8

1 = Cannot do this 5 = Can do this extremely well

Application and Implementation

To determine the extent to which the knowledge, skills, and tools are actually being used and to check the progress of the action plan, a questionnaire was distributed two months following participation in the program. This two-page, user-friendly question-naire evaluated the success of the program at the application level. Table 12-5 provides a summary of the results, which show progress in each of the areas and success using the content. The safety leaders also indicated that this program was affecting other safety measures beyond the three selected for action planning. Typical barriers of implementation they reported included lack of time, understaffing, changing culture, and pressures to get work done. The highest ranked enabler was support from the project general manager. This follow-up questionnaire gave project safety leaders an opportunity to briefly summarize progress with the action plan.

TABLE 12-5. Application Results

Success With:	Rating
1. Conducting safety audits	4.1
2. Providing feedback to employees	3.9
3. Investigating accidents	4.8
4. Solving safety problems	4.9
5. Following safety procedures and standards	4.7
6. Counseling problem employees	4.2
7. Conducting safety meetings	4.6

1= Unsuccessful   5 = Very Successful

In essence, it served as a reminder to continue with the plan, as well as a process check to see if there were issues that should be explored.

Business Impact

Project safety leaders provided safety improvement data specific to their construction projects. Although the action plan contained some Level 3 application data (the left side of the form in Figure 12-6), the primary value of the action plan was business impact data obtained from the documents.

In the three-month follow up, participants were required to furnish the following items:

1. The actual change in the measure on a monthly basis (included in part D of the action plan). This value is used to develop an annual (first year) improvement.

2. A list of the other factors that could have caused the improvement (part E), which is the only feasible way to isolate the effects of the program. As they monitor the measures and observe their improvement, the project safety leaders probably see the other influences driving a particular measure.

3. The percent of improvement resulting from the application of the content from the safety management program (the action steps on the action plan). Each project safety leader was asked to be as accurate as possible with the estimate and express it as a percentage (part F).

4. The level of confidence in their allocation of the contribution to this program. This reflects the degree of error in the allocation and is included in part G on the action plan, using 100 percent for certainty and 0 percent for no confidence.

5. An estimate of the number of months to project completion. This allows for the calculation of the duration of the benefits.

FIGURE 12-6. Action Plan

Name: Roger Gerson Facilitator Signature: _____ Follow-Up Date: 1 July
Objective: Reduce first-aid treatments Evaluation Period: January To: April
Improvement Measure: First-aid visits Current Performance: 22 / Month Target Performance: 10 / Month

Action Steps	Analysis
1. Review first-aid records for each employee—look for trends and patterns.	A. What is the unit of measure? One first-aid visit
2. Meet with team to discuss reasons for first-aid visits—using problem-solving skills.	B. What is the value (cost) of one unit? $ 300
3. Coursel with "problem employees" to correct habits and explore opportunities for improvement.	C. How did you arrive at this value? Standard Value
4. Conduct a brief meeting with an employee returning to work after a visit to first aid.	D. How much did the measure change during the evaluation period? (monthly value) 11
5. Provide recognition to employees who have perfect accident records.	E. What other factors could have caused the improvement? 1. Required OSHA training 2. Project leadership (General Manager) 3. Safety-first program for all employees
6. Follow-up with each discussion and discuss improvement or lack of improvement and plan other action.	F. What percent of this change was actually caused by this program? 60 %
7. Monitor improvement and provide recognition when appropriate.	G. What level of confidence do you place on the above information? (100%=Certainty and 0%=No Confidence) 80 %
	H. How many months to project completion? 18 %
Other Benefits: Greater Productivity	OPTIONAL: Calculate the value (B x D x 12 x F x 9)
Comments: The action plan kept me on track with this problem.	11 x 300 x 12 x 60% x 80% = $19,008

217

6. Input on intangible measures observed or monitored during the three months that were directly linked to this program.
7. Additional comments, including explanations if necessary.

Figure 12-6 shows an example of a completed action plan. The example focuses directly on first-aid visits from participant number five. This participant was averaging 22 incidents per month, and the goal was to reduce it to 10. Specific action steps are indicated on the left side of the form. The average cost of a first-aid visit is $300, an amount that represents a standard value. The actual change on a monthly basis was 11 visits, which was slightly below the target. Three other factors contributed to the improvement. The participant estimated that 60 percent of the change was directly attributable to this program, and is 80 percent confident in this estimate. The confidence estimate frames a range of error for the 60 percent allocation, allowing for a possible 20 percent (plus or minus) adjustment in the estimate. To be conservative, it is adjusted to the low side, bringing the contribution rate of this program to a 48 percent reduction:

60% x 80% = 48%

The actual improvement value for this example can be calculated as follows:

11 visits x $300 per visit x 12 months = $39,600

The number of months to project completion is 18, making it appropriate to use the one-year rule for benefits. In the last three months of a project, most of the employees have left the job. Consequently, a project has to have at least 15 months remaining to use one year of data. Otherwise, an adjustment must be made. For example, a project with 14 months remaining would use 11 months of benefits instead of one year.

Table 12-6 shows the annual improvement values on the first measure only for the first 25 participants in this group. Similar tables are generated for the second and third measures. The values are adjusted by the contribution estimate and the confidence estimate. In the fifth example, the $39,600 is adjusted by 60 percent and 80 percent to yield $19,008. This same adjustment is made for each of the values, with a total first-year adjusted value for the first measure of $320,309. The same process is followed for the second and third measures for the group, yielding totals of $162,310 and $57,320, respectively. The total benefit is $539,939.

Program Cost

Table 12-6 details the program costs reflecting a fully loaded cost profile. The estimated cost of the needs assessment ($5,000) is prorated over the life of the program, which will be with three sessions. The estimated program development cost ($7,500) is also prorated over the life of the program. The program materials and facilitators are direct costs, and the program also includes a book on safety management. Travel and

TABLE 12-6. Business Impact Data

Participant	Annualized Improvement ($ Values)	Other Measures	Other Factors	Contribution Estimate From Safety Project Leaders	Confidence Estimate	Adjusted $ Value
1	5,000	Medical treatment	2	40%	90%	23,400
2	5,500	Property damage	4	25%	70%	963
3	32,800	Disabling injuries	2	70%	60%	13,776
4	21,800	First aid	1	80%	80%	13,952
5	39,600	First aid	3	60%	80%	19,008
6	19,800	Disabling injuries	2	70%	90%	12,474
7	25,000	OSHA citations	3	30%	70%	5,250
8	23,000	Property damage	4	30%	40%	2,760
9	34,500	Medical treatment	1	75%	800%	20,700
10	50,000	Near miss	0	100%	100%	50,000
11	75,000	Disabling injury rate	2	45%	75%	23,313
12	42,350	Medical treatment	3	50%	75%	15,881
13	40,000	OSHA fine	4	25%	80%	8,000

Total this group $209,477

Participant	Annualized Improvement ($ Values)	Other Measures	Other Factors	Contribution Estimate From Safety Project Leaders	Confidence Estimate	Adjusted $ Value
14	59,000	Disabling injuries	3	40%	85%	20,060
15	75,000	Disabling injuries	2	20%	90%	13,500
16	missing					
17	24,900	Hazmat violations	2	40%	70%	6,972
18	25,000	Property damage	5	20%	80%	4,000
19	missing					
20	39,000	OSHA citations	2	60%	95%	22,230
21	13,500	OSHA citations	2	70%	90%	850
22	15,000	First aid	0	100%	90%	13,500
23	1,000,000	Near miss	0	100%	100%	1,000,000 (leave this out of calculation)
24	54,000	Hazardous materials	3	60%	70%	22,680
25	22,000	Property damage	3	40%	80%	7,040

Extreme data was omitted from this analysis.

Total (this page) $110,832
Total First Measure $320,309

Total Annual Benefit for Second Measure is $162,310
Total Annual Benefit for Third Measure is $57,320

lodging are estimates using an average for each participant. Facilitation and coordination costs were estimated, too. Time away from work represents lost opportunity and is calculated by multiplying two days by daily salary costs, adjusted for 40 percent employee benefits factor. The average hourly rate for these leaders is about $50. When adjusted for benefits, the rate is $70, which is $560 per day or $1,120 per participant for the two days. That brings the total to $28,000 for 25 participants, which is the second-largest cost item after travel. The cost for the evaluation was estimated. The total costs of $106,087 represent a very conservative approach to cost accumulation.

ROI Analysis

The total monetary benefits are calculated by adding the values of the three measures, which total $539,939. This leaves a benefits-cost ratio (BCR) and ROI as follows.

$$BCR = \frac{\$539,939}{\$128,067} = 4.22$$

$$ROI = \frac{(\$539,939 - \$128,067)}{\$128,067} \times 100 = 322\%$$

When this actual ROI is compared with the forecasted ROI, a significant difference surfaces. The return is 54 percent less than the forecast, but this is expected because of the optimism experienced at the end of the workshop.

TABLE 12-7. Program Cost Summary

Needs Assessment (Prorated over three sessions)	$1,667
Program Development (Prorated over three sessions)	2,500
Program Materials – 25 @ $100	2,500
Travel and Lodging – 25 @ $2000	37,500
Facilitation and Coordination	50,000
Facilities and Refreshments – 2 days @ $700	1,400
Participants Salaries Plus Benefits	28,000
ROI Evaluation	4,500
Total	**$128,067**

Credibility of Data

This ROI value of more than 300 percent greatly exceeds the 20 percent target value. However, despite being extremely high, the ROI value was considered to be credible. This is because of the principles on which the study was based.

1. The data come directly from the participants.
2. The data could be audited to see if the changes were actually taking place.
3. To be conservative, only the first year of improvements was used. With the changes reported in the action plans, there should be second- and third-year values that were omitted from the calculation.
4. The monetary improvement was discounted to account for the effect of other influences. In essence, the participants only took credit for the part of the improvement related to the program.
5. The estimate of contribution was adjusted for error, which represents a discount, adding to the conservative approach.
6. The costs are fully loaded to include both direct and indirect costs.
7. The business impact does not include value obtained from using the skills to address other problems or to influence other measures. Only the values from three measures taken from the action planning projects were used in the analysis.

The ROI process develops convincing data connected directly to project construction costs. From the viewpoint of the chief financial officer, the data can be audited and monitored. It should be reflected as actual improvement at the project site.

Intangible Data

As a final part of the complete data profile, the intangible benefits were itemized. The participants provided input on intangible measures at two timeframes. The follow-up questionnaire provided an opportunity for participants to indicate intangible measures they perceived to represent a benefit directly linked to this program. In addition, the action plan provided an opportunity to add additional intangible benefits. Collectively, each of the following benefits was listed by at least five individuals:

- improved productivity
- improved teamwork
- improved work quality
- improved job satisfaction
- improved job engagement
- enhanced image
- reduced stress.

To some executives, these intangible measures are just as important as the monetary payoff.

The Payoff: Balanced Data

This program drives six types of data items: satisfaction, learning, application, business impact, ROI, and intangible benefits. Collectively, these data provide a balanced, credible viewpoint of the success of the program.

COMMUNICATION STRATEGY

Table 12-8 shows the strategy for communicating results from the study. All key stake-holders received the information. The communications were credible and convincing and the information helped build confidence in the program. The CEO and CFO were pleased with the results. The data given to employees, shareholders, and future partici-pants were motivating and helped to bring more focus on safety.

TABLE 12-8. Communication Strategy

Timing	Communication Method	Target Audience
Within one month of follow-up	Executive briefing	Regional executives CEO, CFO
Within one month of follow-up	Live briefing	Corporate and regional operation executives
Within one month of follow-up	Detailed impact study (125 pages)	Program participants Safety and health staff • Responsible for this program in some way • Involved in evaluation
Within one month of follow-up	Report of results (1 page)	Project general managers
Within two months	Article in project news	All employees
As needed	Report of results (1 page)	Future participants in similar safety programs
End of year	Paragraph in annual report	Shareholders

LESSONS LEARNED

It was critical to build evaluation into the program, positioning the action plan as an application tool instead of a data collection tool. This approach helped secure commit-ment and ownership for the process. It also shifted much of the responsibility for evaluation to the participants as they collected important data, isolated the effects of the program on the data, and converted the data to monetary values—the three most critical steps in the ROI process. The costs were easy to capture and the report was easily generated and sent to the various target audiences.

This approach had the additional advantage of evaluating programs in which a variety of measures were influenced. The improvements were integrated after they were converted to monetary value. Thus, the common value among measures was the monetary value, which represented the value of the improvement.

DISCUSSION QUESTIONS

1. Is this approach credible? Explain.
2. Is the ROI value realistic?
3. Were the differences in the ROI forecast and the actual revenue per inquiry expected? Explain.
4. How should the results be presented to the senior team?
5. How can the action planning process be positioned as an application tool?
6. What type of programs would be appropriate for this approach?

ABOUT THE AUTHOR

Jack J. Phillips, PhD, is chairman of the ROI Institute, the leading provider of services for measurement, evaluation, metrics, and analytics. A world-renowned expert on measurement and evaluation, Phillips provides consulting services for more than half of the Fortune 100 companies and workshops for major conference providers worldwide. A former bank president, Phillips has served as head of HR for three organizations, including a Fortune 500 company for eight years. Author of the first book on training evaluation in the United States, Phillips has authored or edited more than 75 books in evaluation, metrics, and analytics. He is the developer of the ROI Methodology, the most used evaluation system in the world. His work has been featured in the *Wall Street Journal, Bloomberg Businessweek,* and *Fortune*, and on CNN. He can be reached by email at jack@roiinstitute.net.

13

Measuring ROI in an Operations Manager Development Program

International Nonprofit Agency Group

Caroline Hubble and Chris Kirchner

This case was prepared to serve as a basis for discussion rather than an illustration of either effective or ineffective administrative and management practices. Names, dates, places, and data have been disguised at the request of the author or organization.

Abstract

The Operations Manager Development Program (OMDP) was developed to enhance the performance of the International Agency Group's (IAG) managers who oversee operational centers throughout the world. The program was designed to develop manager capabilities and ensure that the centers adhere to the operational standards of IAG. This program required extensive resources, so there was a desire to evaluate it. The ROI Methodology was selected because it provides a credible and systematic process to identify key program benefits and opportunities for program enhancements. Even though the program's success was complicated due to the diverse locations of participants who were influenced by local cultures, politics, and processes, a positive ROI was realized.

BACKGROUND

The nonprofit International Agency Group (IAG) is an organization that is committed to providing support and services to individuals across the globe. The support they provide ranges from securing funding for health and safety initiatives in underdeveloped countries to promoting better living standards and social progress in all countries. In order to ensure that they achieve their mission and goals, IAG staff is located at operational centers in different parts of the world. Within these operations centers, there are varying levels of staff, from project team members to senior management. The senior managers not only lead the team but also provide oversight regarding the implementation and operations of the various projects and programs. Because each location has a unique set of circumstances, culture, and governmental procedures, it is critical that the staff have the capabilities necessary to manage these factors while staying true to the overarching vision of the company.

Operations Manager Development Program

Following a comprehensive needs analysis, IAG realized that in order for their operations centers to succeed, the performance of managers needed to be enhanced. By developing a program that provided these individuals with specific information related to all areas of IAG's operational practices (such as, finance, risk, controls, HR, and vendor management) and developing their leadership capabilities, the centers would meet the needs of those they serve. Furthermore, the program would favorably impact key measures, such as productivity, waste reduction, and quality. Lastly, since IAG is a non-profit organization, it was very important that costs be reduced in the upcoming year.

To ensure the program realized its goals, it was designed so that the content was covered in both self-directed e-learning modules and face-to-face workshops. Some of the program's overarching objectives were to:

- Increase manager awareness, knowledge, and capabilities regarding IAG's operations procedures and processes.
- Increase manager ability to think strategically.
- Facilitate managerial responsibilities, including increasing accountability for decision making.
- Increase adherence by all staff to IAG's operational protocols.
- Decrease costs across the globe.

Evaluation Purpose

Due to the nature of IAG's operations and the fact that the participants were located across the globe, there was extensive use of the organization's resources to implement the program. Furthermore, since this program was designed to affect key business measures and had high visibility, a comprehensive evaluation was planned. The goal of the evaluation was twofold: to validate whether the program was successful, with the investment in the program being outweighed by the benefits realized; and identify areas for program enhancement.

EVALUATION METHODOLOGY

The ROI Methodology was used to implement the evaluation of the OMDP because the results generated by this simple yet comprehensive process identified the success of the program as well as opportunities for improvement. Table 13-1 shows the five level evaluation framework, which represents the categories of data that are captured throughout the evaluation of OMDP.

TABLE 13-1. Evaluation Framework

Evaluation Level	Measures	Key Questions Addressed
Level 1: Reaction	Stakeholder reaction and level of satisfaction with the initiative	What are the stakeholders' reactions and perceived value of the initiative?
Level 2: Learning	Changes in knowledge, skill, awareness, contacts, and attitudes	What skills, knowledge, attitudes, and so on have changed? By how much?
Level 3: Application	Changes in job performance and application of new skills	Did teams apply what they learned?
Level 4: Impact	Changes in organizational results	Did the initiative produce tangible and intangible business results?
Level 5: ROI	Program benefits compared with costs	Did the monetary benefits of the tangible results exceed the cost for the initiative?

The evaluation followed the step-by-step ROI Methodology Process Model, which included four phases: evaluation planning, data collection, data analysis, and reporting. Additionally, to ensure that the evaluation process maintained credibility and the findings presented were conservative, the ROI Methodology guiding principles (Table 13-2) were also followed.

TABLE 13-2. Guiding Principles

1. When conducting a higher-level evaluation, collect data at lower levels.	7. Adjust estimates of improvement for potential errors of estimation.
2. When planning a higher-level evaluation, the previous level of evaluation is not required to be comprehensive.	8. Avoid using extreme data items and unsupported claims when calculating ROI.
3. When collecting and analyzing data, use only the most credible sources.	9. Use only the first year of annual benefits in ROI analysis of short-term solutions.
4. When analyzing data, choose the most conservative alternative for calculations.	10. Fully load all costs of a solution, project, or program when analyzing ROI.
5. Use at least one method to isolate the effects of a program.	11. Intangible measures are defined as measures that are purposely not converted to monetary values.
6. If no improvement data are available for a population or from a specific source, assume that little or no improvement has occurred.	12. Communicate the results of the ROI Methodology to all key stakeholders.

Evaluation Planning

During evaluation planning, detailed data collection (see Figure 13-1) and ROI analysis plans were developed. The data collection plan outlined the specific program objectives and measures, as well as the data collection instruments, sources, and timing details. The ROI analysis plan identified the key business measures targeted to be improved by the program, the method for isolating the effects of the program, and the method for converting the data to monetary value. Additionally, the cost categories for the program, potential intangible benefits, and a communication strategy were identified. Once developed, these plans served as the framework by which the OMDP was evaluated.

Data Collection Strategy

As noted, OMDP participants came from various support IAG locations across the globe. They were determined to be the most credible source for providing data regarding the success of the program because they not only participated in the program but could speak specifically to how the program's content related to their given operational center. Additionally, because of the complexity of the program, multiple data collection activities were necessary to ensure needed data were collected. Figure 13-2 illustrates how the different data collection efforts aligned to the different elements of the program.

FIGURE 13-1. OMDP Data Collection Plan

Level	Broad Program Objective(s)	Measures	Data Collection Method/Instruments	Data Sources	Timing	Responsibilities
1	**REACTION AND PLANNED ACTION** • Content relevant to job • Content useful • Intend to apply • Provided with new information	• At least 85% agree (4 or 5)	• End of workshop questionnaire • Post-workshop questionnaire	• Participants	• End of workshop • 30 days post workshop 1 and 2	• Facilitator
2	**LEARNING AND CONFIDENCE** • Increase knowledge of operational procedures and processes • Increase awareness and skills regarding ways to manage operations centers in diverse environments	• Increase in knowledge from pre- to post-workshop • At least 85% agree (4 or 5) increase awareness and skills	• Pre- and end of workshop questionnaire • Post-workshop questionnaire	• Participants	• End of workshop • 30 days post workshop 1 and 2	• Evaluation team • Facilitator
3	**APPLICATION AND IMPLEMENTATION** • Use of knowledge and skills from OMDP • Take appropriate action based on IAG's operational protocols	• At least 65% report content is used since attending workshop • At least 4 out of 5 on a five-point scale	• Post-workshop questionnaires	• Participants	• 30 days post workshop 1 and 2 • 90 days post workshop 3	• Evaluation team
4	**BUSINESS IMPACT** • Improve 2 business measures of productivity, quality, waste reduction • Decrease costs/cost savings	• Vary depending on measures and location • Cost savings of 5% (estimated)	• Post-workshop questionnaire	• Participants	• 90 days post workshop 3	• Evaluation team
5	**ROI** 30%	Comments:				

FIGURE 13-2. OMDP Program Evaluation Map

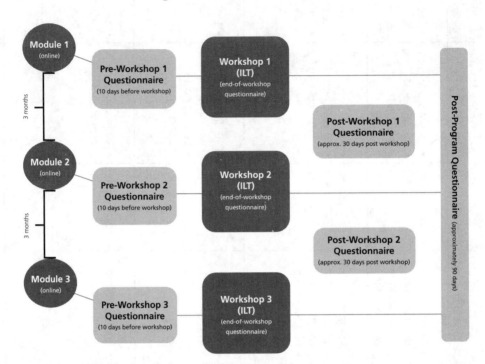

Following the completion of each of the three e-learning modules and approximately 10 days before the workshop, a pre-workshop questionnaire was sent to the participants to establish a baseline to compare future findings. This questionnaire captured their reaction to the e-learning module and identified their current knowledge level regarding the upcoming workshop's content. At the end of the workshop, a post-workshop questionnaire was completed to identify a change in knowledge as well as a reaction to learning from the OMDP.

In addition to the pre- and post-workshop questionnaires, a specific follow-up questionnaire was administered approximately 30 days after the completion of workshop 1 and workshop 2. Approximately 90 days after the conclusion of workshop 3 the participants were invited to complete a final questionnaire, which captured additional application and impact data (Levels 3 and 4) based on the entire program's content.

ROI Analysis Strategy

How business was affected by the OMDP irrespective of other potential influences was essential information for the organization. It was also critical to identify the program's contribution to the identified improvements. In order to do this a variety of techniques were considered. The most traditional technique to isolate the effects of a program is to use a control group arrangement. However, this was not an option because of the nature of the program and the uniqueness of each operations center. Trend-line analysis and forecasting models were also not feasible. If the isolation step was ignored the results would be invalid. Therefore, a process to estimate the contribution of the OMDP was used and the participants were identified as the most credible source for these estimates.

The process involved questions in the post-program questionnaire that were designed to capture estimated improvements attributed to the program. Participants were first asked to identify the extent to which specific measures were improved by applying the knowledge, skills, and information acquired in the program. Once the degree of improvement was identified, the respondents were asked a series of questions designed to capture the details regarding the measure's improvement as it related to OMDP participation. The participants also provided the estimated monetary value of the improvement. Lastly, the participants were asked to provide their level of confidence in the estimates provided. This question provided a means for accounting for the potential error in their estimate. By factoring their confidence into the estimate, the lower-end range was reported, and therefore represents a conservative finding.

Finally, the fully loaded cost of the OMDP was determined by considering all the costs associated with the needs assessment, design and implementation, and evaluation of the program. Based on these elements, including all travel, salaries, and benefits costs by both program owners and the participants, the fully loaded cost of the program totaled $750,200.

EVALUATION RESULTS

Level 1, Reaction

Overall, the participants reacted favorably to the OMDP. More specifically, they provided favorable ratings (agree/strongly agree) on the follow-up surveys and questionnaires regarding the e-learning modules and workshops, as reflected in Table 13-3. Furthermore, at least 92 percent of the respondents agreed that the program was a good use of their time, and at least 90 percent agreed that the program was a good use of IAG's time and resources. Of the 65 respondents who provided data on the post-program questionnaire, 93 percent reported that they would recommend the program to others.

TABLE 13-3. Participants' Reaction Results (percent agree or strongly agree)

	E-Learning Modules (n = 75)	Workshop 1 (n = 75)	Workshop 2 (n = 75)	Workshop 3 (n = 75)
Content covered relevant to job	92% or higher	96.77%	100.00%	94.44%
Content useful	88% or higher	96.77%	100.00%	88.89%
Intend to apply content	85% or higher	96.77%	100.00%	94.44%
Provided new information	95% or higher	93.55%	96.00%	100.00%

Level 2, Learning

The respondents also reported being more knowledgeable in concepts presented in the e-learning modules and workshops, and were more confident in their ability to transfer the knowledge into action. More than 91 percent reported that they had increased their awareness of IAG's operational procedures and how to relate them to their specific operations center.

For all content areas covered in the workshops, 100 percent of the participants experienced an increase in knowledge, based on the pre- and post-workshop questionnaire results. Lastly, the post-program questionnaire respondents (N = 65) reported that they shared information, tools, and resources with co-workers (75 percent), and also agreed that participating in the program fostered more networking (79 percent) and sharing best practices and lessons learned (89 percent).

Level 3, Application

Overall the respondents reported using the knowledge and skills acquired in the OMDP. Table 13-4 provides a summary of three key questions related to the application results from the post-workshop questionnaires.

TABLE 13-4. Workshop Follow-Up Application Results

	Post Workshop 1		Post Workshop 2	
	N	Average %	N	Average %
Percent of job requires content presented in workshop	65	88%	65	92%
Percent proficiency (knowledge and skill) in content increased	65	61%	65	64%
Percent of content applied since workshop participation	65	68%	65	74%

Of the 65 individuals who responded to the program follow-up questionnaire, 92.90 percent indicated that they continued to use the knowledge, skills, and information provided in the OMDP program; 85.71 percent also reported having success using the knowledge, skills, and information.

The respondents were also asked to identify to what extent specific behaviors had improved as a result of program participation using a scale of no improvement (1) to significant improvement (5). The highest average improvement ratings were for monitoring procedures to ensure alignment to operational procedures and protocols, managing staff performance, and empowering others to make decisions.

They were also asked to identify what supported (enablers) and what deterred (barriers) the successful application of the program's content on the job. Using a list of enablers and barriers, respondents were asked to mark all that applied. The enablers noted by the respondents included knowledge and skills acquired, having resources available to complete the actions, program materials, and leadership support. Four individuals noted lack of leadership support as a barrier, while 18 noted a lack of time.

Level 4, Business Impact, and Level 5, ROI

Using a scale of no improvement (1) to significant improvement (5), the post-program questionnaire respondents identified the extent to which specific measures improved as a result of applying the knowledge, skills, and information acquired in the OMDP. Ratings were provided by 55 of the 65 respondents. Productivity increase, cost savings, and waste reduction received the highest improvement ratings (4.21, 3.64, and 3.57, respectively).

To further understand the impact of the program, the respondents' data regarding specific business improvements were also analyzed. As noted, the estimation process was used as an isolation technique to determine how much of the improvement was attributable to the program.

The post-program questionnaire administered 90 days after the completion of the third workshop included specific questions to capture the necessary impact results, including data related to the estimation process. Table 13-5 summarizes the data by the 11 respondents who answered all the necessary questions. The participants noted improvements related to cost savings, time savings, productivity, and quality. After factoring each respondent's estimated annual monetary value, program contribution percent, and confidence percent, the total estimated monetary benefit of the OMDP was determined to be $1,012,980. Based on the fully loaded costs of the program ($750,200), the resulting net program benefit totaled $262,780. Using the net program benefits and the fully loaded costs, an ROI of 35 percent was determined:

$$ROI = \frac{\text{Net Program Benefits}}{\text{Program Costs}} \times 100$$

$$ROI = \frac{\$1,012,980 - \$750,200}{\$750,200} \times 100 = 35\%$$

Intangible Benefits

In addition to the positive ROI, there were other measures affected favorably by the program that were not converted to monetary value due to limited access to needed data or resources. These benefits, called intangible benefits, were identified as improving efficiencies, increasing employee commitment to IAG, improving client and employee satisfaction, and positively affecting the achievement of organizational goals.

COMMUNICATION STRATEGY

The results of this study were shared with IAG management and program stakeholders. Additionally, a two-page summary of the key findings was developed as a tool to share with the participants who were involved in the study. The summary document was also designed to be a marketing tool to help educate others about the program.

Overall, the results of the study were well received by all parties. In addition to the study's findings, the company also reviewed and took action on the lessons learned. This process identified immediate action items to further enhance the program based on the evaluation results, and put further support in place for those areas noted as being successful. Additional action items were identified to further enhance the evaluation process, such as reducing the number of questionnaires administered, increasing communications regarding the program and evaluation efforts, and developing standards for converting impact measures to monetary value.

TABLE 13-5. Post-Program Questionnaire Business Impact Results (N = 11)

One Measure Improved	Improvement in Measure	Other Factors That Caused Measure Improvement	Monetary Value of Measure's Improvement	Definition of Monetary Value	Frequency of Measure	Annual Monetary Improvement	Estimated Improvement Due to OMDP	Confidence	Monetary Value Attributable to Program
Time management and productivity have been dramatically improved.	30%	Coaching.	$800	In terms of productivity and the salary paid.	Per quarter	$9,600	80%	75%	$5,760
Made staff aware of wasted time, which they were informed will be monitored through log.	There has been a 25% reduction in vehicle idle time.	Budget instructions to implement efficiency gains.	$10,000	Calculating amount of time saved.	Per quarter	$40,000	50%	75%	$15,000
Motivation contributed to an increase in team productivity.	A quantitative improvement of about 30%.	Willingness to make a difference has contributed to this improvement.	$1,000	Coordinating combined actions, which has reduced the amount of time devoted to individual meetings versus group ones.	Per quarter	$4,000	25%	80%	$800
More effective meetings.	10%	Feedback from colleagues.	$50,000	More efficient use of resources.	Per day	$50,000	70%	60%	$21,000
Switch from internal source for power to country grid due to understanding vendor relationship.	Gave additional motivation to achieve cost savings and efficiency gains.	Push for cost savings and efficiency gains.	$50,000	Based on previous power bill and new one.	Per month	$600,000	20%	95%	$114,000
Cost savings: I am working hard to identify cost savings and bring them to fruition.	100%	Identified as a priority within the organization.	$500,000	Based on the projects that I am working on, currently I believe this is a realistic estimate of annual savings.	One time	$500,000	80%	100%	$400,000

One Measure Improved	Improvement in Measure	Other Factors That Caused Measure Improvement	Monetary Value of Measure's Improvement	Definition of Monetary Value	Frequency of Measure	Annual Monetary Improvement	Estimated Improvement Due to OMDP	Confidence	Monetary Value Attributable to Program
Error reduction was improved due to workflow analysis and implementation of better systems.	50%	Maturity and position of responsibility.	100,000	By savings done on integrated processes.	Per Month	$1,200,000	30%	90%	$324,000
Spent more time with partners in the country to understand their requirements and work out solutions that adhere to our process, but meet their needs. Was able to find ways to reduce costs.	By at least 25%.	Change in leadership has brought a "can do" attitude to things.	$15,000	The overall productivity and satisfaction has improved tremendously resulting in careful, collegial review of requirements, rationalization of unnecessary requests, and improved streamlined processes.	Per Month	$180,000	40%	75%	$54,000
Improved time management by having shorter but more effective meetings.	A 20% time efficiency gain.	Reinforcement by leadership.	$2,500	Efficiency measured against monthly gross salary.	Per Month	$30,000	15%	60%	$2,700
Projects are completed on time and on budget as a result of better project management.	There have been no overruns in projects since program participation.	Staff taking ownership and lifting the competence of the whole center.	$1,000	Employee hours saved through timelier implementation of projects.	Per Month	$12,000	20%	30%	$720
Cost Savings.	50%	Attention to detail.	$300,000	Savings on claims paid to support programs.	One time	$300,000	25%	100%	$75,000

LESSONS LEARNED

Lessons learned from this evaluation process should be incorporated into future evaluation efforts at IAG. For example, one suggestion that arose was to incorporate a more detailed discussion during Workshop 1 regarding the evaluation strategy. This process should include discussing the alignment between the program and the measures targeted for improvement, as well as the evaluation process (such as the data collection process, what questions will be asked, and so on). This step, and several others that were identified, will help ensure that more comprehensive evaluation data are collected from the participants. As the evaluation strategy continues to evolve and data about the program are retained and analyzed over time, IAG will be able to more comprehensively evaluate the results of the program's success, insights, and overall benefit to the company.

QUESTIONS FOR DISCUSSION

1. One of the pieces of post-evaluation feedback involved the extensive amount of time that participants spent completing the questionnaires. What strategies could be put in place to reduce the number of data collection instances, or reduce the time required to provide the data?
2. How would you make sure that the data required to illustrate the chain of impact were captured?
3. What concerns arise from the business impact data provided by the post-program questionnaire respondents? Is there a concern that only 16 percent provided useable data? Please explain.
4. Overall there were good response rates to the questionnaires for all data collection efforts. However, the response rate was not as successful for the post-program questionnaire's business impact questions. What strategies could be put in place to increase the number of respondents that provide useable impact data?
5. How would you present these data to senior stakeholders in light of the response rate?
6. Without the ability to use a control group technique to isolate the effects of the program, please discuss the following:
    — What other techniques could have been used and why do you think they were not selected?
    — How credible is the estimation process used, and what steps should be taken when communicating the results?

7. In this study the participants estimated the monetary value of Level 4 business impact measures. What issues arise when converting the business measures to monetary value using this process? What other sources or methods would you consider for converting the measures to monetary value?

ABOUT THE AUTHORS

Caroline Hubble is the director of research and consulting services with the ROI Institute. She manages complex program evaluation projects, as well as designs and facilitates various courses on the ROI Methodology. She has significant experience conducting research and evaluation studies in areas such as leadership development, process improvement, and not-for-profit/community related initiatives. Additionally, she provides expert coaching to individuals working toward ROI Certification. Caroline's professional background includes working in financial services, market research, and not-for-profit professional development industries. Caroline holds a BA in psychology from Rollins College and a master's of science in organizational development from Avila University. She is a Certified ROI Practitioner and received ATD's Certified Professional in Learning and Performance credential in 2006. Her publications include *ASTD Handbook of Measuring and Evaluating Training*, chapter 4 (ASTD 2010), *Measuring ROI in Learning & Development: Case Studies From Global Organizations*, chapter 4 (co-authored) (ASTD 2012), "Offering Money for School Pays Off" (co-authored) *Chief Learning Officer Magazine* (2012). She can be reached at caroline@roiinstitute.net.

Chris Kirchner is director of ROI implementation at the ROI Institute and provides educational and research services to clients on the use and application of the ROI Methodology. A 20-year veteran in experiential marketing, Chris's career started in nonprofit cause-related marketing throughout the Southeast, in the development of fundraising programs. After a seven-year career in nonprofit, Chris was recruited to manage experiential events at Lowe's Home Improvement (a Fortune 100 Company) and educational point of sale customer programs in more than 1,000 stores. Chris's career led to an opportunity in a national B2B technology company managing all experiential customer and channel programs, including educational seminars, tradeshows, conferences, and incentive programs. Each of these positions required advance analysis of the performance of programs to identify organizational benefits and improvement opportunities. This led Chris to the use and adoption of the Phillips ROI Methodology for providing a systematic and credible process framework to apply to program evaluations. He can be reached at chris@roiinstitute.net.

RESOURCES

Phillips, J.J. 2003. *Return on Investment in Training and Performance Improvement Programs*. 2nd ed. Boston: Butterworth-Heinemann.

Phillips, P.P., and J.J. Phillips. 2008. *ROI Fundamentals: Why and When to Measure Return on Investment*. San Francisco: Pfeiffer.

Phillips, P.P., J.J. Phillips, and R.L. Ray. 2012. *Measuring Leadership Development: Quantify Your Program's Impact and ROI on Organizational Performance*. New York: McGraw-Hill.

About the ROI Institute

ROI Institute is the leading resource on research, training, and networking for practitioners of the Phillips ROI Methodology.

With a combined 50 years of experience in measuring and evaluating training, human resources, technology, and quality programs and initiatives, Jack J. Phillips, PhD, chairman, and Patti P. Phillips, PhD, president, are the leading experts in return on investment (ROI).

The ROI Institute, founded in 1992, is a service-driven organization that strives to assist professionals in improving their programs and processes through the use of the ROI Methodology. Developed by Jack Phillips, this methodology is a critical tool for measuring and evaluating programs in 18 different applications in more than 60 countries.

The ROI Institute offers a variety of consulting services, learning opportunities, and publications. In addition, it conducts internal research activities for the organization, other enterprises, public sector entities, industries, and interest groups. Together with their team, Jack and Patti Phillips serve private and public sector organizations globally.

BUILD CAPABILITY IN THE ROI METHODOLOGY

The ROI Institute offers a variety of workshops to help you build capability through the ROI Methodology. Among the many workshops offered through the institute are:

- One-day *Bottomline on ROI* Workshop—Provides the perfect introduction to all levels of measurement, including the most sophisticated level, ROI. Learn the key principles of the Phillips ROI Methodology and determine whether your organization is ready to implement the process.
- Two-day *ROI Competency Building* Workshop—The standard ROI Workshop on measurement and evaluation, this two-day program involves discussion of the ROI Methodology process, including data collection, isolation methods, data conversion, and more.

ROI CERTIFICATION

The ROI Institute is the only organization offering certification in the ROI Methodology. Through the ROI Certification process, you can build expertise in implementing ROI evaluation and sustaining the measurement and evaluation process in your organization. Receive personalized coaching while conducting an impact study. When competencies in the ROI Methodology have been demonstrated, certification is awarded. There is not another process that provides access to the same level of expertise as our ROI Certification. To date, more than 10,000 individuals have participated in this process.

For more information on these and other workshops, learning opportunities, consulting, and research, please visit us on the Web at **www.roiinstitute.net**, or call us at **205.678.8101.**

About the Authors

Jack J. Phillips, PhD, is a world-renowned expert on accountability, measurement, and evaluation. Phillips provides consulting services for Fortune 500 companies and major global organizations. The author or editor of more than 50 books, he conducts workshops and presents at conferences throughout the world.

Phillips has received several awards for his books and work. On three occasions, Meeting News named him one of the 25 Most Powerful People in the Meetings and Events Industry, based on his work on ROI. The Society for Human Resource Management presented him an award for one of his books and honored a Phillips ROI study with its highest award for creativity. The American Society for Training & Development gave him its highest award, Distinguished Contribution to Workplace Learning and Development, for his work on ROI. His work has been featured in the *Wall Street Journal, Businessweek,* and *Fortune* magazine. He has been interviewed by several television networks, including CNN. Phillips served as president of the International Society for Performance Improvement, 2012-2013.

His expertise in measurement and evaluation is based on more than 27 years of corporate experience in the aerospace, textile, metals, construction materials, and banking industries. Phillips has served as training and development manager at two Fortune 500 firms, as senior human resource officer at two firms, as president of a regional bank, and as management professor at a major state university.

This background led Phillips to develop the ROI Methodology, a revolutionary process that provides bottom-line figures and accountability for all types of learning, performance improvement, human resource, technology, and public policy programs.

Phillips regularly consults with clients in manufacturing, service, and government organizations in 44 countries in North and South America, Europe, Africa, Australia, and Asia.

Phillips has undergraduate degrees in electrical engineering, physics, and mathematics; a master's degree in decision sciences from Georgia State University; and a PhD in human resource management from the University of Alabama. He has served on the boards of several private businesses—including two NASDAQ companies—and several nonprofits and associations, including the Association for Talent Development and the National Management Association. He is chairman of the ROI Institute, Inc., and can be reached at 205.678.8101, or by email at jack@roiinstitute.net.

Patti Phillips, PhD, is president and CEO of the ROI Institute, Inc., the leading source of ROI competency building, implementation support, networking, and research. A renowned expert in measurement and evaluation, she helps organizations implement the ROI Methodology in 50 countries around the world. Since 1997, following a 13-year career in the electric utility industry, Phillips has embraced the ROI Methodology by committing herself to ongoing research and practice. To this end, she has implemented ROI in private sector and public sector organizations. She has conducted ROI impact studies on programs such as leadership development, sales, new-hire orientation, human performance improvement, K–12 educator development, and educators' National Board Certification mentoring.

Phillips teaches others to implement the ROI Methodology through the ROI Certification process, as a facilitator for ATD's ROI and Measuring and Evaluating Learning Workshops, and as professor of practice for the University of Southern Mississippi Gulf Coast Campus human capital development doctoral program. She also serves as adjunct faculty for the UN System Staff College in Turin, Italy, where she teaches the ROI Methodology through their Evaluation and Impact Assessment Workshop and Measurement for Results-Based Management. She serves on numerous doctoral dissertation committees, assisting students as they develop their own research on measurement, evaluation, and ROI.

Phillips's academic accomplishments include a PhD in international development and a master's degree in public and private management. She is certified in ROI evaluation and has been awarded the designations of Certified Professional in Learning and Performance and Certified Performance Technologist. Patti Phillips can be reached at patti@roiinstitute.net.

Jack and Patti Phillips contribute to a variety of journals and have authored a number of books on the subject of accountability and ROI, including: *Measuring the Success of Organization Development* (ASTD, 2013); *Survey Basics* (ASTD, 2013); *Measuring the Success of Sales Training* (ASTD, 2013); *Measuring ROI in Healthcare* (McGraw-Hill, 2012); *Measuring the Success of Coaching* (ASTD, 2012); *10 Steps to Successful Business Alignment* (ASTD, 2012); *The Bottomline on ROI*, 2nd ed. (HRDQ, 2012); *Measuring Leadership Development: Quantify Tour Program's Impact and ROI on Organizational Performance* (McGraw-Hill, 2012); *Measuring ROI in Learning and Development: Case Studies From Global Organizations* (ASTD , 2011); *The Green Scorecard: Measuring the ROI in Sustainability Initiatives* (Nicholas Brealey, 2011); *Return on Investment in Meetings and Events: Tools and Techniques to Measure the Success of All Types of Meetings and Events* (Elsevier, 2008); *Show Me the Money: How to Determine ROI in People, Projects, and Programs* (Berrett-Koehler, 2007); *The Value of Learning* (Pfeiffer, 2007); *Return on Investment Basics* (ASTD, 2005); *Proving the Value of HR: How and Why to Measure ROI* (SHRM, 2005); *Make Training Evaluation Work* (ASTD, 2004); *The Bottomline on ROI* (Center for Effective Performance, 2002), which won the 2003 ISPI Award of Excellence; *ROI at Work* (ASTD, 2005); the ASTD in Action casebooks *Measuring ROI in the Public Sector* (2002), *Retaining Your Best Employees* (2002), and *Measuring Return on Investment* Vol. III (2001); the ASTD *Infoline* series, including "Planning and Using Evaluation Data" (2003), "Managing Evaluation Shortcuts" (2001), and "Mastering ROI" (1998); and *The Human Resources Scorecard: Measuring Return on Investment* (Butterworth-Heinemann, 2001).

Rebecca Ray, PhD, is executive vice president, knowledge organization and human capital practice lead for The Conference Board. In this role, she has oversight of the research planning and dissemination process for three practice areas: corporate leadership, economics and business development, and human capital. She is the leader of the global human capital practice.

Rebecca was previously a senior executive responsible for talent acquisition, organizational learning, training, management and leadership development, employee engagement, performance management, executive assessment, coaching, organizational development, and succession planning at several major companies. She taught at Oxford and New York Universities, and led a consulting practice for many years, offering leadership assessment and development services to Fortune 500 companies and top-tier professional services firms. Rebecca was named Chief Learning Officer of the Year by *Chief Learning Officer* magazine, and one of the Top 100 People in Leadership Development by Warren Bennis's *Leadership Excellence* magazine. She serves on the advisory boards for New York University's program in higher education and business education at the Steinhardt School of Education and the University of Pennsylvania's executive program in work-based learning leadership. She was elected to serve on the Business Practices Council of the AACSB (Association to Advance Collegiate Schools of Business).

Rebecca received a PhD from New York University and is a frequent speaker at professional and company-sponsored conferences and business briefings around the world. She is the co-author of numerous publications on leadership development, analytics, and engagement, including *Measuring Leadership Development* (McGraw-Hill 2012).

Index

A

Absenteeism, 69
Accountability, 5
Acquisition costs, 71
Action plans
    for business impact data, 49, 51
    case study examples of, 117, 210–211, 217–218
    example of, 51
    goal setting for, 50
    implementation of, 52
    improvements noted in, 52
    isolating the effects of the program, 52–53
    monetary value on improvements, 52
    performance agreements versus, 49
    ROI calculation, 53–54
    summarizing of data, 53–54
    targets for, 50
    unit of measure for, 50
    uses of, 49
Activity-based initiatives, 15–16
Alignment, of leadership development programs with business needs, 27–35
Application and implementation data. *See* Level 3 data
Application objectives, of leadership development programs, 34
Assignmentology, 7
Audience, customizing communication of results for, 80–81

B

Bad news, 107–108
Benefit-cost ratio (BCR), 20, 73–74, 196, 221
Block, Peter, 93
Business databases, 56
Business impact data. See Level 4 data
Business impact report, 83–85
Business needs, leadership development program alignment with, 27–35

C

Case studies, 35–42
    data collection plan, 37–40
    description of, ix
    Fashion Stores Incorporated, 113–135

Global Bank Inc., 179–199
Global Engineering and Construction Company, 201–224
Global Manufacturing Company, 155–178
IAMGOLD, 137–154
International Agency Group, 225–239
ROI analysis plan, 40–41
ROI study results presented to senior management, 85–92
CCO. *See* Chief culture officer
Change, resistance to, 97–99
Change agent, 14–15
Chief culture officer, 13
Climate surveys, 76
Collaborative environment, 13
Communication of results
    audience's opinion, 83
    case study examples of, 133, 151, 178, 223, 234
    cautions of, 82–83
    communication mode for, 81
    consistency in, 82
    guidelines for, 79–82
    hiding of results, 82
    media for, 92–93
    meetings for, 85–86
    neutrality during, 81–82
    options for, 81
    plan for, 40, 42, 94–95
    political aspects of, 82–83
    recommendations from, 83
    to senior management, 85–86
    target audience considerations, 80–81
    testimonials included in, 82
    timeliness of, 80
    tools for, 92–93
Control groups, 62–63
Coordinator salaries, 71
Core values, 13
Costs
    acquisition, 71
    case study examples of, 130–131, 174–175, 194–196, 218, 221
    categories of, 70
    design and development, 71
    evaluation, 72
    implementation, 71–72
    maintenance and monitoring, 72

needs assessment, 70–71
overhead, 72
Crosby, Phillip, 67

D

Data
    application and implementation, 18–19
    business impact, 19–21
    categories of, 18–20
    credibility of, 132–133, 221–222
    databases as source of, 56
    direct reports as source of, 57
    evaluation, 108
    external groups as source of, 57
    hard, 30–31
    intangible, 20–21
    internal groups as source of, 57
    learning, 44
    negative, 93
    participants as source of, 56
    participants' immediate managers as source of, 56
    peer group as source of, 57
    positive, 94
    project input, 18
    qualitative, 43–44
    quantitative, 43
    reaction, 18, 21
    ROI, 19–20
    simplifying of, 93
    soft, 31–32, 69
    sources of, 56–57
    team members as source of, 57
    use of, 108
Data analysis
    converting data to monetary units. *See* Data conversion
    intangibles. See Intangible assets
    isolating the effects of the program. *See* Isolating the effects of the program
Data collection
    accuracy of, 59
    action plans for, 49–54. *See also* Action plans
    case study examples of, 37–40, 119–121, 141, 143, 161–162, 184–186, 206–208, 228–230
    data sources, 56–57
    disruption of work activities caused by, 59
    focus groups for, 48
    immediate manager's time for, 58
    interviews for, 47
    mixed methodology for, 44
    objectives of, 43
    observations for, 48–49
    organization culture effects on, 44
    performance monitoring, 54–55

questionnaires for, 44–47
response rates for, 55, 214
surveys for, 44–47
timing of, 57–59
Data conversion
    case study examples of, 126–128, 193–194
    expert input used in, 68
    external studies used in, 69
    historical costs used in, 68
    to increased output, 67
    management estimation used in, 69–70
    to monetary units, 67–70
    participant estimation used in, 69
    to quality improvements, 67–68
    to time savings, 67
Databases, 56
DDI. *See* Development Dimensions International
Decision making, 5
Design and development costs, 71
Development Dimensions International, 4, 9
Direct reports, 57
Diversity, 76
DNA of Leaders: Leadership Development Secrets, 6

E

Employee engagement, 75
Empowering style of leadership, 13
Evaluation costs, 72
Evaluation data, 108
Evaluation planning
    case study examples of, 158–164, 184–189, 206–209, 228
    description of, 36
Evaluation targets, 101–102
Expert input, in data conversion, 68
External experts, 68
External groups, data from, 57
External studies, in data conversion, 69

F

Facility costs, 72
Fashion Stores Incorporated case study, 113–135
Feedback
    giving of, 93–94
    high-performing culture use of, 14
    on progress, 93–94
    360-degree, 23, 37–39
Focus groups, 48
Follow-up questionnaire, 44
Forecasting, 64–65
Fundamentals of Business Leadership program, 155–178

G

Global Bank Inc. case study, 179–199
Global Engineering and Construction Company
    case study, 201–224
Global Leadership Forecast 2014/2015, 4
Global Manufacturing Company case study, 155–
    178
Global organizations, 10

H

Hard data, 30–31
High-performing culture, 13–14
Historical costs, in data conversion, 68
Human capital, 3–4
Human resource measures, 31–32

I

IAMGOLD case study, 137–154
Immediate managers of participants
    communication with, 81
    data from, 56
Impact objectives, of leadership development pro-
    grams, 34
Implementation. *See* also Level 3 data
    costs of, 71–72
    plan for, 102–103
Input objectives, of leadership development pro-
    grams, 34
Intangible assets
    case study examples of, 90–91, 132, 150–151,
        176–177, 197, 222, 234
    climate surveys as, 76
    diversity as, 76
    employee engagement as, 75
    organization culture as, 76
    organizational commitment as, 75
    stress reduction as, 76–77
    tangible assets versus, 74–75
Intangible data, 20–21
Internal experts, 68
Internal groups, data from, 57
International Agency Group case study, 225–239
Interviews, 47
Invisible observations, 49
Isolating the effects of the program
    action plans and, 52–53
    case study examples of, 126, 188
    control groups for, 62–63
    description of, 61–62
    expert estimation for, 66–67, 188
    forecasting methods for, 64–65
    manager's estimation for, 66
    participant estimation for, 65–66
    trend-line analysis for, 63–64

K

Knowledge transfer, 151
Kravitz, Joan, 86–92

L

Leaders
    importance of, 3
    mindset of, 8
    selection of, for development, 6
Leadership
    characteristics of, 4
    empowering style of, 13
    imperatives for agile business, 5
    importance of, 6
Leadership development
    bottom line results for, 16
    business measures connected to, 8
    expenditures on, 4
    initiatives for, 7–8
    investments in, 4
    leader selection for, 6
    methods for, 7
    reasons for failure of, 8
    ROI Methodology application to, 16–17, 20
    70-20-10 myth, 9
    status of, 6–10
    strategies for, 4–5
    success factors for, 11
    surveys of, 4
    top executive view of, 3–5
Leadership development practitioner, as change
    agent, 14–15
Leadership development programs
    alignment of, with business needs, 27–35
    business impact analysis of, 22–24
    client requirements, 23–24
    costs of. *See* Costs
    dedication to, 6
    global, 10
    goals for, 7–8
    human resources measures relevant to, 31–32
    isolating the effects of. *See* Isolating the effects
        of the program
    level of evaluation for, 21–22
    local, 10
    management interest in, 23
    results-based initiatives aligned with, 15–16
    for ROI analysis, 21–24
    structure of, 7–8
    time commitment for, 23
Leadership development team, 104–106
Leadership skills, 5
Leading, managing versus, 10
Learning
    needs assessment for, 32–33

testing used to measure, 47
Learning data, 44
Learning (Level 2). *See* Level 2 data
Learning objectives, of leadership development programs, 34
Level 0 data, 18–19
Level 0 objectives, 34
Level 1 analysis (V-Model), 33
Level 1 data (reaction)
    case study examples of, 119–120, 123, 145, 161, 165, 185, 189–190, 207, 212, 213, 215, 231
    description of, 18–19
    leadership development programs evaluated with, 21
Level 1 objectives, 34
Level 2 analysis (V-Model), 32–33
Level 2 data (learning)
    case study examples of, 120–121, 123, 145, 161, 165–166, 185–186, 190–191, 207, 215, 232
    description of, 18–19
    leadership development programs evaluated with, 22
Level 2 objectives, 34
Level 3 analysis (V-Model), 32
Level 3 data (application and implementation)
    action plans used to capture, 49
    case study examples of, 121, 123–124, 145–146, 162, 166–170, 186, 191, 208, 215–216, 232–233
    description of, 18–19
    leadership development programs evaluated with, 22
    from participants' immediate managers, 56
Level 3 objectives, 34
Level 4 analysis (V-Model), 30–32
Level 4 data (business impact)
    action plans for capturing of, 49, 51
    case study examples of, 88–90, 121, 125–126, 125–130, 129, 146–148, 162, 170–174, 186, 191–193, 208, 216–218, 219–220, 233–236
    collection of, timing considerations for, 58
    description of, 19–20
    importance of, 21
    leadership development programs evaluated with, 22–24
Level 4 objectives, 34
Level 5 analysis (V-Model), 29
Level 5 data (ROI)
    case study examples of, 121, 148–150, 162, 186, 208, 233–234
    description of, 19–20

leadership development programs evaluated with, 22–24
Level 5 objectives, 34

M
Maintenance and monitoring costs, 72
Management estimation
    in data conversion, 69–70
    isolating the effects of the program using, 66
Management teams, 5
Managing, leading versus, 10
Materials cost, 72
Measures/measurement
    high-performing culture use of, 13–14
    performance, 54
    system created to routinely review, 15–16
Meetings, for communication of results, 85–86
Monetary units
    converting data to, 67–70
    soft data converted to, 69

N
Needs analysis, 27
Needs assessment
    costs of, 70–71
    for learning, 32–33

O
Observations, 48–49
Operational databases, 56
Operations management development program case study, 225–239
Organization climate
    assessment of, 99
    surveys of, as intangible asset, 76
Organization culture
    data collection affected by, 44
    as intangible asset, 76
Organizational commitment, 75
Organizer salaries, 71
Output, increased, 67
Overhead costs, 72

P
Participant(s)
    data from, 56
    feedback given to, 81
    immediate managers of, 56
    salaries and benefits of, 72
Participant estimation
    in data conversion, 69

for isolating the effects of the program, 65–66
Payback period, 74
Payoff needs, 29–30, 35
Peer groups, data from, 57
Performance agreements, 49
Performance measures, 54
Performance monitoring, 54–55
Performance needs assessment, 32
Positive data, 94
Preference needs assessment, 33
Productivity, 75
Progress
    feedback on, 93–94
    monitoring of, 109
Project input data, 18

Q

Qualitative data, 43–44
Quality improvement, 66
Quality improvements, 67–68
Quantitative data, 43
Questionnaires, 44–47

R

Rackham, Neil, 63
Reaction data. *See* Level 1 data
Reaction objectives, of leadership development
    programs, 34
Reporting of results. *See also* Communication of
    results
    meetings for, 85–86
    reports for, 81, 83–85
    to senior management, 85–86
Reports, 81, 83–85
Results
    communicating of. *See* Communication of re-
        sults
    hiding of, 82
    measurement of, 8, 11
    reporting of. *See* Reporting of results
Results-based initiatives, 15–16
Return on investment. *See* ROI
ROI
    briefing on, 106
    client preparation for, 106
    data, 19–20
    definition of, 73
    executive preparation for, 106
    goals and plans for, 101–102
    implementation of, 97, 102
    as learning tool, 104–105
    myths about, 107
    as process improvement tool, 104–105
    resistance to, 97–99, 104

sustaining of, 97–98
ROI analysis, 21–24, 210–212, 221, 230–231
ROI analysis plan, 40–41, 119, 122, 163–164,
    187–188, 206, 209
ROI calculation
    benefit-cost ratio used in, 73–74
    case study examples of, 90, 131–132, 144,
        148–150, 175–176, 196, 212, 221, 234
    description of, 53–54, 72–73
    formula for, 73
    payback period, 74
ROI Institute, 99–100
ROI leader, 100
ROI (Level 5). *See* Level 5 data
ROI Methodology
    case study examples of, 140–141, 159, 204–
        205, 227
    champion for, 100
    cost control for, 98
    data for, 17–21. *See also* Data
    description of, 15
    guidelines for, 102, 104
    history of application, 17
    implementation of, 97–98, 102
    leadership development uses of, 16–17, 20
    obstacles, 107–108
    procedures for, 102, 104
    process model of, 24–25, 205
    progress monitoring, 109
    report used in, 83
    resistance to, 97–99, 104
    roles and responsibilities for, 99–101
    stakeholders and, 17
    strategic alignment and, 17
    task force for, 100–101
ROI objectives, of leadership development pro-
    grams, 34
ROI studies, 105–106
Rothschild, Nathan, 3

S

Safety leadership case study, 201–224
Salaries, 71
Senior management
    ROI study results presented to, 85–92
    ROI understanding by, 17
70-20-10 myth, 9
SMART goals, 50
Soft data, 31–32, 69
Stakeholders
    interviews with, 99
    in leadership development, 17
Strategic initiatives, 22–23
Stress reduction, 76–77
Structured interview, 47

Succession planning, 10
Supervisory Leadership Development Program case
    study, 137–151
Supplies cost, 72
Surveys, 44–47

T

Tangible assets, 74–75
Target audience, customizing communication of
    results for, 80–81
Task force, for ROI Methodology, 100–101
Team members, data from, 57
Testimonials, 82
Testing, for measuring learning, 47
360-degree feedback, 23, 37–39
Time savings, 67
Timing
    of communication of results, 80
    of data collection, 57–59
Travel expenses, 72
Trend-line analysis, 63–64

U

Unnoticeable observations, 49
Unstructured interview, 47

V

V-Model
    description of, 27–28
    example of, 33
    Level 1 analysis (preference needs), 33
    Level 2 analysis (learning needs), 32–33
    Level 3 analysis (performance needs), 32
    Level 4 analysis (business needs), 30–32
    Level 5 analysis (payoff needs), 29
    levels of measurement, 28–35
    schematic diagram of, 28
Volatile, uncertain, complex, and ambiguous
    (VUCA) world, 4